CW00751387

'YOUR CHILDREN ARE NOT YOUR CHILDREN'

Headfort at night

'YOUR CHILDREN ARE NOT YOUR CHILDREN'

The Story of Headfort School

Lingard Goulding

with a foreword by Charles Lysaght

Lingard Goulding [signature]

THE LILLIPUT PRESS
DUBLIN

First published 2012 by
THE LILLIPUT PRESS
62–63 Sitric Road, Arbour Hill
Dublin 7, Ireland
www.lilliputpress.ie

ISBN 978 1 84351 321 6

1 3 5 7 9 10 8 6 4 2

A CIP record for this title is available
from The British Library.

Set in 11.5 pt on 15 pt Garamond by Marsha Swan
Printed in England by MPG Books Ltd, Cornwall

Your children are not your children.
They are the sons and daughters of Life's longing for itself.
They come through you but not from you,
And though they are with you, yet they belong not to you.

You may give them your love, but not your thoughts,
For they have their own thoughts.
You may house their bodies, but not their souls,
For their souls dwell in the house of tomorrow, which you cannot visit, not even
in your dreams.

You may strive to be like them, but seek not to make them like you.
For life goes not backward nor tarries with yesterday.
You are the bows from which your children as living arrows are sent forth.

From 'The Prophet' by Khalil Gibran

The philosopher's guide to education

'Your children are not your children.' Khalil Gibran's provocative paradox stresses that our children are not possessions. And yet how hard it is not to feel possessive towards them – to love completely, completely without attachment; for attachment enslaves. Gibran clearly does not advocate a laissez-faire approach, for 'You are the bows from which your children … are sent forth'. Even after the umbilicus is severed, a genetic chord still ties you to them, but 'seek not to make them like you.'

Point them in the right direction. Take careful aim. But then (to mix the metaphor most horribly), release the apron strings.

Contents

FOREWORD

My links with Headfort and with the author of this book go back to the late 1950s and derived from the game of cricket we both enjoy so much. The school was the home ground of the County Meath Cricket Club founded around that time by local squire and Labour Party activist Jack Whaley. Initially, I went there as a member of visiting teams from the Pembroke Club in Dublin. Soon I was co-opted by Jack to play for County Meath, so enabling me to claim that I had played county cricket in Ireland when persuading Cambridge captain Mike Brearley to give me a trial for the Varsity.

The author Lingard Goulding was another player not resident in Meath whom Jack recruited for his side; our good understanding calling one another for runs developed into an enduring friendship. He had a formidable cricketing pedigree having kept wicket on a Winchester side that included the Nawab of Pataudi, subsequently captain of India. But believing then as now that 'mankind thrives upon flirting with danger', Lingard was diverted by a passion for motorsport from playing regular cricket. Running marathons was a later enthusiasm pursued with the same characteristic single-mindedness.

The presence on County Meath teams of a star wicket-keeper lent distinction to our Meath team and Dublin clubs were pleased to send their best sides to oppose us. We then played on fine wickets lovingly prepared by cricket master Jack Sweetman, who was one of our main bowlers. Jack, a crafty leg-spinner, his son Alan, a former pupil, and masters Duncan White, Neville Wilkinson and Mike Bolton also turned out on our companionable teams. Until 1992, sumptuous teas served under the Big Tree were prepared by Jack's wife Edith. Those summer days at Headfort as the rhododendrons bloomed were some of the happiest in my year over several decades. The presence of the pupils and some of the other masters made me feel linked to the school and gave me a special interest in its progress.

Through our cricket contacts, I was able to observe the author's personal odyssey attempting dutifully at first to bend himself to his inheritance as heir to one of Ireland's foremost business enterprises and then finding his way out of that inheritance to be his own man and embark on a career as a schoolmaster that he has found so fulfilling.

Headfort School, as much as the Goulding family business, belonged to an old order that in the 1950s seemed quite secure. It may be that it had suffered political eclipse with Irish independence but it retained its social position and, to a large extent, the inherited wealth that underpinned it. Living in splendid isolation removed from impoverished nationalist Ireland, the denizens of this still self-confident world saw no need to modify their essentially British allegiances and way of life. Education across the water was an important part of the identity of this community. Headfort was then only one of about a dozen preparatory boarding schools in Ireland preparing boys for English public schools.

The headmaster David Wild, so well described in this book, fitted this world perfectly. He was of a type bred by the great British Empire, combining high standards of personal behaviour and a keen sense of duty with a lofty attitude towards other cultures and a consequent lack of appreciation of what they might have to offer. I relish as so characteristic his justification for installing a television in the 1950s that the boys were 'remote from the mainstream of affairs'. Moving towards the mainstream of Irish life was not an option that would even have occurred to him – or indeed, let it be said, to many of the parents. I recall his dismissing as absurd my suggestion that the boys should be taught some Irish history in their history class so that they would know about the role of their ancestors in that history. But the sense of duty and loyalty exemplified by diving into a river to save a child's life was the positive side of men like David. He also passed the telling test of commanding the esteem of those who served under him. Regardless of the fact that he would derive no personal advantage from it, he prepared his succession meticulously. His choice of the author was a masterstroke.

David Wild belonged to a class and generation of Englishman that in education as in much else wanted to re-create and preserve the pre-war world. It was therefore wholly in character that apart from the introduction of science the essential character of the education provided at Headfort remained the same between its foundation and the recruitment of the author as headmaster-elect in 1973. It was in that year that girls were first admitted – a gigantic step necessitated, it seems, by considerations of financial viability rather than educational preference. From this change flowed many other changes creating, in the author's words, a more couth, civilized community. Upon becoming headmaster in 1977 the ever gentle Lingard contributed to this by abolishing corporal punishment anticipating by some years its general removal in schools.

Succeeding decades have seen changes in the curriculum described in this book with the eclipse of the classics and the shift of emphasis to more useful subjects for the computer age. Religion plays a lesser role and has become œcumenical, reflecting a more diverse student body as well as the spirit of the age. The Irish language has been introduced to fit in with the curriculum in Irish schools for which more children are destined. The manly art of self-defence and shooting have given way to less violent sports. Discomfort and austerity, once regarded as character-building, have been eroded by central heating and better grub. Weekend breaks are commonplace and parents more involved. In the new century under the guidance of Dermot Dix, whom I also first met on the cricket field when he was a boy at St Columba's, day pupils have become an important presence making up one-third of the pupils. Teaching methods have been tilted to introduce more dialogue. With his background teaching in New York and his charming Indian wife Chandana, Dermot has consolidated the cosmopolitan aspect of the school that can be traced back to the arrival of Spanish pupils in the 1980s.

My friendship with the author was founded on the game of cricket so I have observed with special interest the interplay between his career at the school and a growing attachment to the game through his middle years. Until he took over as cricket master in 1993 on the retirement of Jack Sweetman, he was quite lukewarm about it. He had to be coaxed to play and cricket did not figure largely in his conversation. Since then he has played much more, turning out for a variety of teams and astonishing those who encounter him by the standard of his performance and general agility at an age when most cricketers have retired or settled for the travesty known as 'Taverners'. Onlookers sigh and reflect on what might have been had he played seriously when he was younger as he would surely have graced the Irish team. He is a keen follower of first class cricket, a spectator at Tests or Irish internationals and a perceptive and articulate judge of the merits of players. Nowadays he spends our autumn and winter coaching and playing in Australia, where he enjoyed three years as a neophyte businessman in his twenties

As cricket master he had already contributed to the history of the school, producing annually in his *Cicada* enchanting accounts of the season's games;

these Headfort Wisdens will be gold dust to those whose youthful exploits on the field are recorded so meticulously. He still returns with the swallows after his Australian sojourn to oversee the Headfort team so maintaining an important contact with the school beside which he retains a residence. His easy relationship with his successor helping out in this and with various other tasks says much about both men.

The author brings to his subject more than his unique knowledge of the history of the school. He writes the graceful prose of a man nurtured on the classics. He has inherited the individuality that made his father and mother such striking characters in their different ways. He has imprinted on this book as he did on the school his own philosophy of life, which is an engaging mixture of the conventional and the modern. He mocks with gentle irony both the lofty assumptions of the old aristocratic world and some of the silliness of the new political correctness. His insights on education and life, sometimes encapsulated in memorable *bon mots*, are original and stimulating. His decision to mention no former pupils by name in a school history is characteristically idiosyncratic but not without a wisdom of its own. His preference for contemporary sources, such as letters to parents, over the tailored memories of masters and pupils adds to the authenticity of the tale he tells.

A book like this is not easy to write if only because there is much that for one reason or another cannot be published and must be reserved for the oral tradition. The author, with characteristic diffidence, sets his face against glorifying his own considerable role. But it is a case of what we lawyers call *res ipsa loquitur* – the thing speaks for itself. Headfort survived through his tenure while the other preparatory boarding schools on the island disappeared or became so transformed as to be scarcely recognisable. It has done so despite the extra problems posed by the noble landlord, clearly a *bête noire* of the author, and the long years of violence on the border deterring pupils from Northern Ireland. It has had to cope with the decline of the community for whom preparatory boarding school education was traditional and the disinclination of most of those who could now afford the fees to send their children away to school at a tender age. While retaining its patrician and British connections, and some of the character that goes with that, Headfort has reached out into a broader world, albeit still a world of some privilege, and established connections with a broad range of Irish schools. It can no longer be stereotyped just as a British prep school in Ireland. It is something unique situated in a unique historic house whose restoration it has overseen and whose preservation it helps to ensure. As a school, Headfort inspires loyalty and pride among those who have been associated with it.

The author is not responsible for all that has been achieved but it must be doubted if it could have been achieved without him. He now renders Headfort School a further important service by telling its story so well.

Charles Lysaght

PREFACE

A daunting task

When the Chairman of Headfort School Ltd asked me to write a history of the School, the prospect was daunting. I conveniently forgot about it. Catching me in an unguarded, social moment a year later, he gently reminded me of his request. This time I had to reach for my pen.

I am not an historian by training. Maybe this ignorance will absolve me from observing some of the strict rigour and traditional approach with which the professional historian would tackle the task; it will allow me to intersperse the recording of facts and events with some of my educational hobby-horses. These of course will be my own personal opinions, nothing more. Perhaps I side more closely with Titus Livius (Livy), author of *Ab Urbe Condita,* than with Asinius Pollio. Pollio who had crossed the Rubicon with Julius Caesar, been Consul in 40 BC and subsequently fought with Mark Antony in the civil war against Pompey, was a strict historian of the old school. To him, history was purely a record of what happened: how people lived and died, and what they did and said. He felt obliged to suppress his finer, poetic feelings and make his characters behave with conscientious dullness. In his view, any epic theme or digression from the factual merely distorted the record. In contrast, when Livy writes history, he refuses to deny his readers an epic theme merely because such embellishment is deemed to belong to the province of poetry. Instead, he has the citizens of ancient Rome behave and talk as though they were alive today, and his work is the more attractive to read. My aim is to bring the citizens of ancient Headfort to life. When rigid histories grow out of date, they serve only as wrapping paper for fish; whereas those that stray irreverently beyond the factual – whilst still respecting the truth – may perhaps extend their longevity.

As one of the three long-serving Headmasters, and consequently a small part of the history of the School, my principal challenge has been to achieve objectivity. Having been present for only the final three years of David Wild's headmastership, I was naturally less conversant with this most crucial phase of Headfort lore than with the two that followed. Consequently the treatment of the early years is less chronological, more fragmentary, than that of the others, and I have had to depend to a great extent upon the memories and observations of past pupils who lived through those times. It is fascinating to observe how people's memories vary, and how a good story matures over the years. I have tried to establish corroboration for each of the wonderful tales that has been fed to me and to prune it of excessive embellishment, but be aware that they are literally fabulous.

I trust that I have been able to do justice to the monumental pioneering work of David Wild and his early colleagues who set the School upon its eventual course.

No names

The reader will notice that, despite enormous temptation, I have resisted mentioning individual pupils by name in these annals, with the exceptions of those who subsequently joined the staff, the list of acknowledgments and Appendix C (the compendium of all Headfort pupils). This may seem strange: after all, in what does a school subsist, if not in its children? It is customary in school histories to extol those alumni who have made their mark in the world: the prominent politicians, the leaders of industry, heroic sportsmen, talented musicians – even, in some cases, mention is dependent upon nobility of birth; there tends to be no reference to the few who, despite their fine education, end up sleeping rough or languishing in prison. I can assure the reader that most Headfort pupils are steering a straight course through life and leading successful, fulfilling careers. I should dearly love to boast of their triumphs; but I cannot recount the life history of each one, and it would be invidious to cite just the most gifted or those who are in some respect special.

Certainly we have had past pupils of distinction. Were I to name any, I should wish firstly to acknowledge those many who have won academic scholarships and exhibitions from Headfort to their secondary schools; then I should pay tribute to our leading musicians, artists, dramatists and sportsmen. The School may claim more immediate input to their success than to those who blossomed later in life. Of the latter category, we have produced leaders of industry, members of the armed forces – both male and female – prominent educationalists, publishers, doctors, journalists, giants of the bloodstock (what a horrible word) world and those who bask in the groves of Academe. In the arena of sport, I think, in chronological sequence, of a six-times winner of the British Open squash tournament; a long-term member of the Irish men's hockey team; an Irish National Hunt champion jockey; an Irish ladies' cricket captain, veteran of three World Cups.

I think of a boy, and two girls, with the voices of angels. I think of an Incorporated Association of Preparatory Schools (IAPS) chess champion, undefeated over two years in the Prep Schools' Congress, despite playing against future grandmasters. I think of an actor who is gracing the international stage professionally... and many, many more.

I think of students from Spain and Mexico, from France, Italy, Germany, the United Kingdom, Russia, South Korea, South Africa, the Bahamas, the United States of America, Canada, Australia, New Zealand, Poland, Nigeria, Monaco and Malta who have contributed widely to the cultural cross-pollination that is Headfort Today.

Each one of the almost two thousand children who has experienced a Headfort education so far has made his or her impingement upon the history of this great School. I do not wish to select my own personal 'honours gallery', and that is why I choose to avoid using names, even though the omission may be unique within the genre of school histories. Any pupil's name that appears in the text is a pseudonym. The diligent past pupil, however, will find no difficulty in detecting the identity of the protagonists who feature in anecdotes relating to his or her particular era.

Genesis

Shortly after World War II, Elsie (christened Elise), Fifth Marchioness of Headfort, was finding her stately, four-storey mansion, Headfort House, too unwieldy for the sole occupance of a single family. Together with her husband, Terry, the Fifth Marquis, she struck upon the notion of founding a school: they themselves would retire with their family to the east wing, known as Headfort Court, leaving the main body of the spacious house to the education of young people. She also founded the Headfort Golf Club and leased land to the Club.

Elsie, Fifth Marchioness of Headfort, founder of Headfort School
and *Terence, Fifth Marquis of Headfort*

Opening its doors in April 1949, with fees of fifty guineas per term, Headfort School has flourished through the intervening years, filling a small, but significant, niche in the Irish educational market. It has not been an easy passage, however, and, although now in 2012 the School runs on a sound financial basis, the Good Ship Headfort has sailed through inimical waters along the way. This brief history aims to trace the course of a very special seat of learning.

After its first year of operation, three Headmasters have steered the School through the subsequent sixty-two years, with the exception of a brief hiatus in the academic year 2001–2. These Headmasters were David Wild, Lingard Goulding and Dermot Dix. It will be convenient to treat the School's history in discrete segments to coincide with each of these Headmasters' reign. We shall examine in turn:

Part One   THE EARLY YEARS
Part Two   THE MIDDLE YEARS
Part Three   HEADFORT TODAY

Although I am treating the history of Headfort more or less chronologically, many of the topics covered could well have featured in any of these three Parts: I am thinking of headings such as the IAPS, Common Entrance, runaways, homesickness, bullying, coeducation, religion, Sports Day, political correctness, summer nostalgia, other Irish IAPS schools – all of these are fairly randomly positioned within the body of the work.

When I asked Dermot Dix to expand upon the changes that he has implemented during his tenure of office, he expressed the fear that to do so might imply criticism of the previous era. I had experienced a similar fear in the treatment of changes that occurred in my time. But there is no cause for such apprehension. Each generation evolves inevitably from its predecessor, and change is an essential ingredient. If a new Headmaster did not introduce some improvements, he would not be worth his salt. Although the Headfort of 2012 holds much in common with the Headfort of 1949, were it to run along exactly the same lines today, it would of course have ceased to exist.

In my treatment of the Middle Years I have quoted quite extensively from the termly newsletters that I wrote to parents. I wanted to show how I was feeling about issues at the time of writing, rather than depending upon my fallible memory many years later.

Some past pupils will doubtless rue the omission of events that were important to them during their time at the School; indeed, I may even have failed to acknowledge a revered member of staff. If so, I apologize. A history was written of St Peter's College, Adelaide in 2010. For this purpose the school employed an archivist for nine years to research the background and write the book. I have spent nine months.

A convention: the Marquess of Headfort is a title in the Peerage of Ireland. It was created in 1800 for Thomas Taylour, Second Earl of Bective. Despite the official title, the family unfailingly uses the alternative rendering, Marquis of Headfort, and this is the spelling that I shall employ throughout the book. The names of Staff and Board members are styled in capitals on first reference.

We shall begin the discovery of our School with a 'mood' piece that appeared in *The Irish Times* property section at a critical moment in Headfort's history. It aims to convey a feeling for the mystery of Headfort House, that majestic environment in which generations of children have happily passed their early schooldays.

W.L.W.G.

April 2012

THE SPIRIT OF HEADFORT

She is grey and somewhat austere nowadays, as befits a lady of her years, and she exudes an aura of permanence and mystery.

I am fortunate to pass my working life in one of those mansions that Virginia Woolf described as, 'comfortably padded lunatic asylums which are known, euphemistically, as the stately homes...'. One cannot fail to personify the old girl – the house, I mean, not Miss Woolf – just as a sailor reverentially attributes human qualities to his ship.

She was born around 1760. It was a difficult birth, labour being protracted until the end of the decade. By 1758 Sir Thomas Taylor, later Earl of Bective, had placed an order for over half a million bricks and 14,000 slates arrived the following year. In 1771 Robert Adam was commissioned to decorate five of the principal rooms. It was a time of tension and turmoil in Ireland: the Penal laws and coercion acts, imposed by the Westminster* parliament, suppressed Catholics and ensured that Ireland was unable to compete with England in terms of trade. Across the water, England was engaged in frenzied colonial aggrandizement: Clive was securing control of India at Plassey; Wolfe's capture of Quebec wrested Canada from the French; while, further south, Captain Cook helped himself to the whole of Australia and New Zealand. Into such a world Headfort House sprung upwards.

Infinite character is steeped in those old bricks and mortar. It may be that nowadays her joists creak a little, rheumatically. I know the feeling. But she is wise and harbours her manifold secrets discreetly. One may conjecture romantic dalliances and indiscretions that she has seen down the ages. Such foibles were, and are, as habitual to the aristocracy as to those of lower station, but we are talking, of course, of more refined and deferential days when the tabloids respectfully forbore to call a spade any such thing.

---

* Charles Lysaght corrects me here. It was the Irish Parliament, rather than the Westminster government, that imposed the Penal Laws.

In 1930 Winston Churchill wrote, with a hint of petulance, I fear, that, 'Headmasters have powers at their disposal with which Prime Ministers have never yet been invested.' Quite correct, Sir Winston: very proper. Yet to be Headmaster of Headfort is a humbling experience. It is a joy to share its gracious surroundings with receptive young minds. In summertime, the magnificence of the edifice, the blaze of rhododendrons, the somnolent hum of bees, the dignified strutting of pheasants and the scent of nectar in the labyrinthine gardens bestow upon the girls and boys an appreciation of our heritage. The so-called 'Eating Parlour' which we now term 'the Ballroom', that magical double cube with its gorgeous ceiling and handsome, twin Adam fireplaces, in which we assemble each morning and where we produce plays and concerts, is the first target to which past pupils swarm when they return to see us. The old lady leaves her mark upon all who visit her.

There are of course mild disadvantages to living in an old house. It requires more maintenance – care for the elderly, I call it. The wonderful high ceilings that afford light and a sense of freedom also make the building difficult to heat. Certainly we live a few degrees cooler than do dwellers of modern, 'two-up-two-down' abodes, those suffocating, hermetic saunas that are heaven-sent playgrounds for active, young viruses with reproductive tendencies. We wear an extra layer of clothing and, I contend, are healthier. There are, betimes, episodes of incontinence, as gutters become blocked and water finds its way under roof tiles; and we may suffer more false, nocturnal fire alarms than do the inhabitants of today's houses. It is a small price to pay.

A 230-year-old building must inevitably titillate students of the super-natural. Well, the 'Dean's Ghost' is a benign, grey apparition that may haunt receptive psyches of a dark evening; while the more fervent ghoul-watchers among Headfort children speak with awe of a bizarre spectre, sporting the sobriquet, 'Headless Harry'. This is an altogether different proposition and not to be contemplated by those prone to weaknesses. I am glad to report that I have been favoured with a sighting of neither spirit.

Headfort displays two personae. During term time, when full of children, she is warm and interactive. She communicates in concerto form: children make a statement, high in pitch and volume, and the old building reverber-ates her kindly response in rich, resonant tones. She loves to be lived in. By contrast, when the children go home at the end of each school term, she undergoes immediate, schizoidal change. The geist has fled the building, and she becomes like Oscar Wilde's Selfish Giant at his frostiest. Those weeks represent the nadir of my existence as I struggle to write reports in a soulless, unwelcoming house. Concerto form evaporates, and the mocking groans that the ancient timbers now emit are mournful, minor key and disturbing. She is pining for the children whom she loves.

Lingard Goulding
February 1993

Watching cricket at Clontarf

'YOUR CHILDREN ARE NOT YOUR CHILDREN'

PART ONE

The Early Years
1949 until 1977

I. PRELUDE

The setting – Skeletons in the cupboard – Other Irish prep schools

The setting

Kells (*Ceanannus Mor* is the Irish version) is a market town and urban district of County Meath in Ireland, on the River Blackwater. The town was originally a royal residence. In the sixth century it was granted to the missionary, St Columba, who founded a community there and Kells became a centre of learning. It was appointed a bishopric around 807, uniting with that of Meath in the thirteenth century, and St Columba's house was converted into a church. Near the present Church of Ireland church is a round tower, and several ancient crosses still stand in the locality.

The Book of Kells lends eminence to the town. A masterwork of Western calligraphy, it is an illustrated manuscript of the four gospels of the New Testament. It takes its name from the Abbey of Kells that was its home for much of the medieval period. The date of production of the manuscript is the subject of debate among scholars. What is certain is that it is not the work of Columba's own hand; palaeographic evidence points to a composition date of around 800, long after the Saint's death in 597. This date would seem to be corroborated by the fact that Viking raids on Iona began in 794 and eventually dispersed the monks and their holy relics to different parts of Scotland and Ireland. There are numerous theories as to where the work was produced: currently the most widely accepted belief is that it was begun at Iona and continued at Kells. The Book of Kells was certainly produced by Columban monks closely associated with the community at Iona.

Kells Abbey was plundered and pillaged by Vikings many times in the tenth century and it is something of a miracle that the book survived. The Abbey of Kells was dissolved due to the ecclesiastical reforms of the twelfth century and was converted to a parish church in which the Book of Kells was treasured. The book remained in Kells until 1654, the year that Cromwell's cavalry was quartered in the church there. The governor of the town wisely sent the book to Dublin for safekeeping. The bishop of Meath presented the manuscript to Trinity College in 1661 where it has remained ever since. A facsimile is situated in St Columba's Church of Ireland church and also in St Columcille's Roman Catholic Church in Kells.

The modern Headfort House was built during the 1760s and early 1770s by Sir Thomas Taylor, Third Baronet. It is an imposing, if austere, edifice that was described, prophetically, by George Hardinge in 1792 as, 'more like a college or an infirmary' than a stately mansion. To relive the story of the protracted growth of this spectacular Georgian edifice, and to delve into the history of the exotic Headfort family, the author commends to you the book, *Headfort House,* by M.D.C. Bolton, published in 1999 (obtainable from the School).

Skeletons in the cupboard

All the best families keep a skeleton or two in their cupboard and the Headforts are no exception. Thomas, First Marquis of Headfort, was stationed at Limerick with his Meath Militia in 1803, near the home of The Rev. Charles

Massy of Summerhill and his attractive young wife Maria, née Bomford. A liaison developed between the much older peer and Mrs Massy, and he swept her off to England one Sunday, shortly after Christmas.

Now, His Lordship had an enormous income, estimated at £30,000 a year, and so The Rev. Massy claimed £40,000 damages against him for 'seducing and taking away' his wife. The trial at Ennis Assizes excited wide publicity; many were the splendid and even scurrilous speeches by learned council on both sides. The jury brought in a verdict for £10,000 damages in favour of Charles Massy. It is not known whether the cuckolded rector welcomed back his errant wife after the brief affair. One might surmise that he had no need to do so, because he took unto himself a further three wives before he died in 1822.

A century later London society gasped with astonishment to learn that the Fourth Marquis and Marchioness of Headfort had been invited to one of the most important balls of the season – one at which King Edward VII and Queen Alexandra had consented to be present.

LONDON SOCIAL SENSATION

Marchioness of Headfort at Grosvenor House Ball.

Duchess of Westminster's Invitation to the ex-Chorus Girl Means That Society Will Receive Her.

What was so strange about this? Well, a couple of years previously the young Marquis, not yet of age, had created an immense sensation in smart society by declaring his intention to marry Miss Rosie Boote, a chorus girl in the Gaiety Theatre, London. The Marquis was a first lieutenant in the First Life Guards, one of the crack British regiments, and he was warned that, if he married the actress, he would have to resign his commission. Even the King tried to intercede, commanding Prince Edward of Saxe-Weimar, Colonel of the First Life Guards, to prevent the marriage. The Colonel ordered the Marquis to hold himself in readiness to go to South Africa on active service. However Lord Headfort would not give up his fiancée: refusing to go to Africa, he married Miss Boote instead. A year later a son, Terence, was born.

The wiseacres in English society shook their heads over the disgrace that the young nobleman, head of an ancient house and the possessor of considerable wealth, had brought upon himself. It was thought that the marriage would not last, and the *New York Times*, in its edition of 2 August 1903, suggests that it might not have done, had Miss Boote been:

> ... a Gaiety chorus girl of the ordinary type, but as a matter of fact, she was a quiet, refined woman, a devout Catholic, and there was nothing against her except the fact that she did not belong to the upper classes, and gained her living on the stage.
>
> The entrance of Lord Headfort and his wife was of course the sensation of the evening and, in spite of what must have been a most trying ordeal, Lady Headfort bore herself in a manner which everybody declared to be perfect. Her gown was one of the most beautiful of all the beautiful costumes seen at the ball; her appearance was as striking and, if anything, her manners were better than those of the *grandes dames* who crowded around her inquisitively.
>
> Now that the Duchess of Westminster has received Lady Headfort, other hostesses will of course follow suit, and the ex-chorus girl will not only have the nominal, but the actual, position of a Marchioness. Plenty of peers have married actresses before, but English society has in almost every case ostracized both husband and wife.

Little had been heard about Lord and Lady Headfort since their marriage. Then, out of the blue came the invitation from the Duchess of Westminster who had

> ... become a notable figure in London society, and takes as much care as any other hostess over her invitation lists. The presence of the Headforts at Grosvenor House could mean only one thing – that London society was ready to receive the chorus-girl Marchioness.

The Fourth Marquis converted to Roman Catholicism in support of his wife whose parents were English, but who had been educated at the Ursuline Convent in Thurles, County Tipperary. Subsequent members of the family have adhered to that faith. It is perhaps anomalous that, despite this fact, the School should have begun with a Protestant ethic.

Rosie Headfort became a hugely popular figure in the Kells area and lived until 1958, although it is thought that, as the Dowager Lady Headfort, she did not approve of her daughter-in-law's treatment of the house and its transition to a school.

The farmyard in the 1950s

Other Irish prep schools

In the 1950s there were twelve preparatory schools in Ireland, six in the North and six, including Headfort, in the Republic. The other schools were:

ARAVON

Aravon is by far the oldest of the Irish prep schools. It was founded in 1862 and for its first fifty years of existence catered for boys up to the age of eighteen. In 1912 it was decided to discontinue the secondary stage and by 1917 the older children had gone.

The school's name derives from, and is the reversal of, Novara House in Novara Road, Bray, County Wicklow, where the school was sited until 1984 when it moved to its present, attractive location on Ferndene Road, just outside Bray. Former Headmasters include Charles Mansfield and Freddie Cooper; the present Headmaster is Kevin Allwright.

BRACKENBER HOUSE

Brackenber House School opened in 1930 on the Malone Road in South Belfast. John Craig was a long-standing Headmaster. The school closed in the late 1970s.

BROOK HOUSE

Founded by Peter Ross in 1952, Brook House was originally located at Monkstown, County Dublin, but in 1973 it transferred to Killarney Road, Bray, County Wicklow. It accepted both day pupils and boarders. Peter Ross's son, Mark, was Headmaster for a few years before he accepted a teaching post, and eventually a headship, in England. Chris Macdonald, subsequently Assistant Headmaster at Headfort, became Headmaster during its final years before the Ross family sold the property and the school closed in 1991, being subsumed by Castle Park.

CABIN HILL

Cabin Hill was acquired in 1924 as the preparatory school for Campbell College at Knock, in east Belfast. It was the largest of the Irish prep schools with some 400 boys at its zenith. Uniquely among those schools that were still extant in the 1980s, it never accepted girls. Most of its pupils progressed to the senior school. It closed in 2006 when Campbell College started its own preparatory department. Luther Vye was Headmaster for many years, followed by Chris Dyer.

CASTLE PARK

Castle Park was established in 1904. Situated at Dalkey, County Dublin, by the 1970s it was a flourishing school of some 120 pupils, all of whom were boarders. Palmer Carter was Headmaster from 1962 until 1989 when Carl Collings succeeded him. He left in 2004 and the present Headmaster is Denis McSweeney.

ELM PARK

Elm Park, at Killylea, County Armagh, was founded in 1920 by two gentlemen who had served in World War I and subsequently taught at Rockport. They were Captain H.E. Seth-Smith and Mr Willoughby Weaving. Seth-Smith was a man of some means and he underwrote the annual loss that the school made. During World War II there were between fifty and sixty boys at Elm

Park. Seth-Smith died in 1946 at the early age of fifty-nine and the school was unable to survive. Michael Williams became Headmaster in the final years. The school closed in 1954.

GLOUCESTER HOUSE
Gloucester House was the preparatory school for Portora Royal School in Enniskillin, County Fermanagh. John Mills was Headmaster for many years. The school closed in 1983.

MOURNE GRANGE
Mourne Grange was a much-loved, proprietary prep school at Kilkeel, County Down in the southern foothills of the Mourne Mountains. It was founded at the beginning of the twentieth century by Allen Sausmarez Carey. The school was renowned for its high standard in classics and drama. The Headmaster from the 1950s was the founder's son, Patrick Sausmarez Carey. The school's demise in the early 1970s was partly a consequence of the political difficulties in Northern Ireland, because Mourne Grange used to recruit pupils from England and the Republic, as well as locals.

ROCKPORT
Rockport in Holywood, County Down on the Ards peninsula was founded in 1906. It is situated in an attractive setting on the banks of Belfast Loch. Recent Heads include Eric Tucker, Michael Williams (ex-Elm Park), John Agg Large, Graham Broad, Heather Pentland and Clare Osborne.

ST GERARD'S
St Gerard's in Bray, County Wicklow was founded in 1918. However, it was only a prep school for a short period in the 1960s and early 1970s when it used the Common Entrance Examination and sent children to HMC schools. Before and after those dates it accepted secondary pupils. J.C. Maher, Colum O'Cleirigh and Michael O'Horan were Headmasters during its prep era.

ST STEPHEN'S
St Stephen's School, Dublin existed from 1946 until 1963. It is enshrined in Headfort folklore because a Headfort bowler captured all ten of St Stephen's wickets for twenty-one runs in their 1952 cricket fixture. The Rev. Hugh Brodie was the school's only Headmaster, assisted by his wife, Mrs Lettice Brodie.

In the early days, the majority of Headfort's sporting fixtures was contested with the other Irish prep schools. Sadly, many of these have now disappeared, while others have changed their style. Today Aravon is the only prep school with whom Headfort competes regularly. Instead, the School now looks largely to the junior departments of secondary schools for competition.

1958 First XI with Jack Sweetman & David Wild

2. THE PRIVATE SCHOOL ETHOS

Foundation & values of IAPS – Privilege & snobbery – Professionalism –
Traditions & initiation ceremonies – Your children are not your children
– Boarding

Foundation and values of the IAPS

In March 1892, there met at the Golden Cross Hotel, Charing Cross in London, a group of fifty Preparatory School Headmasters to discuss the burning issue of the size and weight of a cricket ball best suited to the boys in their schools. That historic gathering gave rise to the organization that today comprises some 600 boarding and day schools, looking after more than 150,000 children, both in Britain and in what were then her Dominions. It was the foundation of the IAPS.

The building of 'character' was the primary ideal of those early Headmasters. This, they held, depended upon three themes: religion ('divinity', as it was called), the classics and team spirit. The life of the school, therefore, tended to revolve around the chapel, the teaching of Latin and Greek – to which all other subjects were subordinate – and to the playing of cricket and football, in which a boy learnt to accept hard knocks and to subjugate his personal glory to that of the team. When the author was at his own prep school, Ludgrove, some fifty years later than that inaugural meeting in London, and shortly before Headfort was founded, the end-of-term document that was sent to parents listed the ranking of each boy in every subject that was taught. It is significant that the sequence in which these subjects were listed – in other words, their perceived importance – began as follows: i) Old Testament History; ii) New Testament History; iii) Latin; iv) Greek. Other subjects deemed to be of lesser significance followed, such as Mathematics, English, History, Geography, French, et cetera.

Things had not changed much from the 1890s, and perhaps they still have not changed altogether. Recently a little boy who was due to bat next in a practice game of cricket on the Headfort square asked the author whether he might stand as the square-leg Empire (sic) until he was required at the crease. Empire and Umpire have much in common in the world of private education. The umpire is always right, even when he is palpably wrong; and the rationale behind the public school system was to prepare boys to fight *pro deo et patria* and to defend the British Empire in its far-flung outposts. After all, this Empire at one time controlled a quarter of the world's population and assumed that it had the divine right and duty to civilize the world. The sense of certainty that the most important thing to do in life was one's duty to God and Country remained unshaken until the late 1960s, although Wilfred Owen had striven to debunk the fatuous theory in his memorable lines of 1917:

> My friends, you would not tell with such high zest
> To children ardent for some desperate glory,
> The old lie; Dulce et Decorum est
> Pro patria mori.
>
> ('It is a sweet and proper thing to die for one's country'
> – taken from an ode by Horace).

Headfort School grew into this tradition of the ideology – even idolatry – of Empire, albeit shortly after the British Empire had virtually collapsed. Most of Ireland had been independent for three decades and India had acquired independence just two years previously. Nevertheless, prep and public schoolboys were still expected to become the next rulers of the reduced Empire.

The indoor games that children played in those days reflected the times in which they lived. Board games with a military overtone such as L'Attaque, Dover Patrol and Tri-tactics were in vogue and thoroughly stimulating.

To be educated privately in the 1950s was still a rather austere journey – less cruel certainly than a century earlier, but nevertheless harsh. Children, sentenced to trimensual internment, were subjected to a muscular form of Christianity: they were not expected to question their elders, and breaches of conduct would surely lead to chastisement. One boy described how his parents chose the appropriate school for him. It was a school that was known to prepare boys successfully for Eton by the generally accepted combination of brutality, boredom and slow torture. However, the ultimate criterion was that the Headmaster was 'the most famous dribbler in England'. Not showing any interest in football, the boy had not previously been led to regard dribbling as an especially desirable domestic accomplishment.

Dr Thomas Arnold, Headmaster of Rugby School from 1828 until 1841, maintained that, 'a sermon is the greatest of all means of moral discipline at a schoolmaster's disposal'. Dr Arnold had no interest in sport: he was more concerned with a boy's soul than his body, and sought to mould Christian gentlemen. Somehow the imposition of sermons fails to embrace the enthusiasm of modern youth who prefer to be offered rational argument, followed by discriminating debate, before they will accept a proposition. But Dr Arnold was also concerned with the intellectual life of the school to a greater degree than was common in Victorian England.

At Headfort, too, regulations were strict: for instance, during David Wild's reign, silence was imposed upon the children before they walked upstairs to their dormitories at night, and they might not speak again until after 'grace' had been said at breakfast the following morning. Bedtime is a period when children like to unwind, but that did not accord with the regime of the day.

Yet a degree of courtliness was ever present in these early schools. George Biddle, a revered Mr Chips-style figure from Mourne Grange and latterly Brook House, was once asked whether he had ever taught a particular pupil. He replied, 'Far be it from me to suggest that I ever taught anything to anybody; but that young gentleman was sufficiently gracious to sit in my classroom.'

Another memorable colleague of the author at Brook House's first home in Monkstown in the early 1970s was Bill Monk Gibbon, 'The Grand Old Man of Irish Letters'. Already in his mid-70s, Monk Gibbon would cycle to the school once or twice a week to teach English to the Upper Sixth. He was treated with considerable reverence in the school community. He boosted the sales of his delightful autobiographical novel, *The Seals,* by prescribing it as Christmas holiday reading for his pupils. *The Seals* is a highly philosophical work and the twelve-year-olds did not find it easy reading. One day Monk Gibbon was talking to the boys about collective nouns; he returned to the Common Room and asked his colleagues to provide a collective noun for prostitutes. Some rather feeble efforts were attempted, whereupon Monk Gibbon offered the following four:

An anthology of prose
A jam of tarts

A novel of Trollope's
A flourish of strumpets

In its Early Years Headfort tended to be, to a certain extent, a receptacle for the sons (girls had not yet been invented) of the Anglo-Irish landed
gentry who would, stereotypically, indulge a spot of huntin', shootin', fishin',
alongside controlling the tenantry. It was an essentially British model that
chanced to be implanted into rural Ireland. Of course, nowadays most of the
poor dears can no longer afford the fees and the pattern of the School's clientele has altered radically over the years, both during Mr Wild's tenure and,
increasingly, in the two that followed, as more parents from the professional
classes and beyond discovered the benefits of sending their sons, and eventually daughters, to a boarding school that catered for all of their extracurricular
requirements, as well as the purely academic.

Many of the early masters at Headfort were veterans of World War II, from
all three services; in consequence, they were unlikely to seek to alter the public
school ethos of character building – an ideal that had seen themselves emerge,
at least partially unscathed, from situations unimaginable to later generations.

Privilege & snobbery

There is no doubt that privilege and snobbery were prevalent within private
education in those days. Robert Tabor, Headmaster of Cheam School in the
middle of the nineteenth century, actually went to the trouble of devising a
graduated mode of salutation, dependent upon the social station of the pupil
whom he wished to address: were the boy a young peer of the realm, the
greeting was, 'My darling child'; were he merely the son of a peer it was, 'My
dear child'; whereas a commoner was simply, 'My child'.

In *The Story of Ludgrove* Richard Barber tells a delightful tale about
Colin Ingleby-Mackenzie that he has kindly granted me permission to repro-
duce here. Colin was an exceptional schoolboy cricketer; subsequently, he
became the inspirational, last amateur captain of Hampshire County Cricket
Club between 1958 and 1965, and later President of the Marylebone Cricket
Club (MCC) from 1996–8, a period in which women were first admitted to
membership. He was a pupil at Ludgrove a few years before the author. His
family owned a battered old Wolseley motoring car. As they arrived at school

on the first day of term, Colin besought his father, Vice-Admiral Sir Alexander Ingleby-Mackenzie, not to drive the Wolseley up to the front door of the school, in case it should compare unfavourably with the stylish limousines of his classmates. He would prefer to be left at the gate and allowed to walk up the drive. However the Admiral replied robustly that not only would he drive his car up to the front door of Ludgrove, but through it too if he wanted to.

Today Ludgrove is one of the most highly esteemed modern prep schools. It is a school of its time, but it was also a school of its time sixty years ago and that was a very different time. The announcement of the first fourteen past pupils reported killed, wounded, missing or taken prisoner in the early months of World War II, included seven who were peers of the realm or baronets. There was also inevitably a strong military influence shortly after the War. The parental XI in the Fathers' Match of 1949, the author's second year at the school, comprised four peers, a general, a brigadier, three colonels and two humble civilian commoners. The place was awash with nobility: if a boy did not bear a title, his surname would surely be double- or treble-barrelled.

Children are less snobbish than adults, but they are not free from the infection. In those days local children were known disrespectfully as 'VKs', short for 'village kids' or even 'oiks'. Some thirty years ago a series of television programmes revealed life at Sunningdale, another prominent English prep school that sent many boys to Eton. The interviewer fired all manner of leading questions at staff and pupils. One young gentleman was asked whether the local butcher's son would be welcomed, were he to attend Sunningdale. The little chap was horrified: with a disdainful curl of the lip, he replied, 'Oh, no, that would not do at all.'

The social attitudes of the landed gentry in Ireland were no different to those across the water. The author recalls playing country cricket at Bagenalstown in County Carlow during the 1950s. The home team's batting order appeared to be determined strictly in accordance with social standing. It is not surprising, therefore, that the first Headfort prospectus of 1949 sported a panel on the inside cover, bearing the names of the eight Governors of the School: five peers, two baronets and a solitary commoner, J.K. Roxburgh, founder and first Headmaster of Stowe School.

Professionalism

Inevitably there tended to be a lack of professionalism in some schools during these early post-war days. A small number of brilliant and inspiring people maintained a level of academic excellence in most of them, but many of the masters, returning home when the guns stopped firing, were completely unqualified as teachers. Headmasters were happy to employ anybody of reasonable character who was sufficiently desperate to accept work for long hours at low pay. A Dip. Phys. Ed. (Abu Dhabi), for example, would qualify a man to teach French and geography; attendance at a public school before the war was adequate qualification to join the Common Room.

One such inspiring teacher was Ken Morrison who used to sing Harrow songs with the author's grandmother whose husband and son were Old Harrovians. Known as 'The Toad', Ken was a learnèd classicist, who taught the author Latin and Greek at Ludgrove in the late 1940s and early 1950s. He used to rail against the use of the bastard word 'television' that is a hybrid of Greek and Latin. He maintained that the medium, which was of course in its infancy – the Gouldings did not yet have a set at home – should be termed 'teleopsis', 'tele' being the Greek for 'distant', and 'opsis' meaning 'sight' or 'spectacle'.

The author of this book joined Brook House for his first teaching assignment in 1970. At the staff meeting a few days before the beginning of term, the Headmaster announced,

'Mr Goulding, you will teach English and Latin to Form V, and biology to the Upper VI.'

'But Mr Ross', came the reply, 'I don't know any biology'

'Oh,' said the Headmaster, 'that is a disadvantage. Well, take this book; you will know some by Monday.'

And so those unfortunate children were taught biology throughout their final year at prep school by a master who had no knowledge of the subject whatsoever, but who always kept a couple of chapters ahead of them in the Nuffield Biology course. It was certainly not attributable to their biology teaching that one boy won the top scholarship to Shrewsbury School and the other (there were remarkably only two members of the Upper Sixth that year) an exhibition to St Columba's College.

This was the pattern at prep schools for several more years. It was only by the middle of the 1980s that parent power began to demand that those who taught their children should be properly qualified to do so.

In the twenty-first century prep school teachers receive a fair salary, commensurate with those who teach in state primary schools, although they still work longer hours and play a greater role in the lives of the children. Perhaps a partial compensation for the lack of professional expertise of some earlier prep school teachers was the sense of vocation that they demonstrated. They were content to spend many hours outside the classroom, enthusiastically sharing their interests and hobbies with the children.

Traditions & initiation ceremonies

Unlike the great 'public schools' (nowadays termed 'independent secondary schools'), prep schools do not include among their customs alarming traditions and initiation ceremonies that are prevalent at the senior level. In the 1660s, for instance, smoking was compulsory at Eton as a prophylactic against the plague, and any boy who did not light up in the morning would receive a hearty flogging. Later, a brothel was opened for the gratification of Sixth Form students. In 1810 the boys of the Lower Fifth were late for chapel. The Headmaster, Dr Keate, a Mephistophelean character who might be expected to use his whip with equal ease on his horses, his dogs and his women, publicly birched all one hundred of them. Some of the boys threw eggs at Keate; his task of flogging, while sploshing about in burst eggs, became farcical, and he had to summon assistant masters to patrol the crowd with birches whilst he beat the remaining eighty-odd boys. Keate was only five feet tall, but he was massively strong. In contrast, when Dr Heath birched a mere seventy boys in 1796 (ten cuts each), he had to take to his bed for a week with strained ligaments and muscles.

There was a riot at Harrow in 1771 because the Governors failed to appoint a popular don as Headmaster. Despite being a favourite among the boys, this man was partial to flogging; however, he also had a sense of fair play to the extent that, when the urge to flog came upon him, he would offer to whip boys in advance and then excuse them their next transgression. To the best of the author's knowledge, this concept of 'credit beating' has not been practised elsewhere in the world of education.

At St Peter's College, Adelaide, tradition decreed that each new boarder be 'roasted' by being held in front of an open fireplace for as long as he could bear it, ideally until he fainted. It is an initiation ceremony that is first found in Thomas Hughes's *Tom Brown's Schooldays.* In June 1912 a fourteen-year-old boy at St Peter's struggled against his tormentors while receiving this treatment and, slipping from their grasp, he fell onto the live coals, to the considerable disimprovement of his posterior. The poor child was conveyed to the infirmary where he observed the expected schoolboy code of honour, refusing to 'sneak', and declaring that he had inadvertently sat upon a hot brick, a deception that convinced nobody. He was then sent home for further treatment. His father, a doctor, was outraged by what had happened to his son and sued the school, although he later withdrew the suit. *The Adelaide Advertiser* gleaned news of the story and printed the dramatic headline, 'Roasting a College Boy'. The Headmaster sought to defuse the scandal by declaring that the incident, although unfortunate, was 'not an immorality of the worst order'; he did not even trouble to visit the boy.

On another occasion four senior boys went into a city hotel and became drunk. The same Headmaster, in his report of the occurrence to the school Council, wrote that, 'they were remarkable afterwards in the streets of Adelaide. I have caned the four.'

At Winchester College, new boys had to run the gauntlet down St Giles's Hill on the first Sunday of their first term, while those one year their senior, whose role ironically was to serve as their protectors, pelted them with limestone rock. The 'protégés' could use their 'strats' (straw hats) in an attempt to protect their faces but, since the descent was steep and slippery, many of them would fall and roll down the hill, such that they were easy prey for their tormentors.

Your children are not your children

In the early days parents would traditionally hand over their child to the school for every aspect of his education, the parents themselves abdicating that responsibility; indeed, parents were certainly not welcome at the school, apart from at the beginning and end of term when they might deliver and collect their child, like a product presented to be processed. They could also visit the extraordinary birds that they had hatched once a year on Sports Day in the Summer Term, when they were expected to appear in a respectable carriage (a Daimler or Bentley would suffice – a Rolls-Royce was perhaps a trifle ostentatious), and bearing a Fortnum and Mason or Smyths on the Green hamper. It was assumed that the curious creatures really lived, learned, expressed themselves and developed at school: they merely existed at home. 'Your children are not your children' – they were the School's children during term time.

As one who was despatched to another country, England (Headfort had not yet been founded), at the age of eight, the author experienced a degree of isolation for a while; however most children are tolerably resilient beings, and the boarding life inevitably teaches them independence

The early independent schools tended to share Philip Larkin's attitude to the input of parental influence, as expressed in his poem 'This Be The Verse':

> They fuck you up, your mum and dad.
> They may not mean to, but they do.
> They fill you with the faults they had
> And add some extra, just for you.

They might not have phrased it quite as indelicately. 'Remove boys from the noxious influence of home', was the way the Headmaster of one school described it. Parents were seen as interfering amateurs. A visiting lecturer at St Peter's College Adelaide, where the author works for six months each year, recently promoted his book, entitled *Crap Parenting*, that transmits the same idea.

Toiling in the fields at Cabra College, Adelaide

Even at Headfort the attitude was not entirely foreign. On 4 April 1957 David Wild wrote to parents as follows:

> As the petrol situation is now so much easier, I do not propose to place any restrictions on visiting next term. I would, however, remark that too much visiting is not good, and that the less a boy goes out with his parents, the more settled he will be and the better he is likely to do.

FROM THE HEADMASTER TO PARENTS OF NEW BOYS

Headfort,

Kells,

Co. Meath.

13th May, 1966.

Long Sunday this term is on the 22nd May. On this day boys may be taken out from 9.30 until their bedtime (in the case of young boys 7 o'clock).

On other Sundays boys may be taken out after church (Anglican 12.30, Roman Catholic 12.15) and must be back by 6 o'clock. Boys should not be taken out too often and may not go out with their own parents on two consecutive Sundays.

Half term: Sports Day is on Friday, 24th June and boys are allowed to go home for the week-end after Sports, returning the following Monday evening.

D. P. W.

It is only in recent years that schools have come to realize that parents really do have the right and the ability to contribute significantly to their children's education.

The concept of boarding is anathema to many continentals; and over the past half century more and more English and Irish people have chosen to play a greater part in their children's education, sharing their extracurricular pursuits and enjoying every element of their sons' and daughters' development. The obvious way to achieve this ideal is to keep the children at home and send them to school as day pupils; but, even in the case of those whose children are boarders, education has become a more evenly shared responsibility between school and home. Modern parents are welcomed at the school and many of them contribute richly to the life of the community.

Boarding

As late as 1986 the Headfort prospectus claimed:

> Uniquely among Irish Preparatory Schools, Headfort does not take day-pupils. Thus we are free from the divisiveness that a mixed boarding/day system tends to engender. Also, the monitoring of a child's work is greatly facilitated under such a regime. The children do their evening 'prep' together, under supervision, which yields more reliable and uniform results than 'home-work.'

Until well after the middle of the twentieth century virtually all prep schools catered exclusively for boarders. This was the case at Headfort and also at its leading Irish competitors. Quoting again from the 1986 prospectus:

> Companionship is the essence of the boarding life. Children are impelled into experience. How else could a boy who feels like a game of football, for example, find twenty-one others with a like inclination at the same time? But companionship means more than the availability of playmates: it involves learning to abide by the rules of social co-existence; it involves forming friendships and taking account of other people's wishes.

Boarding still has its place in society, even at the preparatory level. Many couples, and also single parents, especially those who live in rural areas, cannot find the time amongst their hectic lives to transport their children to sports clubs or music academies after the school day finishes. At boarding school all of these facilities may be found on campus. Headfort remains predominantly a boarding school – indeed, it is the only Irish prep school that accepts a significant number of boarders – but around one-third of its clientele consists of day pupils in 2012.

There is no doubt that seven-day boarding facilitates the logistical side of running a school. If all of the children are present all of the time, it is a relatively simple task to schedule the full range of activities. However many modern parents deem the compromise of a slight loss in efficiency to be a moderate price to pay for the joy of experiencing more of their children's lives. It is the School's duty to minimize 'the divisiveness that a mixed boarding/day system tends to engender.'

A rainbow sets over the games field. The hockey pitch is in the foreground, the cricket square in the middle distance and a rugby match is in progress in the background

3 . HEADFORT SCHOOL OPENS

The first year – David Wild & the founding fathers – The importance
of games – The forts

The first year

Lady Headfort's initial intention was that Headfort should become a public school (a misnomer for what is really a private, fee-paying, school). It would be structured along the lines of the famous English secondary schools – an Irish Eton perhaps.

T.J. McElligott who wrote several books on secondary education in Ireland claims in *This Teaching Life* to have worked briefly at Headfort in 1947.

He writes that the Headmaster, a Group-Captain Watkins, MC, DSO, employed him 'to teach subjects likely to be offered for Trinity Entrance, take games and supervise study.' He writes in flowery terms of the splendour of the estate and traces the history of the Taylors, soon to become Taylours, who hailed from Sussex. There were only five students in the School that year, all of them of secondary-school age, and he names each of them. He acknowledges that Headfort afterwards began as a preparatory school in 1949 under its first Headmaster, Romney Coles. This must have been Lady Headfort's first attempt to launch the concept. Mr McElligott's final recollection of his time at Headfort was of an evening when Michael, Earl of Bective, shortly to become the Sixth Marquis of Headfort, returned home for his holidays from Stowe School in England. He packed everybody into a 1921 Clyno motoring car and, 'proceeded to hurtle round the estate at a speed expected only of Formula One drivers, to the accompaniment of simulated cries of terror from the boys and at least one very genuine adult squeal.' Sounds authentic.

The prep school proper was due to open in September 1948 and staff were engaged, including the first Headmaster, ROMNEY COLES, from Carmel College, Newbury. There were delays and it became apparent that the concept of running Headfort as a secondary school was not practicable.

Romney Coles, Headfort's first Headmaster

5 May 1949 saw the arrival of fifteen children, ranging in age mostly from seven to eleven, but with one older boy of fourteen, for the modern Headfort's very first term. The earliest prospectus and the magazine, *Headfort Chronicle, Vol. 1, No. 1* (*No. 2* did not emerge for a further eight years), each pay sycophantic tribute to the Marquis and Marchioness of Headfort. The Chronicle bears photographs of the couple and also a full-page portrait of the suave, handsome Mr Coles, adopting something of a film star's pose. Mr Coles begins his encyclical with the sentence, 'It falls to few people these days to open a new Independent School.' He goes on to describe the excitement of the first day of term, and then pays generous tribute to his two right-hand men, Mr Stuart-Mills and Mr Ross. He continues, 'I feel that this brief record would not be complete without a list of the boys here this first term...'. The list of 'boys' includes the name of Mr Stuart-Mills's daughter who attended the school as a day pupil. She, and later her sisters, were the only female pupils at the School for almost three decades. The Headmaster concludes,

> When this Chronicle is a valued document in the School Library a century or so from now, it will be a matter of interest to look back and read the names of the happy little band of boys [sic] who today are our 'freshmen', but who have already developed a corporate spirit and who are now laying the foundations of our future traditions. You, who come after and read this many years hence, will treasure these as the very spirit of your School.

Headfort in 1949

This prospectus bears the marvellous sentence: 'Corrective exercises are given to any boy without additional charge if his physique appears to warrant it.'

A past pupil recalls being allowed to play Cowboys and Indians in the woods in Romney Coles's time. He is horrified to recall the treacherous wooden spears, daggers and swords that the boys used to fashion in the carpentry shop. He believes that David Wild put a stop to this.

BILL STUART-MILLS ('Pilch') was educated at Oxford and served in the Royal Air Force during the war, attaining the rank of Wing Commander. He was a courteous, scholarly man and a wonderful schoolmaster: tolerant and patient, he shared his great love of the classics with his pupils and was a revered figure at Headfort for thirty-one years.

He also coached hockey, ran the scout troop, played the clarinet and wore a kilt. He had the gift of being universally popular, without being populist. One of Bill's duties in the Early Years was to travel to England at the beginning and end of each term to escort English boys across the Irish Sea in the B & I ferry, stopping off at the Isle of Man to pick up others, and thence continuing by public transport to Kells. He became Senior Master when Peter Ross left two years later. He composed the Headfort School grace that was recited before meals for many years, either by a member of staff or a senior pupil:

Benedicat, omnipotens deus, et nos et haec sua dona
quae de manibus eius benignis iam sumus accepturi.

(Bless, all-powerful God, both us and these his gifts
which by his kindly hands we are about to receive).

To the pupil he was fair-minded, caring, inspiring – slow to chide and swift to bless. His scholarship was monumental and he possessed the talent to transmit his love of learning to others, even to the less gifted. He was a quiet gentleman, a gentle man, who seldom raised his voice, yet no schoolmaster commanded greater respect. As a colleague he exuded wisdom.

Several past pupils fondly recall Bill's influence in communicating his passion for classical music. On certain evenings he would talk about particular compositions by Mussorgski, Ravel, Sibelius, Dvorak, Mozart and Beethoven in the Library and then play selected movements on his gramophone.

Bill's wife, KATE STUART-MILLS, was the School's first music teacher and presented concerts, featuring the children's work, for many years: a cheerful, energetic woman, she had rowed for her college at Oxford where she met her husband who served as cox. An oar with the names of the crew inscribed upon it used to adorn a wall in their house and is now a treasured possession of their eldest daughter.

Bill and Kate Stuart-Mills

PETER ROSS, the school's first Senior Master, was a man of resolve and valour. A fine footballer while at Repton School, he graduated from Trinity College, Dublin, and became a troop commander in General Bernard Montgomery's Eighth Army, winning the Military Cross for gallantry at the El Alamein campaign.

That first *Headfort Chronicle* is a charming document that paints a lyrical picture of an idyllic family-style school. The initials W.P.M.R. (Peter Ross) appear under most of the articles. In his editorial he too looks to posterity: 'How interesting, we think, will this first number be to those who refer to it a hundred years hence! How careful we must be, for are we not setting the fashion for generations of successors?'

Yes, indeed. He quotes Dryden's encouragement to all pioneers: 'Mighty things from small beginnings grow'.

This first edition acknowledges the gift of a three-inch refractor telescope from Lord Headfort; tells of a visit to the Boyne Furniture Works in Navan; declares the Library to contain 123 books; records the business of the debating society; and gives reports of an end-of-term tea party, a concert, a visit to the cinema, cricket, tennis, Cowboys and Indians, physical training and athletics. For the final assembly of the term, the Headmaster called upon Miss Swords, 'a charming visiting teacher from Australia', to dispense the prizes. Apart from academic prizes, awards were made to two boys for, 'never having complained at meals and for having appreciated all that was set before them.' Included in the magazine is a poem by Mr Ross, entitled 'Personalities', that makes reference to every pupil. One stanza reads:

> When I consider Moore and Mitchell*
> At lunch, I often wonder which'll
> Burst
> First.

Is this politically incorrect? Maybe, but it was a different world and, in some ways, a happier one.

The idyllic picture of this first year is corroborated by a past pupil who writes with enormous fondness of the School and all – or almost all – of those who taught therein. He describes Romney Coles as a delightful, gentle man. 'It was said that his wife did not see eye-to-eye with the then Lady Headfort

---

* The only instance in the main body of this work, apart from those who subsequently taught at the School, where pupils' names are mentioned.

(pretty formidable she was), hence their brief rule.' Here we have a possible reason for Mr Coles's early departure.

This pupil recalls being bidden to tea, together with his parents and his brother, by the Headforts before the start of his first term.

> It was a very starchy affair, taken in the main hall with considerable ceremony and halting small talk. I still have a vivid picture of the house parlour-maid and the butler in attendance, rather à la *Downton Abbey*. I imagine it was a kind of appraisal, possibly to consider whether the children of a linen manufacturer from the north of Ireland would make appropriate pupils for a prep school like Headfort.

He remembers that, when David Wild took charge, rhododendrons and azaleas from the walled garden regularly adorned the Front Hall and the Library.

HEADFORT CLOTHES LIST

Name _____ Date of Return to School _____

Article	Number Required	Sent to School	Matron's Check	Added at School	Sent Home
Navy Gaberdine Raincoat	1				
*Blazer	1				
*Cap	1				
Grey Flannel Suit—Jacket and Shorts	1				
Pairs Grey Flannel or Corduroy Shorts	2				
Grey Pullovers, V neck, with Sleeves and loop for hanging	2				
Grey Pullovers, V neck, Sleeveless	2				
Grey Flannel Shirts, with collars attached	3				
Pairs Grey Stockings	5				
Vests	3				
Underpants	3				
†Ties	2				
Handkerchiefs	12				
Dressing Gown	1				
Pairs Pyjamas	3				
Pair Bedroom Slippers (soft soles)	1				
Pair Black House Shoes (rubber heels) or Sandals	1				
Pairs Black Walking Shoes	2				
Pair Gym Shoes	1				
Pair Gumboots	1				
Sponge	1				
Hairbrush	1				
Combs	2				
Pair Nail Scissors	1				
Belt	1				
Braces—Pair	1				
Garters—pair	1				
Overcoat (medium grey herringbone Winter Terms only)	1				
Carpentry Apron	1				
Laundry Bag	1				

Article	Number Required	Sent to School	Matron's Check	Added at School	Sent Home
LINEN, Etc. (Left at School during holidays)					
Pairs Single Sheets	2				
Pillow-cases (marked on outside)	3				
Towels (coloured, with loops for hanging)	4				
Table Napkins	3				
Table Napkin Ring	1				
Travelling Rug	1				
Cash's Name Tapes					
Coat-hangers (with bar)	1				

MARKING OF CLOTHES

Parents will understand that it is essential that boys' clothes, combs, brushes, etc., are clearly marked, preferably with Cash's woven name tapes.

Boots and Shoes must be marked inside with the boy's name.

Sufficient gear for the first two nights of the Term should be brought in a hand-case.

Parents are requested not to send trunks or play-boxes to School, but to send a suit-case.

Every boy should be provided with a Bible and a Hymn and Prayer Book.

Part of Headfort's original clothes list

David Wild & the Founding Fathers

Romney Coles left Headfort after three terms, ostensibly because he had been led to believe that Headfort would become a secondary school and he now realized that this would not happen. He had previously been Head of Science at The King's School, Canterbury and was essentially a secondary school man. David Wild was appointed to succeed him.

Peter Ross remained at Headfort for two further years before leaving in 1951 to establish his own prep school, Brook House, in the Dublin area. Brook House opened the following year with just four boys, two of whom were the Headmaster's own sons; the other two followed him from Headfort. It developed into a successful school until, after the retirement and subsequent death of its founder, it closed in 1991.

Thus it was that DAVID WILD began his life's work at Headfort when he succeeded Romney Coles in the Summer Term of 1950. An Englishman, he was educated at Beaudesert Park School, Cheltenham College and Worcester College, Oxford; he taught at Neville Holt (which sadly closed as a prep school in 1998) for three years before the war, during which he served in the Royal Navy from 1940 until 1946, attaining the rank of Commander. He remained in the Navy for two years after the war, living in Sydney, then returned to teach at Neville Holt until he answered the call of County Meath. When he assumed the reins at Headfort, he developed from scratch the structure and routines of the new School, many of which remain in place to this day. He was elected a member of the IAPS, bringing his school into association with some 500 other prep schools, principally in Britain. It is an anomaly of that organization that it is the Headmaster, rather than the school, that is in membership. In those days there were five other prep schools in the Republic and six in Northern Ireland.

David Wild was a man of high principle and great dignity who displayed, and expected, propriety in all things. To be a visitor at Headfort in his era, one felt rather special. As do all good schoolmasters, he loved children and he understood them. He could be quite stern, but was always fair. He had a love of music. Monteverdi was one of his favourite composers; he would play the great 1610 Vespers on an antique gramophone in the Front Hall of an evening at high volume; the music reverberated profoundly up through the bowels of the building to the children who were trying to sleep at the top of the house, as they did in those days.

The Summer Term used to extend deep into July and it remained light until ten o'clock; there were no curtains in the dormitories: these were a luxury awaiting a later age. Several years afterwards, a boy recalled to the author how he had acquired his lifelong fondness for classical music from listening to the soaring tones that emanated from Mr Wild's gramophone, while he awaited the onset of sleep. What a wonderful gift.

The gentrification of the boys was ever a priority. Dermot Dix recalls that David Wild would invite his thirteen-year-old pupils to meet his dinner guests and engage them in intelligent conversation. They were also taught that one drank dry sherry, rather than sweet.

These were formal times. The Matrons used to wear full nursing uniform; the Chef donned a toque, his hat of office; and the domestic staff, four of whom lived on the premises above the stable yard, wore aprons and waitresses' headgear when they served Mr Wild his dinner, a meal that was taken privately each evening in the office, opposite the study. It is impossible to overestimate the importance to the School of the domestic staff through the ages. They have not always received the recognition that they deserve but, without them, the very fabric of the place would have crumbled. Academic staff sported gowns at Morning Assembly and mortar-boards on formal occasions.

A menu, in certain eras written in French, was provided on every table at lunchtime. It bore the Winchester College and New College Oxford motto, 'Manners Makyth Man'. A past pupil writes:

> A pity that the cooking was not on a par with the ceremony. Egg Mornay was a particularly vile concoction – hard-boiled eggs coated in a congealed sauce made with (I'm guessing here) a revolting powdered mustard and processed cheese. Refusing to eat was not an option that the teaching staff entertained.

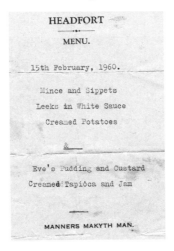

An early Headfort menu

Mr Wild's other great passion was gardening, and very expert he was. Most mornings he would wander up to the Walled Garden between classes to discuss growth with TOMMY HARTEN and WILLY SHERIDAN who used to cultivate fruit and vegetables, some of which would be consumed by the School; other produce was sold to local people. Raids on the kitchen garden to garner apples and strawberries were amongst the daring exploits that the braver Headfort boys would undertake in the summer months. Sometimes the Headmaster would take groups of boys to the Great Island to inspect his favourite Wellingtonia or *Sequoiadendron Giganteum*, the giant redwood.

Many memories of 'Boss Wild', as he was known, have been relayed to the author. The most spectacular is of when he dived, fully clothed, into the river to rescue a boy who was in difficulties. Today this 'boy' claims that he would surely have drowned, were it not for the gallantry of the Headmaster who, he recalls, was wearing brown, suede shoes.

This boy arrived at Headfort at the age of seven, 'too young to be beaten', according to David Wild who, as the respondent remembers, made up for the omission in later years. However, he did not know that the boy was already well used to a good flogging from his father.

One past pupil remembers that the stern man in the smart suit or blazer was omnipresent. Being sent to his study, and waiting in the small, dark, alcove outside, was the closest he ever reached to experiencing abject fear. On the other hand, receiving a lift in Boss Wild's car to the old swimming area was a major triumph, as otherwise the boys had to run all the way.

The old swimming area

A less attractive memory of David Wild concerns his noisome Old English Sheepdogs: there was no need for one boy to keep '*cave*' (beware), if a misdemeanour was being perpetrated: an olfactory trauma offered advance warning of the Headmaster's approach. Later he had an equally loathsome mongrel called 'Ellie', whom he called 'Ellie boy' (Ellie was a bitch). After Ellie's span on earth was completed, an indentation was detected on the hockey field one day: for some years afterwards this was referred to as 'Ellie's grave'.

David Wild had two exceptional lieutenants with whom to liaise in those early days, Bill Stuart-Mills, already mentioned, and Jack Sweetman.

JACK SWEETMAN served Headfort faithfully for forty-one years. He taught history and geography and coached rugby and cricket rigorously. A fine, all-round sportsman – he has been described as one of the best rugger players never to represent Ireland – he was a stickler for discipline and proper conduct. Upon Bill Stuart-Mills's retirement from the role, he succeeded as Senior Master in 1971. The triumvirate of Wild, Stuart-Mills and Sweetman was paramount in establishing the procedures of the emerging school. As is the case with several of the characters who feature in this history, Jack Sweetman's working life revolved entirely around Headfort.

Jack Sweetman

A past pupil recalls that, in the early days, while wooing the School Matron, Jack Sweetman's euphoria would sometimes induce him to croon Frank Sinatra songs during history or geography classes, while the children were writing. Absent from his broad range of accomplishments was Aoide, the Muse of singing, and consequently these solo performances were audibly painful to at least one member of his audience. An accomplishment that Jack did possess in abundance was expertise in the preparation of cricket pitches. He tended the Headfort square lovingly for forty years, and Headfort wickets were renowned for their excellence. He instituted the practice of requiring the members of the First XI, and others on Top Game who were close to the team, to roll the cricket pitch each morning after breakfast in the Summer Term, by hauling the giant manual roller over the square. Through becoming involved in the preparation of wickets themselves, the children learnt that cricket is a labour-intensive game and that they should not take all the work for granted.

This routine continued for several years after Jack Sweetman retired, but became impracticable with the advent of day pupils in 1996 when the rescheduling of the School day did not leave sufficient time between the end of breakfast and the beginning of class.

EDITH SWEETMAN (née MORTON), who arrived at Headfort a term after her future husband, served as Assistant Matron and Matron, and eventually as Housemother to the girls. After their marriage, she retired for a couple of years, as was the custom in those days, before returning to play an important role in Headfort's history. A warm-hearted, maternal lady of great charm, she was a source of reassurance and comfort to generations of children and their parents. Any task undertaken by either of the Sweetmans was invariably performed with absolute thoroughness and efficiency.

The importance of games

Young limbs need to be flexed and extended. Therefore, sport in some guise has always played an important role in the lives of Headfort children. A minority of children do not enjoy formalized sports and the School has generally tried to vary the programme for these as far as possible; however, some form of physical exercise is a prerequisite to good health. Games form the highlight of many children's waking hours. And, of course, sport and religion have long been recognized as the principal palliatives to sexual experimentation in the young.

Headfort cricketers adopt the Humphrey Bogart pose

From the beginning, games – garrison games, although at Headfort rugby replaced association football – were an integral part of the boys' lives. These games were well taught and, as soon as the fledgling School was large enough, matches were played with other schools. A pupil who arrived in Headfort's second term recalls the ignominy of an early away cricket match. The opposition expressed disappointment that they had only scored about 150 runs; then Headfort batted and were all out for eight in the first innings, and something similar in the second.

Rugby was the principal game in the Christmas Term, hockey in the Easter and cricket in the Summer. This is still the boys' programme today. However tennis was also enjoyed, as was squash on the School's stone-floored court, whereupon a subsequent champion would play his early games (he subsequently won six British Open titles between 1967 and 1973, at a time when the British Open was effectively considered to be the world championship, before the World Open was inaugurated in 1976. He was surely one of Headfort's finest athletes). Football, the world's most popular sport, has always been played at Headfort on an ad hoc basis in leisure hours. For a time in the Middle Years the southern Irish prep schools used to hold a football tournament for both boys and girls.

Headfort on the attack against Aravon in 1975

Croquet hoops would be erected during the long summer evenings: this tended to be the aesthetes' game: the 'hearties' rarely participated. In the early days, boys had to run beyond the New Bridge, half a mile away, in order to swim in a tributary of the River Blackwater, near the mausoleum. Later Mr Wild bought a small, circular, plastic pool that was located by the ha-ha on the south side of the house and, later still, the present pool was built amongst the rhododendrons on the edge of the games field.

Mr Wild would attend the School matches and encourage the boys from the touchline: 'Go on, my jungle bunny', he would shout as Manning major streaked down the wing at hockey or rugby.

While being driven to matches by Mr Wild in his Austin Cambridge, whenever the car stopped at a junction, the passengers would be asked, 'Anything to port or starboard?' Their response to this naval question would determine whether the car would proceed or no.

There were other seasonal crazes that the boys indulged. Mighty 'conker' battles were waged at 'break' and the sale of shoelaces would surge. Marbles virtuosi clashed horns on the circle outside the house during 'morning walk' after breakfast and at break. Roller-skating on the rink was popular in all seasons, later to be superseded by roller-blading. Strangely these worthy activities have fallen into desuetude in recent years. In the 1950s and early 1960s Bill

Stuart-Mills used to acquire balsawood gliders for the boys, and fierce aerial battles were engaged of an evening in the skies over the games field at the front of the house. These gliders would continue to fly, even after suffering massive collision damage. It was The Battle of Britain all over again. Anybody who flew his glider with pacific intent would have to keep his craft out of the war zone on the north side of the house, and fly in safety over the lawn instead.

From 1953 until the end of the Middle Years, excepting the years of 'the troubles', the IAPS North v South representative cricket match was held during the Summer Term, alternately at Headfort and Mourne Grange. With the demise of the latter, the match was held each year at Headfort.

Headfort in 1957

The forts

The forts are a series of primitive dwellings that the children build in the woods on the north-west side of the house. They constitute an important element of Headfort folklore. Children form 'syndicates' to construct wigwams of varying degrees of complexity, using whatsoever materials that they are able to scrounge. Over the years some quite sophisticated forts have been erected, including two-storey 'mansions' built surrounding a tree, and even tunnels interconnecting one fort to another.

The social intercourse demonstrated in the forts is a microcosm of the adult world of tribal convention and property ownership. Membership of a particular fort's syndicate is a measure of a pupil's esteem in the jungle, and boundary rights are zealously guarded. Forts owned by younger pupils are generally tolerated, indeed respected, by their elders, provided that they are not situated on prime estate. Occasionally dealings become fractious and a judiciary system must be invoked to resolve property disputes.

The forts are a liberating influence in the life of the School because they are unable to be as closely monitored by staff as are the open playing fields. When a group of friends retire to their fort, they are free to be themselves, do what they will and discuss whatever they choose. Of course, Headmasters always exhort staff to watch the forts closely, for nefarious happenings may occur there. Past pupils tell lurid tales of battles, fought with bows and arrows, swords, spears and knives; certainly one or two accidents have befallen fort dwellers. One boy dropped out of a tree – up which, of course, he should not have been – and incurred a savage leg wound. Another was poked just above the eye with a stick. But, as has been written elsewhere in this book, a modest degree of risk is a necessary concomitant to children's healthy development. Recently Robert Pelant has built an outward-bound course in the area.

The forts have given a cherished breathing space to generations of children in an environment that is otherwise quite tightly controlled.

The Forts – a happy refuge for generations of children

4 · A SCHOOL ESTABLISHED

David Wild's achievement – Early staff – An unusual evening – A digression –
More staff – Television – County cricket – Science laboratory –
Staff of the early '70s – Company structure – Religion – Letter writing – Pigs! –
Exeats – Riding upon horseback

David Wild's achievement

This chapter covers a quarter of a century, the majority of David Wild's reign. It is inevitably fragmentary, as it describes a series of events that took place as he built the numbers in the School from an initial trickle – there were thirty-eight boys by September 1950 – into a viable quantity that oscillated over the years. He had to overcome numerous hurdles, including legal issues with the landlord, the Sixth Marquis of Headfort. He kept in his desk a drawer entitled 'battle files' that contained reams of quasi-litigious manoeuvring. He remained in charge of Headfort for almost twenty-eight years and the vast majority of past pupils remember their time at the School with affection and nostalgia.

Early staff

Jack Sweetman tells of interesting personalities who served in the Early Years, including EILEEN ARMSTRONG (née WILLIAMS) – she was the first Matron and she set the tone for others to follow; JOAN GAITSKILL, a relative of the British Labour Prime Minister, Hugh Gaitskill; she was David Wild's secretary and also taught art. She drove a boy to the dentist in Dublin on one occasion and afterwards took him to lunch at Jammet's, one of the smartest and costliest restaurants in town. At the end of the meal, the boy noticed the remnants of a worm on Miss Gaitskill's plate that she had delicately placed to one side.

Other early staff members include the first riding mistress, ELIZABETH CLARKE, a daughter of Lady Headfort by her first marriage to Sir Rupert Turner Havelock Clarke; LIZANNE MUSGRAVE, sister to Sir Richard, who succeeded her; in turn, SARAH PERRY who had two brothers in the School replaced Miss Musgrave; JANE BALDING, an early Cook; CATHERINE HAZARD, Housekeeper in the early 1950s – according to Jack Sweetman, she lived up to her name behind the wheel of a car – she subsequently worked at Brook House; MARY SIMMS, niece of the Lord Archbishop of Armagh, who survived the sinking off Donegal of the liner *Athenia*, carrying refugee children to Canada. TOM O'DONNELL, later to become a government minister and eventually an MEP, taught mathematics; THE REV. JOHN 'KIT' CARSON, Rector of Kells, taught scripture and senior mathematics in the mid-1950s (a past pupil answered all questions correctly in a mathematics test, but was given 99 per cent – when he remonstrated at the loss of a mark, the good clergyman replied, 'Only God is perfect'); HAROLD BRODIE-IND, a descendent of the brewing firm, Ind Coope, also taught mathematics to those who chose to learn, but he sometimes nodded off to sleep during class; yet another clever mathematics teacher, NOEL STEWART; MICHAEL GARDINER, former actor, taught English, and actually made walks popular by telling the children enchanting stories; RICHARD DAVIES taught general subjects in the 1950s – his brother, Philip, was an English rugby international who subsequently became Headmaster of an IAPS school.

MISS ROONEY, a former governess (not to be confused with the later Mrs Rooney), was a much-loved Form One teacher upon whom the children played all manner of fiendish pranks, including the production of a pyrotechnic display, achieved by purloining sugar from the dining room table and fertilizer from a steel drum found underneath the stairs – when she took children for walks, she would carry an umbrella with which to prod the slow and wallop the wicked; MONSIEUR JEAN PRUDOR who came from Brittany and had been in the French resistance – 'twas rumoured that he had been awarded the *Croix de Guerre* and the *Legion d'Honneur*; his was an unusual, and likeable, presence in the Irish midlands; also, he was said to be a dab hand at marbles and would frequently 'clean up' when challenging the children; BILL KIRWAN, Lady Headfort's chauffeur, did maintenance work for the School. Amongst his duties was to prepare and light the open fires that heated the classrooms in winter. Kirwan also served as David Wild's chauffeur on occasion: smartly clad in the formal uniform of his craft, as prescribed by Lady Headfort, he would drive David Wild to dinner parties. A ten-shilling note would change hands, with the instruction that he should have something to eat and return at half past ten. Kirwan would betake himself to the nearest pub, sink as many pints of Guinness as the note would procure and return to collect his master. He would snap smartly to attention and open the back door of the car. David Wild would slide into the back seat and immediately fall asleep; whereupon Kirwan somehow managed to negotiate the inevitably narrow gateways and safely navigate his slumbering cargo back to Headfort.

MICHAEL GABRIEL, a French and English teacher, used to park his beautiful Lanchester motor car in the stable yard in the 1950s. On one occasion a couple of devilish boys gained entry to the car and drove it all around the yard on the starter motor until they had run the battery flat and had to push it back to its resting place.

One of the more exotic Headfort teachers tended to suffer from malaria. When he did not appear in class, the Matron would be sent to the staff sleeping quarters to find him. She would report back that his malaria was troubling him. It was universally known that his particular strain of 'malaria' was transmitted not by the nip from a mosquito, but by the nip from a whiskey bottle.

JIM MCALEESE taught at Headfort from 1954 until 1964; he was a fine teacher and a man of wide culture and enormous charm. Educated at Belvedere College, he read English and Psychology at University College Dublin and took his Higher Diploma in Education at Cambridge University. He taught both in England and Ireland before joining Headfort. A colleague of his on the staff was the riding teacher, JILL FISHER. A romance blossomed and they shared thirty-eight years of happy marriage. They were wonderful friends to the School over many years; indeed, their two sons, and later their grandchildren, became pupils. Jim and Jill were an exceptionally united pair who shared many interests, and their warmth and gift for friendship were infectious. Jim would burst into song at the slightest opportunity, rendering lyrics, both sacred and very profane, in a deep, gravelly voice with a dramatic, musical sense of timing. He was a boisterous sportsman who played rugby and cricket with verve. At one time he and Jill kept a pack of otter hounds at Williamstown. They were enthusiastic beaglers and Jill served The Pony Club for twenty years. Jim was a public-spirited man who contributed to numerous civic causes, from environmental groups to the Tidy Towns competition;

from assisting the parish water scheme to mowing the church lawns. A keen conservationist, he was Chairman of the Newtown Graveyard Restoration Society where he now lies. He was a member of the Irish Georgian Society and Chairman of the Meath Branch of *An Taisce*. He and Jill believed strongly in the right of country folk to hunt with hounds, and they travelled to England to march against the Blair government's declared intention to ban fox hunting.

Jim McAleese was an unpretentious intellectual. His knowledge of literature and history, his kindly wisdom and native wit made him the most enchanting company. Possessed of a rich command of the English language, he wrote a volume of children's stories as well as his uproarious novel, *The Kilbeggan Touch,* that was published in 1998. He found an improbable fascination in the British social hierarchy – it tickled his sense of the bizarre. One past pupil describes him thus: 'He was a complete all-rounder. Honest to a fault, actor, comic, buffoon, musician, literature maniac, and true sportsman.'

Jim McAleese with his son

Jill was a marvellous riding teacher who possessed a profound under-standing of children. She returned in 1980 to look after the riders for another four years. It was a surprising anomaly of the riding teacher's job specification at Headfort for many years that she was required to relieve the Matron on two nights a week. Jill was a great favourite on these occasions but, when children misbehaved, they were given her 'SS treatment'; this stood for 'shovelling shit' and involved spending their afternoon cleaning Headfort's Augean stables. The 'Jillkhana' was an eagerly awaited event each Summer Term.

An evening spent in the McAleese household would replenish the spirits for a long while. They were avid members of the 'Dig it and Dung it Society' and Jim wrote the recitative for the Society's anthem that was sung (ir)rever-ently to the air of 'The Bold Thady Quill' at each of the Society's events. An item from the 2001 AGM reads, 'There is a long roll of bereavements this winter, including Echiums, Escalonias... and Fuschias. Members remember the list of the fallen. We hope that we may be re-united in the great garden in the sky.'

Jill McAleese with Lynn Temple at Two Old Farts' 130th birthday party
(Jim's seventieth, the author's sixtieth) at Headfort in 2000.

A tree was planted to commemorate each of them when they died, much too soon, in the early 2000s; one tree flourishes on the fringe of the games field near the long-jump pit and the other on the south lawn. Jim and Jill are sorely missed throughout the Royal County and at Headfort in particular.

PAT SHERLOCK taught riding on two occasions, firstly in the 1960s and then for a second term from 1972. She was a knowledgeable horsewoman and enthusiastic teacher. The three Misses Sherlock, Esmé, Letty and Pat, were spinster sisters who lived together near Carlanstown. They were archetypal

Ascendancy figures who knew all the 'right' people. In later years, these ladies would often kindly invite the author to luncheon during term time. Their company was delightful, but their guest had to return home on these occasions and de-fumigate himself before afternoon classes, because each of the three old biddies would light a new cigarette virtually before the previous weed had been puffed into oblivion.

VIVIENNE POTTERTON was the Headmaster's secretary in the 1960s. She too had to perform the Matron's duties two nights a week; and she was expected to teach scripture, coach hockey and eat with the children.

PETER ARMSTRONG taught French during the second half of the 1960s and, together with David Gamble, introduced the notion of annual plays. He later transferred to Rockport.

Three junior mistresses, TERESA 'TITS' McCORMACK, EDIE THOMPSON and VALERIE HILL worked during the 1960s. Miss McCormack was quite commanding; Miss Thompson was mild-mannered and rather nervous; and Miss Hill was a 'progressive': she taught knitting and liked to have the children sit around her in a ring while she read to them – they certainly ran rings around her.

Another important figure was DR PADDY BRANGAN who visited the School regularly, prescribing potions, suturing wounds, burning verrucas and injecting young bodies with chemicals in a manner that became increasingly shaky as age enfeebled him. Tall and thin, he was a charming, cultured man and an expert in oriental artefacts. He was a close friend of David Wild and, both before and after David's retirement, he would sometimes stay behind for a glass of whisky when he had treated his patients.

A well-known racing journalist who was a pupil at the time writes of the flow of teachers who populated the School in the 1960s, 'Other characters came and went, some of their own volition, others booted or hounded out; habitual prep-school chancers of the *Decline and Fall* type: a few endearing eccentrics, several splendid incompetents, one or two monsters.'

An unusual evening

Dr Brangan had to execute an unusual duty one evening in the late 1950s when Lord Headfort held an exotic birthday party for his first wife, Liz Nall-Cain, daughter of the Second Baron Brocket. He had bought her a boat, a substantial vessel designed for cruising on the wide midland lakes. However after a few drinks had been consumed, this boat was designated the 'Flagship of the Headfort Navy' and His Lordship determined to launch it in the tributary of the River Blackwater on the south side of the house, near the small island where several of his ancestors are buried. For this purpose Captain Nigel Naper of Loughcrew, a father and subsequently grandfather of Headfort children, was appointed Admiral of the Fleet; several of the outdoor staff were immediately promoted to the rank of Midshipman and ordered to convey the vessel to the appointed launching pad. The entire party, comprising the bulk of 'the quality' of County Meath, sallied forth en masse towards the river for the formal launching of the craft by the breaking of a bottle of champagne over her bow by the birthday girl, Lady Headfort.

Jack Sweetman and Jim McAleese witnessed some of the bizarre antics that took place on that extraordinary evening, and Lord Headfort visited Bill Stuart-Mills's house, carrying a gun, and tried in vain to induce him to join the gathering. Lord Headfort barked hysterical commands; 'officers' and guests fell into the river, for the ship was far too large to be manhandled into the Blackwater. Captain Naper initially played along with the lunacy (one assumes that the moon was full that night) and perhaps even encouraged it, but he gradually realized that the occasion was moving beyond a joke and indeed degenerating into something thoroughly dangerous. He tried to extricate himself from the role to which he had been assigned, but Lord Headfort branded him 'a deserter' and ordered that he be shot on sight. It is alleged that Lord Headfort captured him on the avenue and held him at gunpoint. His Lordship was partial to arresting people: it is even said that on one occasion he arraigned a set of Headfort parents who were returning their child to School, at a time when he wished to remove the School from his estate.

As the party descended into utter turmoil that evening, Dr Brangan, who was among the guests, followed the Supreme Commander throughout the campaign and eventually took the opportunity to sedate him with a needle that contained a fairly potent brew. The Sixth Marquis disappeared for a period of rest and recovery.

A more serious incident was alleged in August 1965 when Lord Headfort was escorted from the Scilly Isles by police, after what was reported by *The Daily Telegraph* as an abortive attempt to murder the British Prime Minister, Harold Wilson. A waiter called Ray Youngman who was working at the Atlantic Hotel in St Mary's, the largest of the Scilly Isles, told police that he had been approached by 'a tall, sandy-haired man' who had asked to be rowed out to the uninhabited island of Samson. On the way, the man grilled Youngman about his political views. 'He asked me if I could use hand guns and said he had a .38 revolver which he would bring with him the following day for me to practise with on the island,' Youngman told *The Daily Telegraph*. 'After referring to the Prime Minister and asking if I thought Britain was safe in his hands, he wanted to know if I would kill for a fee. He asked if I would kill the Prime Minister without question. I said I would if the money was right.' Youngman claimed that he agreed to work for him and was given £5 on account.

But Youngman soon got cold feet and decided to inform the police about his passenger's 'strange proposals'. Shortly afterwards the police escorted the Marquis from the Scilly Isles, taking him to St Lawrence's Hospital, Bodmin, whence he was later discharged. The following day, from his home in Ireland, Headfort denied Youngman's account of the incident, although he admitted to hiring the boat. His neighbours in Kells described how Headfort, wearing a Stetson, had once fired three blanks into the ceiling of a local pub during a party. 'No one takes much notice because he is known for his practical jokes,' one said. 'The Marquis is regarded as a crack shot.'

The author never really regarded Michael Headfort as dangerous; however, when fuelled with alcohol and beset by his demons, he was – how you say in English? – unreliable.

A digression

The Sixth Marquis of Headfort's half-brother's grandmother created 'The Ashes' that have been contested by English and Australian cricket teams for 130 years.

Elizabeth Clarke, Headfort's first riding mistress, was the sister of Major Sir Rupert William John Clarke, AM, MBE, Third Baronet of Rupertswood, a title to which he succeeded at the age of seven, upon the death of his father on Christmas Day 1926. He was Michael Headfort's half-brother. Born in Sydney, Sir Rupert became a distinguished soldier, pastoralist, businessman and philanthropist. When his widowed mother married Terence, Fifth Marquis of Headfort, in 1928, the young Rupert came to England and excelled, both scholastically and athletically, at Eton and Magdalen College, Oxford. In 1940 he was commissioned in The Irish Guards, and the following year was appointed Aide de Camp to General Earl Alexander of Tunis, while Alexander was General Officer Commanding, Burma. He remained with Alexander in the campaign to push Rommel's forces out of North Africa and, subsequently, in the invasion of Sicily and the long slog up through Italy. He was awarded the MBE and mentioned in despatches.

When King George VI visited the troops, Clarke was given the task of finding a bath for him. Having 'liberated' one, he placed it under some trees near HM's caravan, fetched hot water from the cookhouse and, knocking on the door, announced, 'Your Majesty, the bath is ready.' He subsequently received a rocket in the Mess because the King had found olive leaves in the water.

After the war Sir Rupert returned to Australia and, since Rupertswood, the original family seat, had been sold in the 1920s, he restored another mansion, Bolinda Vale in Victoria, where he entertained on a grand scale. Gregory Peck, Rex Harrison and Showa, the Emperor of Japan, were among his houseguests. His business interests were expansive and he held director-ships in many of Australia's most prominent international companies. In 1976 he became the Honorary Consul-General for Monaco. He received the *Legion d'Honneur* from President Mitterand in recognition of the assistance that he had given France over many years. He was also commemorated by the Melbourne Racing Club, in the naming of the Rupert Clarke Stand at Caul-field in March 1991. Honoured both by Australia and England, Sir Rupert died in 2005 at the age of eighty-five.

Sir Rupert's grandfather, Sir William Clarke, was created a baronet by Queen Victoria, the only Australian-born man to be so honoured. The baron-etcy of Rupertswood is the solitary, active, hereditary title in an Australian family. As President of the Melbourne Cricket Club, he took his family to England in 1882 to watch the Australian team, led by Billy Murdoch, defeat England, under the captaincy of A.N. (Monkey) Hornby, by just seven runs at the Kennington Oval in London in the sole Test Match of that summer. Their victory was achieved, despite the presence in the England team of Dr W.G. Grace, largely due to the Australian fast bowler, Fred 'The Demon' Spofforth, who captured fourteen wickets for ninety runs in the match. The shock of England being defeated by a colonial side for the first time on home soil prompted *The Sporting Times* to publish a mock obituary of the death of English cricket: 'In affectionate remembrance of English cricket which died at The Oval on 29th August, 1882. The body will be cremated and the Ashes taken to Australia.' This much is well known: what follows is not.

Sir William Clarke and his family returned to Australia on the same ship as the 1882–3 English touring party and invited the eight amateurs amongst them to spend Christmas with him at his fifty-room palatial mansion, named Rupertswood after his eldest son, at Sunbury near Melbourne. The Clarkes entertained lavishly at Rupertswood, their guests arriving in their hundreds by train at his private railway platform. Lady Clarke recorded that on 24 December a social cricket match was played against a local side, comprising guests and workmen of the Rupertswood estate, followed by a grand dinner and dancing in the impressive ballroom. Naturally the English team won the match and, as a congratulatory gesture, Lady Clarke and Miss Florence Morphy, a close friend and music teacher to the Clarke children, hit upon the notion of arranging for a cricketing item – it chanced to be a bail – to be burned, and its ashes placed in a small, ceramic urn that would then be presented light-heartedly to Ivo Bligh (later Eighth Earl of Darnley), the English captain, as a personal memento of his visit. Perhaps the butler and housemaids were summoned to fabricate this bijou and insert it in the urn that may have previously contained perfume, and was taken from one of the ladies' dressing tables. There was almost certainly a flirtatious element to Miss Morphy's participation in the whimsy, because she and Bligh became engaged during the tour, and in 1884 he returned to Australia to marry her at St Mary's church, Sunbury. The wedding reception was held at Rupertswood and Sir William Clarke gave the bride away. Upon Darnley's death in 1927, his widow, Florence, Countess of Darnley, presented the urn to the MCC, in whose museum at Lord's it has resided ever since, whichsoever country technically 'holds the Ashes'.

The Bligh family had a seat in County Meath. One of them, John Bligh, First Earl of Darnley, represented Athboy in the Irish House of Commons from 1709 until 1721. Ivo Bligh's father, John Stewart Bligh, Sixth Earl of Darnley, played once for the Gentlemen of Kent in 1848 and was later President of the MCC. He died at Athboy in 1896 and was briefly succeeded by Ivo's elder brother, Lord Clifton, who also played first-class cricket.

More staff

In the late years of his Headmastership David Wild had two reliable secretaries in LORNA SHIER (1968–72) and PAMELA POTTERTON (1974–9). Pamela overlapped with the next Headmaster for his first two years in office and led him patiently into his new responsibilities. She was a fine pianist and organist and taught music in the School.

Later characters include LIEUTENANT-COLONEL ROBERT GOING, a kindly man who became the School's only male riding teacher; HAZEL ANAG-NOSTARAS, a colourful art teacher, riding mistress and welcoming hostess who arrived in 1973, and MARY LEFTWICH, sister to Kate Stuart-Mills, who was the School's first wardrobe mistress. A perfectionist, Miss Leftwich had worked with the BBC and dressed some of the most distinguished actors of her day. DOROTHY BREWSTER – known as 'Tick, Tock' because of her bulky hearing aid that was powered by a battery worn in her breast pocket, with cables heading earwards – was a much-loved Matron during the 1960s. She was a gentle, kindly lady who was inclined to take boys at face-value, being ever willing to sign the 'off-games' book for a boy who was disinclined, rather than too ill, to disport himself on the field of play. She fought a long battle against multiple sclerosis with fortitude. JIM BRUNNOCK taught mathematics on a part-time basis during the early 1970s.

Television

Television was rarely condoned, but past pupils vividly remember watching the coronation of Queen Elizabeth II in the Ballroom, and also the funeral of Sir Winston Churchill. A past pupil recalls:

> At weekends we were allowed to watch TV, BBC being Boss Wild's channel of choice – definitely not RTE. *Sooty and Sweep*, *Dixon of Dock Green* ('Evenin' All'), *The Three Musketeers* (with the dashing Jeremy Brett as d'Artagnan and Berlioz's 'Symphonie Fantastique' as the musical introduction), the dramatization of *Kidnapped* by R.L. Stevenson – wonderful stuff.

An excerpt from a letter to parents from the Headmaster, dated 20 December 1957, reads as follows:

> I have until very recently been against television in schools. It now seems to me that television can be very useful in broadening a boy's outlook and general knowledge, and that this may particularly be the case in Ireland, where boys are brought up remote from the main stream of affairs. I have, therefore, had a set installed, but the use of this will be controlled, and it will not normally be available for entertainment, which is something that, in this age, more than ever, boys must learn to provide for themselves.

County cricket

On certain Sunday afternoons during the summer months, the Meath County Cricket Club would play matches on the Headfort square. In 1970 the fixture list contained no fewer than thirteen matches against other counties, clubs and schools. That year the Marquis of Headfort was the Patron of the Club and David Wild the President. The County side comprised schoolmasters, farmers and other local enthusiasts. It was they who presented the School with the scorebox that still embellishes the games field. The scorebox was renovated in 2010. In later years many past pupils became 'County cricketers' – on one occasion, as many as eight played in a single match. Sadly, the Club barely survives today, although it reconstitutes itself to challenge occasional touring sides.

With apologies to John Masefield:

> Though wayward Time be changeful as Man's Will,
> We have the scorebox on the Headfort Oval still;
> And still the Pigeon Wood adorns the farther end,
> And still the sun shines and the rain descends.

Science laboratory

In 1966 the science laboratory was built in the old stable under the library. For the past few years there had been copious discussion at IAPS meetings about the introduction of this subject into the prep school curriculum.

Locusts in the laboratory

DAVID GAMBLE was Headfort's first science master: he is described as portly, pompous, but pleasant, and a good teacher. He and Peter Armstrong were relatively young and, according to one past pupil, they 'brought a bit of life to the place'. He also had a large drum kit that the boys were occasionally permitted to bash. He emigrated to Australia, and ARCHDEACON GIFF, who apparently was not an exemplar of all the Christian virtues, succeeded him. Science became a Common Entrance subject a few years later.

Work in the laboratory

Staff of the early '70s

In the early 1970s four prominent Headfort figures were appointed: JOHN LEYDEN, AMANDA LEYDEN (née KELSO), VICTOR DE RAEYMAEKER and PETER BAMFORD.

John Leyden, a Welshman and Oxford graduate, taught English, mathematics and, later, Latin; also scripture to the Roman Catholics. He is the consummately versatile prep school master who can turn his hand to anything. For many years he assembled the teaching timetable and the duty roster, as well as writing a booklet of procedures for the benefit of new staff. Later he was to be appointed Senior Master. Amanda, his wife, is a specialist at teaching children to read. Many a Headfort pupil over the years owes her a debt of gratitude for getting him or her up to standard in terms of literacy. It was significant that no stigma attached to a pupil who took 'extra reading': rather, it was something that was looked forward to. The Leydens are the only members of staff who have traversed all three eras of Headfort's history, such is their teaching longevity.

Victor de Raeymaeker, a Belgian citizen, gave twenty years of his life to Headfort from 1972. He was a magnificent teacher of French and a wise and cultured man. When he first arrived at the School, he was bemused by Headfort customs. Watching boys walk down the classroom corridor, he could not

Victor de Raeymaeker's representation of Brian Lara

'Il neige, il pleut'

understand why they would suddenly whirl their arms over their shoulders in a violent, cascading motion (he had yet to discover cricket). He gradually grew accustomed to the idiosyncrasies and the patois of the place. He was a brilliant cartoonist: he adorned the walls of the Music Room and the Remedial Room with magnificent caricatures of classical musicians, in the one case, and aids to spelling, in the other. He kept a library of French literature and, on the last night of term, every child would take to bed a copy of *Asterix* or *Tintin*. The School was weakened when he returned to his native Bruges in 1992.

Victor de Raeymaeker

Peter Bamford was a native of Kells. He served in the war and subsequently worked for an oil firm in Kuwait. In his middle years he returned home and Mr Wild appointed him to teach science. He was not a qualified scientist, but a practical one, and he was dynamic in the classroom.

Peter Bamford

With prominent, bushy eyebrows and booming, plummy voice, he enthused the children with a love for his subject. The laboratory was a treasure trove – a source of enlightenment for children and visiting parents. Every square inch of shelving and wall space was decorated with scientific drawings or samples; children would bring hideous specimens – snakes, millipedes and worse – to add to the collection; and the slides that he drew for his overhead projector were works of art. One summer term in the mid-1970s he despatched children all around the estate on their bicycles, armed with pedometers and instructions to measure distances between remote landmarks. Armed with these rather imprecise dimensions, he painted a fine, illustrated map of the estate on the wall of Fourth Form that was on the bottom corridor in those days. When that room subsequently became a girls' dormitory, the walls required redecorating, but the map was faithfully preserved.

Another teacher who served during the latter part of Mr Wild's tenure was his brother, Bill. THE REV. MAJOR WILD had been a naval chaplain and, despite having suffered a stroke that impaired his mobility, he taught Latin to beginners. Affectionately known as 'Chiefy', he was the butt of numerous pranks; indeed, demonic children would oftimes absent themselves from his classroom through the window that led into the moat, returning in time to hand in their blank exercise books at the end of class. He would rarely deign to notice but, when he did, a volcano would erupt.

JULIET LONG was appointed in the early '70s and served as Matron for six years. A friendly, capable person, she ruled her domain from the Sewing Room, her 'engine room' at the top of the house, where members of staff were welcome to take coffee as she repaired children's clothes after her charges had retired for the night. On evenings when a boy had washed his hair, he would return to the Sewing Room and lie on the floor in front of a two-bar electric fire until his hair was dry. One wonders what the Health and Safety people would think of such a procedure today.

THE REV. VICTOR CRAWFORD taught mathematics in the early 1970s and also coached Top Game hockey. Having been a good player himself, he was assiduous in penalizing every minor infringement which, at schoolboy level, meant that there was little continuity to the game. The story has it that some boys tried to claim an entry for him in *The Guinness Book of Records* as the umpire who had blown his whistle the most times in a single match.

In the subterranean regions of the building, sway was held by those spicily and herbaceously named ladies, VIOLET PEPPER and MONA FENNELL. They provided solid institutional fare. When Mrs Pepper retired, she was replaced by ANNA GILLIC who was renowned for her 'seed cake' that was greedily demolished at break. They all rendered valuable service over a number of years. EDDIE LITTLE worked under Mrs Gillic for a while and then assumed the senior mantle. He was a loyal servant. A past pupil recalls that he sometimes chased errant pupils down the corridor, hurling obscenities at them, and that he harboured designs upon a lady member of the teaching staff.

JOHNNY GRIMES tended the School's part of the estate for a quarter of a century. He began at the age of fourteen, assisting Willy and Tommy in the kitchen garden, but graduated to the role of groundsman and general factotum. He was a loyal, hard-working colleague who was highly regarded by everybody. JOSIE HORAN taught carpentry and also ventured onto the roof of the house every week to clear leaves from the gutter. This latter activity was worrying because he was not always entirely stable on his feet, having enjoyed a tincture or three the previous evening. He worked for Lord Headfort as well as for the School, and was the most obliging of men.

NAN BYRNE, the tall, white-haired lady who worked in a menial capacity at Headfort for a long time, cleaning dormitories and performing any other task that presented itself, was a sensitive person of great charm. She also taught swimming for many years. During the holidays she travelled the world, visiting her far-flung children. When Nan Byrne retired, SUE PHILLIPS taught swimming. In those days swimming lessons were compulsory for all children until they had proven their ability to complete two lengths of the pool, whereafter lessons became optional. SHEELIN STEPHENSON was Housekeeper for a short period in the early 1970s.

The racing journalist again: 'The Headfort of the '60s still had a curiously colonial air, out of tune with its Irish surroundings, and people were only half-joking when they said that Wild saw it as an outpost of Empire.'

Company structure

From the beginning, the School existed as a tenant of the family company, Headfort Estate. During Mr Wild's Headmastership there was a dual structure of management. The School was a limited company, the principal shareholder being Lord Headfort himself. The Board of Directors, comprising Lord Headfort, his elderly uncle Lord William Taylour, the Headmaster, an accountant and a solicitor, convened just once a year to approve the accounts. There was also a Board of Governors, a body that consisted principally of titled gentlemen. Their names, appearing prominently on the inside cover of the School prospectus, were supposed to lend colour to this seat of learning. They appeared for luncheon with Mr Wild once a year during the Summer Term and afterwards graced the playing fields, bestowing their benison ubiquitously. BILL NEWPORT was the meticulous Company Secretary for a couple of decades, both in David Wild's time and also his successor's.

A stalwart of the School throughout its history was SIR RICHARD MUSGRAVE. His father, Sir Christopher, at one time rented Headfort Court; he and Lady Musgrave took a keen interest in the School. Later Dick and his wife Maria became fervent supporters and sent three of their children to Headfort.

Sir Richard frequently used to come to lunch in the School dining room and afterwards played ping-pong with the boys or bowled to them in the nets, according to the season. He had a delightful rapport with children and was a hugely popular visitor. A past pupil, perhaps Snodgrass by name, recalls how one day, while sitting next to the Headmaster at lunch, Sir Richard inquired,

'Which one is Snodgrass?' The said Snodgrass was duly identified and rapidly acquired the hue of a beetroot when Sir Richard roared down the table, 'Have your parents fixed that bloody hole in their roof yet?' He then regaled the entire table – and neighbouring tables that had grown silent in order to listen – with the tale of how he had stayed with the Snodgrasses when torrential rain had cascaded through their roof and ceiling; he claimed that he had had to wear his mackintosh all night long. Young Master Snodgrass emphasizes that there was a degree of hyperbole (a word that he had probably recently learnt) to Sir Richard's account.

He also recalls, 'My mother still pales visibly thirty years on when she recalls the time her car broke down at Headfort and you gallantly towed her car to Dublin … at sixty mph.'

Religion

During the Early Years, Headfort was a predominantly Protestant (Church of Ireland) foundation, despite the Headfort family being Roman Catholic. The first prospectus stated categorically 'RELIGION. Headfort is a Protestant School. Religious Instruction is a daily feature of the Curriculum.' David Wild himself was a fervent Christian. CANON AIDAN OLDEN, the rector of Kells, was a personal friend of Mr Wild. He was a compassionate man and a fine orator. He would visit the School weekly to rehearse the Church Choir that sang in St Columba's Church every Sunday. At the end of each Summer Term the soi-disant 'Headfort School Service' was held in the church, at which pupils would read the lessons, provide the music and even practise their campanological skills, before the advent of electronic bell-ringing technology much later. These services were moving occasions, focussing especially upon those who were leaving Headfort that year; however, as the years rolled by, the School Service became really half a School Service as more Roman Catholic children populated the School; they were not included in this celebration of their years at Headfort.

The Church Choir was not universally popular. Although membership was nominally voluntary, in practice it was difficult to effect one's egress. Boys would use the pretext of a sore throat to croak the hymns a semi-tone flat in the hope of persuading the Canon that their voices were breaking. One boy achieved exodus in an unusual way: he was expelled from the choir for scratching his ear during a service. He performed this simian manoeuvre rather publicly by extending his right arm over his head to reach his left lobe. The action was deemed forgivable in the case of even a higher primate, but it was certainly not befitting a Headfort boy.

On one inauspicious occasion, when Mr Wild chanced to be away, the choir revolted. Behold, a spectacular revelation: the revolting leader, latterday Che Guevara, a boy of otherwise exemplary reputation, would one day, some thirty years later, become Headmaster of Headfort School.

If one sat in the Church of Ireland choir stalls, one commanded a grandstand view of the congregation processing up the aisle to take their seats. The vision could be spectacular, even competitive. The Marchioness of Headfort, a Protestant despite her husband being Roman Catholic, naturally outshone all others in terms of righteousness, splendour and eminence. She was often accompanied by a companion or a secretary, walking a few respectful paces behind her. In close competition followed David Wild, exuding gravitas with his slow, dignified gait. Captain and Mrs Nicholson of Balrath favoured a measured pace, bestowing gracious serenity to left and right, their daughter Patricia trailing along behind.

In the 1950s Roman Catholics were served either a fried egg or else a piece of fish (the piece of Cod that passeth all understanding) at Friday lunchtime, instead of the universal late animal that their Protesting brethren consumed. Much inter-religious bartering was conducted, according to pupils' gastronomic preferences that were not governed exclusively along doctrinaire lines.

There was a small troop of Presbyterians who attended their own church once or twice a month. Periodically they were entertained royally to lunch or tea by local farmer Jimmy Wilson. Wilson also used to take parties of boys to Bettystown on the County Meath coast. He would cast bunches of bananas off a cliff into the sea and the children would swim far out to claim them.

There was ever the suspicion of a degree of religious bias at Headfort. Everybody used to walk to church on Sunday mornings, but it seemed to many to be more than a coincidence that the Protestants were generally given a lift home after the service, whereas the Catholics often had to trudge. However, in one period there was a set of Catholic twins whose father owned a Rolls-Royce and this capacious vehicle would sometimes devour a shoal of boys and return them to School in style; otherwise, if fortunate, they might be scooped up in Moller's or Rudd's horsebox. Another ploy was to feign illness in church. The art was to persuade Mr de Raeymaeker or Mr Leyden that one of their number was about to faint. If either of these kind gentlemen showed the slightest trace of compassion, the 'fainting one' would surely be transported home by vehicle, accompanied by his numerous solicitous 'nurses'.

On more than one occasion the Church Choir (as opposed to the all-embracing School Choir) was invited to perform on national television. A coach would escort the choristers to the RTE studios in Donnybrook; everybody would receive the attention of make-up artists, and Morning Prayer would commence. Boys, well rehearsed, would read the lessons quite beautifully and the Choir sang the anthems and led the hymns.

Harvest Thanksgiving was a special event in St Columba's Church. Headfort generally supplied a member of the Church Vestry and he or she – generally she – would decorate the church with sheaves of corn, baskets of apples and vegetables from the kitchen garden and rhododendrons from the estate. The choir, comprising Headfort pupils, plus one or two tone-deaf, elderly gentlemen and a couple of trilling ladies, would sing lustily. A past pupil recalls: 'One middle-aged lady of the choir who had a loud, coarse soprano voice sang the psalms with a careless abandon, producing a sound like that of a screeching banshee.' Everybody would pray for the rich to be impoverished, the proud to be humbled and the mighty to be brought low. Which was probably not really what they wanted.

In later years, the religion of a new pupil was not always clearly established. One boy who had never previously entered a church undertook a little research before declaring his denomination. He discovered that the Protestant church involved a walk of one and a half miles, whereas the Catholic church was a mere one and a quarter miles distant. He elected to associate himself with Rome.

A past pupil tells of how he was surprised, while kneeling at the altar during his confirmation service, to hear his friend and neighbour, upon being asked by the Bishop, 'Do you renounce the devil and all his ways?' reply, 'I shall give the matter some thought, Your Grace.'

On the way back to School, a visit to McCarthy's was de rigueur. Mr and Mrs McCarthy ran an old-fashioned sweet shop in Farrell Street; the Headfort trade was an important source of their revenue. Their shelves contained large glass jars full of bonbons, Cleeves toffees, mint humbugs, boiled sweets, love hearts, sugar mice, sherbet lemon, lollipops and jelly babies. Mr or Mrs McCarthy would measure out and weigh the delicacies before pouring them into small brown paper bags. The secret was to position oneself at the rear of the 'crocodile' upon leaving the church; drop off the end of the line, dive into the shop and rapidly transact one's business before sprinting to rejoin the peleton, hopefully without detection by the master on duty. The McCarthys were fond of children and they would often add a gobstopper into the bag of a small boy who looked as though he were unhappy at the prospect of returning to school.

Letter writing

In the days before visiting became more common, letter writing was an important lifeline with home. After breakfast on Sundays the children would clamber up the stairs to their classrooms where the master on duty wrote a list of suggested topics on the blackboard. Each child would produce a first draft and present it to the master for inspection to ensure that it was of sufficient length and quality.

These letters were fairly stereotypical. Little boys tend not to write 'an heir was born to…' to indicate the birth of a baby, unless they are copying it from somewhere. Food was a common theme that found its way into most letters. The Sunday letter was a formal, approved School document but, if a child wanted to write a letter that was entirely private, he was at liberty to do so at any other time of the week.

'An heir was born'

The importance of food

Pigs!

David Wild devised an ingenious system for handling wastage from the kitchen. Each term he would acquire a couple of bonhams from the local butcher and appoint two 'pig boys' to serve as their custodians. Their duty was to visit the kitchen after each meal and carry the slops out to the pigsty that was situated in the stable yard. They were required to keep the porcine quarters pristine. At the end of term the 'improving' piglets were sold back to the butcher and the pig boys were given any profit that accrued. This splendid exercise in animal husbandry came to an end in the late 1970s when the butcher lost interest in the project.

Exeats

In the early days there were few opportunities for children to escape the School premises. The weekends were very much school days. Parents might take their children out every third Sunday, but not until after Church (a quarter to twelve for Catholics: half past twelve for Protestants, if the sermon was brief) and they must be returned to School by six o'clock. For those parents who travelled from the distant ends of the country it was a very short time to spend with their children.

Parents who lived remotely from the School frequently wished to spend the night nearby. The Park Hotel, Virginia, formerly the Headfort hunting lodge, became a favourite haunt for visiting families at weekends. Expertly managed by Mrs Helen McDonnell, whose son became a Headfort pupil, the Park is merely a dozen miles from Headfort. A liberal sprinkling of Headfort families used to enjoy lavish Sunday luncheons in the Park's attractive dining room with Jack Yeats's paintings adorning the walls.

Plague

During the 1950s and '60s, and to a lesser extent into the '70s, Headfort was visited with plague most winter terms. David Wild would write to parents advising that there were cases of scarlatina, measles, german measles, whooping cough, chickenpox or mumps and that accordingly the School was in quarantine. Sometimes up to seventy children would be in bed at the same time and visits from parents were halted. These were hard times for the Matrons in particular, but also for other members of staff who might be feeling below par themselves.

```
FROM THE HEADMASTER
                                        Headfort,
                                           Kells,
                                              Co. Meath.

                                 3rd March, 1966.

     We have seventeen cases of influenza in the school and are
therefore returning to purdah.  There will be no more visiting
this term.

                                              D. P. W.
```

Riding upon horseback

Throughout the School's history, horse riding has been a popular, extracurricular activity available to pupils. Meath is a 'horsey' county: many of the traditional Headfort families have been involved in racing and training, and there have been several wonderful riding teachers over the years.

From the outset, children were allowed to bring their ponies to School: ponies were kept in livery at Headfort on the understanding that other children might also ride them at the riding teacher's discretion. Virtually all of the girls, and many of the boys, have been enthusiastic riders. To bring one's pony to Headfort meant that a child would have a little bit of home with her at School. She could visit her pony during free time and pamper him. Each pony was revered in much the same way as Caligula's stallion, Incitatus. The dotty Emperor was so extravagantly fond of Incitatus that he appointed him a senator and nominated him for Consul. The animal had his own house where he lived with his wife, the mare Penelope, attended by a team of servants and grooms; he had a marble bedroom and an ivory manger with a golden bucket to drink from. Whenever he won a race, Incitatus would dine at the Emperor's table. Headfort ponies are granted almost similar status by their adoring owners.

A girl's best friend

In the winter terms the more proficient riders were taken for a day's hunting, and the annual gymkhana in the summer has always been a key day in the School's equestrian calendar. It remains as popular today as ever.

'Archbishop Desmond Tutu' at the Headfort Gymkhana

One day in January 1962 the trainer Tom Dreaper, whose son was a pupil at the time, met Jack Sweetman at Navan races; during the conversation, Jack suggested that Dreaper's favourite, Kerforo, ought to win the next race. When they parted, Dreaper told him that he was not sure about Kerforo, but that he had another horse in the race that would be a useful performer in the fullness of time and might be a good each-way bet that day. The animal's name was Arkle and it won easily for Jack at twenty to one. A year later Arkle won the first of his three Cheltenham Gold Cups. Kerforo won the 1962 Irish Grand National.

5. WICKED CHILDREN!

Pheasant hunting – Overseas adventures: chess, a second Daniel, squash

Pheasant hunting

Many past pupils' anecdotes concern their interaction in the woods with pheasants.

Lord Headfort bred pheasants and held regular shoots during the season. The keeper, Sam Holt, a master of his trade, fed these birds a surfeit of grain. Thus, the brave, heavily camouflaged warriors were enabled to massacre the beautiful creatures in their hundreds; they were so bloated (the birds, not necessarily the warriors) that they could scarcely leave the ground (the latter certainly couldn't). Sometimes the marksmen would shoot the telephone cables in error; on one occasion the telecommunications people refused to repair the lines because they claimed, quite reasonably, that they would be shot again. Children would discover spent cartridges – and occasionally live ones – around the estate and, if they were fortunate, they might find the body of a pheasant that the dogs had missed.

Sunday mornings on shoot days were devoted to the slaughter of duck on the island. A good day's haul might yield 400 pheasant and between 150 and 200 duck between the eight guns, although the duck had to be protected to some extent. The Emperor Claudius considered that the slaughter of 300 lions and 100 bears in the amphitheatre at Rome constituted a successful games that would propitiate the gods.

A past pupil from Botswana recalls how Mr Bamford would sometimes take a carload of boys on a 'pheasant hunt'. They would hare around the minor roads surrounding the estate on shoot days and, when an exhausted bird appeared on the horizon, Mr Bamford would accelerate hard and try to 'wing' the wretched creature. He would screech to a halt, boys would dive out of all the doors, scoop up the bird in its final agony, throw it into the boot and then they would make their escape before being intercepted by the fearsome Sam Holt. The boys would then share the ill-gotten birds. In the final class of the Summer Term Peter Bamford would bring into the classroom his Gurkha uniform that he used to wear in the North African campaign. His fearsome, Nepalese kukri was a weapon not to be trifled with. He had a 'Desert Rat' insignia on his yellow Ford Escort (actually, so this informant declares, it was a gerbil).

This same pupil – let us call him Howley – was very proud of a handsome new pair of desert boots. Little boys can be cussed creatures and it became a source of amusement to a few of his form-mates to cast mud upon the elegant footwear. One day, while they were playing, illegally, in the woods, Howley became displeased and lashed out at the perpetrators. The following morning at Catholic prayers (prayers were segregrated in those days) Mr Leyden exhorted divine assistance as follows: 'Lord, we beseech thee, bring peace in Northern Ireland, an end to famine in Africa and give protection to Howley's holy desert boots.' There were of course howls of laughter and the issue was defused.

The woods were strictly out of bounds. Nevertheless, Poddles major and a brave associate found themselves in the middle of the woods one day while a shoot was in progress. Lo! A winged pheasant (also, of course, wingèd) dropped to earth before them. It squawked and struggled. What should they do? They decided that the humane response would be to put the wretched bird out of its misery – but how? Each little boy made an attempt at neck-wringing, but they were not proficient in the art. All the while the big guns were firing, and shrapnel – well, shot perhaps – was falling through the trees upon them. The trenches in World War I were as nothing compared to the plight in which these boys found themselves. Headfort pupils are taught to be resourceful and so they resolved that death by drowning had now become the fitting end for the afflicted one. Schoolboys of that era, like good boy scouts, always carried string and a penknife in their pockets; they took it in turns, like a pair of nervous thurifers, to carry the struggling victim as they fought their way through the battlefield to the nearest river, where they attached a large millstone to the already somewhat mauled neck and cast the poor fowl into the depths. By now they were besmirched in gore, and whom should they meet on their way back to the School, but Mr Wild? They quaked with fear, expecting that their fate would be only marginally less extreme than that of the pheasant. However Mr Wild, seeing the blood about their bodies, was entirely solicitous:

'My poor boys,' quoth he; 'whatever has befallen you?'

'Sorry, Sir, we fell, while playing in the forts.'

'Dear me. Go and wash yourselves and then let Matron check that you are all right.'

A narrow escape, indeed. Nowadays Poddles views the incident with some alarm, but declares that the only serious injury that befell him while at Headfort was when he was dropped by a teacher in the library.

Another past pupil recalls standing around a small fire in front of the mausoleum beyond the New Bridge during 'playtime', assisting his classmates to stuff a dead pheasant into a rusty old kettle, feathers and all. The bird was boiled: the result may not have satisfied the gourmet, but it certainly engendered lusty gourmandize and much merriment.

Rupert Bear was Captain of the School. He was a pillar of rectitude. Nobody had ever known him to break a School rule; however, when one grew to know him well, it became apparent that he was a supremely spirited, warm-hearted and courageous little boy. Bear used to bribe his father to travel the long journey from home to take him out for lunch with the promise of procuring a brace of pheasants for him. For the consideration of a few sweets, he would coerce a friend to assist him in the execution of his sophisticated technique that involved one boy hiding behind a tree and making pheasant-like noises, while disturbing the undergrowth in a seductive manner. At length, a gullible pheasant would approach timorously until it was within range of the second poacher who would stun it by pelting it with stones. The gruesome task completed, they would take the captured birds to a secret location and hang them for several days, such that they were suitably 'high' for father's visit. On one occasion, shortly after Bear had left Headfort, he and his father came to stay. While their host's back was turned, the naughty Bear took his father poaching. They had a successful mission but, just as they were about to leave, Lord Headfort came screeching across from the airfield in his private fire engine, with two boys hanging out of the side, ringing the bell at full volume, as though there were a national emergency. Lord Headfort expressed an interest in the van that Father Bear was driving and asked whether he might look inside the boot, 'just to see how large it is.' After much prevarication, the boot was opened to reveal a couple of brace of pheasants hanging in the back. 'Thought so,' muttered His Lordship.

Mrs Agatha Plunckington-Bills was the mother of four pupils at the School. She was a great favourite at Headfort. A member of the Board of Directors, she was a colourful and artistic lady with a sense of style. One weekend she came to collect her youngest son, Aurelius. She chanced to notice a pheasant pecking grain near the back of her car. She nonchalantly reached down, wrung its neck and popped it into the boot. 'Mr Bills enjoys a pheasant for his supper now and then,' she told the admiring group of small boys who were mesmerized by her daring.

Overseas adventures
CHESS

In the late 1970s the School used to study the game of chess analytically, and on three occasions between 1976 and 1978 Headfort's leading 'grandmasters' travelled to England for a week in the author's car during the Easter holidays to participate in the IAPS Chess Congress. The team of five players would cram into the ancient Renault 8 and sail across the Irish Sea to the Dragon School, Oxford on two occasions, and Dean Close School in Cheltenham on another. The competition was challenging: Colet Court (the St Paul's prep school), Danes Hill and Brentwood were amongst those schools that took their chess very seriously, but the Irish boys were well prepared. In 1976 Headfort won the coveted Hodgson Cup, the winning team prize, from among the twenty-three schools that were competing; our two leading players finished third and fourth individually in a field of 124 players, and the other three members of the team lent noble support, ranking well up the field. The following year, our champion was actually joint winner of the individual award from among 129 boys – one of Headfort's most remarkable accomplishments. In 1977 and 1978 he did not lose a single game in the Congress; in 1978 he came second, just half a point behind the winner who was a member of the British junior squad. These two drew their individual encounter. Two of those who played in the Congress during those years subsequently became International Grandmasters.

Chess has a language all of its own. At that time parents might have heard their children cry out,

'Tee, hee! You've fallen for the Noah's Ark!' (a trap, first entered by Noah in a game on Mount Ararat some years ago) or,

Gormanston v Headfort chess match, 1976. The Irish Times demonstrates a finesse with the black pieces by the Headfort player.

'You shouldn't fianchetto in the Bogo-Indian, O Dumkopf' (the Bogo-Indian is a defensive system for Black, named after Ephraim Bogolyubov who suffered the indignity, at Hastings in 1922, of having three queens sacrificed against him in a game with Dr Alekhine. He resigned before Alekhine could promote a fourth pawn).

Alexander Pushkin once wrote to his wife, 'Thank you, Darling, for learning to play chess. It is an absolute necessity for any well-organized family.'

Those sorties included activities other than chess. Once the party watched a stirring performance of *A Midsummer Night's Dream* by the Royal Shakespeare Company at Stratford-upon-Avon, after spending the afternoon punting on the river. Once they attended a football match at Highbury between Arsenal and Leeds, a team supported rabidly by one of the delegates. This was an anxious occasion for the party leader: even in those days football crowds did not always practise drawing room decorum and so, like a mother hen, he gathered the five boys protectively about him and did not permit them to move out of his sight. They of course found the environment hilarious, and gleefully counted as 116 of the less couth supporters were rounded up by police – before the game had even started.

A SECOND DANIEL

Another year the Renault wended its way into the Windsor Safari Park that eventually closed in 1992. This was the stuff of adventure. After one valiant little boy, sadly no longer with us, was licked in the face by a giraffe in the Serengeti Zone, the group meandered into the lions' enclosure. Here the kings of the jungle were free to wander right up to the cars: indeed, one was so indelicate as to lift its enormous leg against the side window of the venerable vehicle, that was not entirely water-tight. 'We received a valuable biology lesson that day: that big cats pee backwards,' recalls one of the boys, several decades later.

Another of the boys in the jumble – jungle – in the back of the car (there were, of course, no seat belts) wanted to take photographs. The most advantageous location from which to focus one's camera was the front seat; this he sought to occupy. To this writer's undying horror, he suddenly noticed the back door of the car open and one of the boys emerge directly into the lions' den (well, enclosure) with a view to transferring to the passenger seat of the car. With a roar that would have impressed any lion, your correspondent swivelled around and snatched the errant boy savagely back into the car and attempted to close the door (a feat that was not simple because it was held together with wire). [One of the first ten boys to attend the author's prep school in 1892 was consumed by a lion on his father's Norfolk estate.]

He who escaped the lions that day is now a middle-aged gentleman with children of his own. He considers the most remarkable thing about those adventures was that the Renault transported the squad safely to and from Ireland.

SQUASH

On two occasions, in 1978 and 1982, Headfort contested the IAPS Squash tournament at Chelmsford in Essex. Many of the local boys wore T-shirts bearing the caption, 'Surrey Junior Squad' or 'Essex Junior Squad'. Why did Headfort not think to have 'Meath Junior Squad' T-shirts printed? The Irish team was not fully competitive with the top schools, but finished in a respectable upper-mid-field position. Heading home through the centre of Wales,

Accomplished play in the squash court

en route for Holyhead in the middle of a Sunday night, the party had been unable to find petrol for a hundred miles and, although the Renault would run on merely a sniff of the stuff, it was growing increasingly thirsty. In desperation, the car stopped at a filling station at about midnight. All was dark: not a soul abroad, not a light. The guilt-ridden driver prepared to knock on the door and plead a sob story, when his front seat passenger, a rare Captain of the School, piped up: 'You stay in the car, Sir. A child is more likely to arouse the sympathy of the petrol pump owner'. Out he hopped and bravely approached the house. He did not succeed, and the little car spluttered safely into Holyhead with a bone-dry tank, but his action struck the driver as one of remarkable maturity.

Headfort Bridge

6. DAVID WILD'S FINAL YEARS

David Wild contemplates retirement – Coeducation – Classroom fires –
IAPS Branch Meetings – Common Entrance – Relationship with St Columba's
College – Competition – David Wild retires

David Wild contemplates retirement

By 1973 David Wild was considering retirement. He had already run the
School successfully for twenty-three years and there were ominous signs on
the horizon, in the form of dwindling numbers and a militant Fire Officer.
He chose LINGARD GOULDING, an assistant master at Brook House, as
his successor. The position was not advertised: the interview was conducted,
not before an intimidating pack of directors in a board room, but rather over
an excellent luncheon at a gentlemen's club – such was the way of the world.
After a second glass of port, the Headmaster asked Goulding to join Headfort
in September 1974 and work under him for one year before succeeding to
the headship in 1975. Subsequently, the Headmaster-elect was introduced as
a fait accompli to the company Chairman, a delightful old gentleman called
GODFREY SKRINE (brother to the novelist Molly Keane). Mr Skrine said,
'Well, Lingard, there are not many children in the School at the moment, and
I don't know whether the business is viable in the long term, but you are still
a young man and, if it doesn't work out, you can always find something else
to do.'

Your author duly joined Headfort in September 1974, initially teaching
mathematics, English and Latin under David Wild. At the beginning of that
term Mr Wild announced his impending marriage to Miss Barbara Lever. He
later declared his revised intention to remain at Headfort with Mrs Wild for
two further years until July 1977. Lingard Goulding was appointed Deputy
Headmaster in 1975 and was subsequently elected to membership of the IAPS

Coeducation

At the end of 1974 David Wild asked his successor whether he would be happy if the School were to accept girls during his final two years. This plan was eagerly embraced by Goulding who stated that he had intended to open the School to girls in any case when he assumed office. Thus, a squad of four brave little girls – sent by their braver parents – arrived at Headfort in 1975 and Barbara Wild took a special interest in them.

David Wild's decision to accept girls at that stage of his career was primarily pragmatic, as indeed it was at many other similar schools where numbers were dwindling. One suspects that he would have preferred to complete his days running an exclusively boys' school, but he had the vision to realize that girls would help to boost numbers and hence keep the School viable. The presence of his wife was a prime factor in persuading him to accept girls and Mrs Wild immersed herself in the venture and played an important role in the lives of Headfort's first intake of young ladies.

The Editorial of the 1975 *Headfort Chronicle* (written by John Leyden) reads prophetically: 'Should the history of Headfort ever be written, it may well seem to the historian that the past academic year has been one of the most decisive in the history of the School.' And so it was.

Coeducation needs no defence. At all other stages of life, both before and after school, one lives in a mixed world, and to segregate at the seven-to-thirteen age level seems artificial. The combined presence of boys and girls at this age is surely the most natural preparation for the advent of adolescence and adult life. Coeducation involves more than the joint instruction of boys and girls in the classroom; it enables them to grow together on terms of comradeship in the performance of common duties, and to share together membership of the school unit. While most facets of school life benefit from the complementarity of boys and girls, there are some areas in which the children do not choose to share; where each sex prefers to keep its own company. Coeducation allows for this; rather, it helps them to recognize the essential differences between the sexes and so develop mutual respect.

The arrival of a handful of little girls in the School was a startling event. 'What on earth are these peculiar creatures that have been thrust amongst us?' was the initial cry from the bemused boys. There was, of course, the excitement of claiming a girlfriend; but very shortly that became frightfully old hat and rather poor form – besides there were only four of them to be shared among the whole School! Also, the girls had been given the two most cherished dormitories, The Zoo and The Dean's Room on the first landing, and this gave rise to jealousy.

And so, for a little while, integration was laboured. Indeed, there was even a sense of gender-driven apartheid: if a girl sat next to a boy on one of the long benches in the dining room, the boy would adopt a serpentine motion and slither shiftily away as far as possible, fearful of contracting a spot of female-induced leprosy. It was not until after a couple of years, when new children arrived into a School that was already mixed, that coeducation became the natural thing and, ever since, boys and girls have been the best of friends and some touching friendships have been formed.

It did not take long for the girls to establish themselves in virtually every area of School life, although they were never permitted to join the rugby team. By 1980 the first girl had come top of the Upper Sixth; girls rapidly excelled at music, drama and upon horseback; they won academic scholarships; in 1984 a girl became Junior Victor Ludorum, in competition against the boys – in subsequent years boys and girls were separated for athletics, such that a Victor and a Victrix Ludorum would be crowned in both senior and junior categories; during the 1980s and 1990s several girls captained the First XI at hockey; in 1994 a girl captained the First XI at cricket before, just four years later, joining the national side; and in 2007 a girl opened the batting,

1994 First XI

and became the highest run scorer, in that year's cricket side. Another girl was a champion distance runner: she was the freest spirit imaginable and simply loved running. She was much faster than most of the boys over the 1.9 mile 'Slow Cows' course; however, there was one boy in the School at the time who was even faster than she. Although the two were firm friends, she used to inveigh against the injustice whereby top male athletes tended to be faster and stronger than top female athletes. 'It is just so unfair!'

By 1989 Headfort had its first female Captain of the School. In later years the practice arose to appoint joint Captains of the School, a Head Girl and a Head Boy. In the Christmas Term of that same year a girl came top in each of the first five forms.

Although pupils from the Early Years might not like to hear it said, the author's clear view is that the new, mixed Headfort became a more couth, a more civilized, community.

Classroom fires

During the two winter terms, firstly Bill Kirwan and, after him, Johnny Grimes would set and light fires in each of the classrooms in the two lower storeys of the west wing. This involved carrying coal from the cellar in the moat under the front steps, and logs that they would have to cut from trees on the estate and store in one of the rooms in the stable yard. Fire-lighters would complete the job. It was a considerable task to generate fires in seven divergent classrooms and also the downstairs staff room every morning. Each classroom was permitted one extra bucket of coal per day and as many logs as the children could bring in from the yard. The quantity of logs that was available at any time depended to some extent upon the level of malconduct in the School, because Victor de Raeymaeker devised a system of punishment for minor offences that involved children gathering logs from around the estate. A boy or girl who was late for class, for instance, would have 'five logs' or 'ten logs' awarded against him or her. This meant that, on their free afternoon, the miscreants would be required to carry a given number of logs from the woods to the stable yard. On bad days a whole train of children could be seen bearing armfuls of logs through the grounds. Of course, as with many sanctions, 'logs' involved work for the lawmakers as well as the criminals. John Leyden would station himself in the woods with a chainsaw while de Raeymaeker would control the operation and determine how many logs each offending child must carry. This was one of the more sensible, because useful, systems of punishment. Although the children would naturally complain when they were given 'logs', they actually rather enjoyed the chore, perhaps recognizing that it was an action performed in the common weal.

After morning assembly on cold days, the children would hasten to their classrooms and huddle around the sparkling fire to warm themselves before the lesson began; and at the end of break they would betimes toast marshmallows on their mathematical compasses (and sometimes plant conkers, and even tightly sealed boiled sweet tins, in the fire in order to induce dramatic explosions during the course of the following lesson).

Naturally the upstairs–downstairs transformation in 1983 put a stop to classroom fires; of course one could not burn open fires in dormitories. Henceforth, storage heaters would regulate the temperature in the new classrooms upstairs and, for a while, there was no heating in the dormitories. Children simply dressed and undressed more rapidly and put extra blankets on their beds. Young people's circulation is efficient.

During his final term, David Wild received a letter from the local Fire Officer, demanding a swathe of safety measures, the cost of implementing which would have bankrupted the School instantly.

IAPS Branch Meetings

The Irish IAPS schools used to hold a Branch Meeting each term to discuss matters of mutual interest. There would generally be a guest speaker, often an official of the Association from the mainland. These meetings were sometimes held in the North, sometimes in the Republic, and frequently at an hotel near the border. On these occasions the several Headmasters rejoiced in their freedom and tended to behave like schoolboys who had escaped for the day. They arrived at the venue at half past ten, some of them boasting that they had already taught a class, and several would ingest a gin-and-tonic or two before proceedings commenced at eleven o'clock. The Chairman was expected to declare a luncheon intercession not later than a quarter to one – although this tended to creep earlier and earlier – whereupon the naughty boys would hie them to the bar once more to sneak in a couple of pre-prandial quick ones. Luncheon was a hearty repast: badinage flowed as lustily as the wine, and several points were scored or settled. The afternoon session was brief and did not command the attention of all of the delegates, several of whom succumbed to the somnolent state. At the conclusion of the meeting, there might be 'one for the road' and then these august gentlemen, whose jobs entailed enormous responsibility throughout the working week, would aim for their motoring cars and glide happily homewards. [Perhaps it should be conceded that this paragraph is more of a caricature than an accurate historical description – Asinius Pollio would not approve – yet it is not totally without foundation.]

Common Entrance

From the School's inception, the principal academic goal for all pupils, apart from those who sat scholarships to individual public schools, was the Common Entrance Examination (CE). This was, and is, the gateway to the great English secondary schools to which a majority of Headfort children progressed. CE examines an extensive syllabus, far wider than is required by Irish secondary schools, the majority of whose pupils will not have attended a preparatory school. Gradually, from the end of the Early Years, all the way through to Headfort Today, the number of Headfort children receiving their secondary education in England or Scotland has diminished, as modern parents wish to see more of their children and, besides, the cost for those who live and work in the Irish Republic of sending children abroad rose alarmingly when Ireland broke away from the sterling standard. Several boys and girls still cross the Irish Sea each year, but nowadays the majority of pupils complete their education on home soil, and so Headfort Today follows a dual teaching programme.

Relationship with St Columba's College

From the very beginning Headfort has enjoyed a close relationship with St Columba's College, a Headmaster's Conference (HMC) school, set in the foothills of the Dublin mountains. In David Wild's time a majority of those children who remained in Ireland when they left Headfort progressed to St Columba's. As with other HMC schools, St Columba's used CE as its primary means of selection. The examples of the correspondence that are quoted here between David Wild and Martin Argyle, Warden of St Columba's at the time, show how close the relationship was between the two schools. Note the formal style of address.

The relationship with St Columba's remains close to this day, although Headfort continues to send children to other secondary schools in Ireland and England as well.

In 1981 St Columba's began to accept girls from the age of twelve. This event was of significance to Headfort because it was now possible to offer education for all the family together from the age of eight until eighteen at these two schools

5th November, 1951.

The Warden,
St. Columba's College,
RATHFARNHAM.

Dear Argyle,

Sir ▮▮▮▮▮▮ has asked me to write to you about his eldest son, ▮▮▮.

▮▮▮ will be fourteen in April so would have to go to you next September. He is not a bright boy but is not stupid and should manage the Common Entrance all right if he takes it in the summer. He does not shine at anything but is a perfectly sound boy and one that I can recommend.

I know that you have no vacancies, but I thought that perhaps a chance place might be found for young ▮▮▮.

The father is a ▮▮▮▮▮ baronet and, though at first aquaintance he may strike you as uncouth, he is, in fact, a simple well-meaning fellow and no trouble at all. He will be writing to you shortly.

Yours sincerely,

From THE WARDEN,

COLLEGE OF ST. COLUMBA,

RATHFARNHAM,

Co. DUBLIN

18th June, 1952.

Dear Wild,

Just a line to confirm my telephone message to your secretary yesterday that though ▮▮▮▮ was definitely not up to Scholarship standard we were able to award him a small Exhibition of £15 on his English and General paper. This is mainly due to the fact that competition was not too strong this year. We thought also it might be an encouragement to Headfort as a whole. I know what these things mean to a Preparatory School.

If possible I shall get over for an hour or two on Friday.

Kind regards,
Yours sincerely,

[signature]

D. P. Wild, Esq.,
Headfort School,
Kells,
Co. Meath.

The value of an Exhibition in 1952

28th July, 1952.

The Warden,
St. Columba's College,
RATHFARNHAM.

My dear Argyle,

I am glad to hear that Air-Commodore ▓▓▓▓▓▓
has at last been to see you. I have been badgering him
to do this for the last four terms.

By the same post that brought your letter about
▓▓▓▓▓▓, I had a distraught letter from Mrs.
saying that ▓▓▓▓▓▓ had been expelled for making a
bomb. She asks me to write to you on ▓▓▓▓'s behalf.
Naturally I would be only too glad to do anything I can
for the boy, because I know that for all the bad streak
in him he has also a great deal that is good, but I do not
see what I can say except to express complete confidence
in your judgment and the natural hope that you have not
given up the boy altogether.

Yours sincerely,

Competition

In the 1970s there was a prevalent, loony, left-wing attitude that competition was 'uncool' and antithetical to the new age because, just as competition generates a winner, it must also, ipso facto, spew forth a loser; and to tar a precious plant with the label 'loser' is frightfully damaging to the psychological health profile, don't you know? What piffle!

This theory maintained that children should not compete, merely cooperate. However, in the author's opinion, if they are to grow up realistically, they must learn to pit their skills against others in a competitive environment, and that to lose with dignity is the second most important lesson in life – after the knowledge that life is unfair.

That wise old owl, Bertrand Russell, wrote in *The Conquest of Happiness* that man, like the other animals, possesses within his biological makeup an instinct to compete, to engage in the struggle for life; consequently, anybody who is sufficiently powerful to satisfy all his wants without competition or effort is deprived of a fundamental element of happiness. The corollary is that happiness is only achieved when one is not happy – a nice paradox, indeed.

There is merit in the thesis. It is the chase that excites: realization is anti-climactic. Courtship stirs the blood more than conquest. Children, and adults too, derive satisfaction from struggling with a problem and solving it to the best of their ability, preferably better than their peers. It may have become fashionable in some educational circles to denigrate competition. Not so at Headfort: the School has always thriven upon it.

David Wild retires

David Wild left Headfort in July 1977 in a wave of goodwill, having estab-lished a fine school and steered it successfully through its first twenty-seven and a half years.

David Wild's last School Service, 1977. Back row: David Gibbs, David Wild, Barbara Wild, Bill Wild, Canon Aidan Olden, Pamela Potterton (organist)

PART TWO

The Middle Years
1977 until 2001

7 . A CHANGE AT THE HELM

*Some new procedures – Corporal punishment please! – Crises of the Middle Years
– Fire practice – Latin–Irish – New appointments – The confessions of a rebel –
Strikes – Public schools & IAPS*

Some new procedures

The new Headmaster began his tenure in September 1977 with fees set at £405 per term. A few changes in procedure were made immediately: others were introduced gradually. From the start of the new era, children were permitted to talk at bedtime; boys were allowed to wear long trousers if they wished – eventually they all did so; corporal punishment was abolished; academically, the practice of 'streaming' pupils into Remove or Fifth Form after Fourth Form was discontinued: henceforth, every child would have to pass through the Lower Sixth, the Common Entrance form, before he might progress to the Upper Sixth that was nominally a scholarship form. Nevertheless children still rose through the ranks according to the joint criteria of ability and age, the idea being to achieve relative homogeneity within each class; thus the academically brighter ones would attain the Lower Sixth, and thence the Upper Sixth, more rapidly – to win a scholarship to a major public school, a pupil would generally need to spend two years in the Upper Sixth.

The end-of-year 'School service', an exclusively Protestant celebration in St Columba's Church, continued to be held for a few more years, but a full School valedictory assembly was now held in the Ballroom for all of the pupils, replacing 'Mark Reading'. An ancient minibus was purchased for the first time. It was a sixth-hand vehicle that ran on gas and tended to consume its pistons, but it afforded a flexibility that had not previously been available. Three further minibuses were purchased in subsequent years; the latest, acquired in 2000, was financed largely by a Race Night in the ballroom: it was an hilarious evening in which companies and sporting parents sponsored a series of horse races that were run on film.

A newsletter was despatched each term to parents, together with the school reports, to recall the salient features of the recent term and to serve as a medium for broadcasting educational ideas. The current Headmaster preserves this practice.

Groups of children visited theatres and art galleries most terms. Another innovation was the introduction of a 'carrot and stick' approach to discipline. A 'treat' was awarded twice a term to those whose conduct had been satisfactory, as determined by their not having been in 'the Book' more than twice. The Book was a system of punishment, introduced to replace 'whacking'. Children who accrued more than ten 'points', or committed a sufficiently heinous offence, would earn a booking that involved some form of detention or public service during their free time.

Gradually over the following few years the use of surnames as the accepted mode of address gave way to that of given names, although surnames are still used in official documents. Also, the teddy bear population in the School grew exponentially and their keepers extended up the age range. The prep school world was becoming more humane.

Although children continued to be taken to their respective churches on Sundays, Headfort ceased to define itself as a Christian, let alone a Protestant, institution. The majority of Headfort families were still at least nominally Christian, and progressively more Roman Catholic, but the new prospectus made it clear that any religious faith, or none, was respected equally, for

> The tsunami doesn't stop to ask people
> About their beliefs.
> Neither does the mountain stream quiz the rocks
> On their opinions
> On its way to the sea.

From Rudra Nua (Tim Goulding), *The Viper Lounge*

Morning assembly was now held for everybody in the Ballroom – actually this had been the case for the previous two years; before that, the small band of Roman Catholics had been despatched to an insalubrious small room that was otherwise employed for modelling aircraft.

In general, the hope was to accelerate the representation of girls in the school and indeed to increase the overall numbers. There was also the conscious objective to integrate the School more closely with its environment; to which end Headfort entered debating competitions, quiz competitions and other inter-school activities in Kells.

In 1978 a limited amount of weekly boarding was permitted, from lunchtime on Saturday until Sunday evening, to accord with many parents' wishes.

Corporal punishment please!

The discontinuation of corporal punishment was not at first popular with all of the staff. For a while the new Headmaster's perceived weakness was blamed when misbehaviour took place. However, it had always seemed to him unnatural for a fully-grown person to smite a half-grown one; there had to be other ways of instilling discipline. Some years later the practice was outlawed in any case.

One weekend in the first term of the new regime the children were disporting themselves gaily around the estate. The sun shone, the birds sang, and all was well in Headfort's little kingdom until a member of staff sent two spirited boys, regular recidivists, to the Headmaster for punishment. The passage of time has cast a mist over the nature of the boys' heinous offence – probably menacing pheasants in the woods, or some such. The Headmaster assumed a stern mien and, upon finding the evidence for the defence unconvincing, pronounced sentence: 'You will go to bed early with the juniors this evening.' The boys looked crestfallen; there was a considerable stigma attached to retiring with the 'untouchables'. The two prisoners walked disconsolately away. Suddenly, one of them turned around, bravely retraced his steps and asked, 'Sir, will you beat us instead?' His wish was not granted, but the incident demonstrates that the level of corporal punishment exercised in the Early Years was far from sadistic.

Crises of the Middle Years

Three crises manifested themselves during the Middle Years:

i) Coping with the Fire Officer's demands,
ii) Combating falling numbers when the lease expired in 1978, and
iii) Combating falling numbers when the estate was put on the market again in 1993.

The immediate problem was to hold the Fire Officer at bay. Some of his demands were sensible: others were not.

The first essential task was to replace with proper external fire escapes the open ladders that abutted the east and west walls of the house. This was done in the first year at the enormous cost of £9000 and, although unsightly, they enabled one to sleep more comfortably at night. Many were the horrific stories of past pupils venturing down the open ladders from the top landing in the small hours of a Sunday morning. Other modifications were undertaken, little by little, but it was a case of playing the Fire Officer like a fish: make an improvement here, a modification there; mollifying him thus, one could buy a little time. This process continued for almost six years.

Fire practice

In the Early Years the fire assembly station was the Front Hall, whither children would wend their way for practices. This seemed to the author to be a strange site for the purpose because, should a real inferno occur, the Front Hall might well be ablaze. And so in the Middle Years the squash court, a concrete building that is separate from the main house, became the new assembly point, and remains so to this day. Peter Bamford was appointed School Fire Officer, a role that is currently held by Michael Bolton; it was his job to administer and keep written records of drills. In one of the early nocturnal practices using the new external fire escapes, having supervised the safe descent to the south side of the house of all those children who resided in the easterly dormitories, Peter Bamford, seeking a mud-free passage through the undergrowth to the squash court, managed to lose his bearings in the darkness. The children, clad in pyjamas and slippers, had no such compunction about slithering through the mud and, like homing pigeons, they reached the sanctity of the squash court without delay. Everybody was present and correct when the Headmaster took the roll call from the balcony of the court – except for Mr Bamford.

On another occasion, the roll call revealed that one pupil had 'perished'. A search party was sent to look for him and eventually found him in the dining room. He was an eight-year-old who, when rudely awoken by the fire alarm and the clanging of a hand bell at half past ten pm, thought, in his confused state, that it must be breakfast time and, instead of donning dressing gown and slippers and heading for the squash court, he had clothed himself fully and went in search of his morning porridge and toast.

Latin–Irish

The Latin language had been staple Headfort fare from the beginning, but Irish had not been taught. Now it was offered as an option. Latin and Irish were timetabled under the heading 'Latish', and Jim Brunnock, a peripatetic teacher, was the first teacher of Irish; he visited from Kells once a week after tea. Parents had to make the choice as between Latin and Irish. That remains the situation to this day.

In the state sector, Irish remains compulsory more than thirty years later. It has always been a political issue and neither of the two principal parties is willing to break the mould. The author respects the learning of Irish as a cultural pursuit, but he does not respect the obligation to learn it.

Latin used to command a far more important role in private education than it does today. In Common Entrance, there was a Latin verse paper, as well as the prose paper. This consisted of three questions: the first one asked pupils to scan a set of given dactylic hexameters and pentameters; the second question required them to rearrange a passage of Latin into the form of elegiac couplets; and the third question had them translate a passage from English into Latin and assemble it into verse form – that was a demanding task that would fall well beyond modern thirteen-year-olds. Today Latin has had to give ground in terms of timetabling to subjects such as science, information technology and computing.

Whilst acknowledging that Latin must cede its place of prominence in the modern world, the author nevertheless regards its study as a valuable pursuit. It is his finding that, although the converse is not true, a pupil who is good at Latin correlates closely with what is generally understood by 'intelligence'. In other words, he has never known a Latin scholar who is not intelligent. Proficiency in the language is an excellent indicator of a high Intelligence Quotient; it also assists in the correct usage of English. Kennedy's Latin Primer deserves its place in history.

Bill Stuart-Mills used to teach Greek to the more academic boys. In the early days of prep school praxis the purpose of learning Greek was to enable pupils to 'read the Holy Scriptures in their original tongues.' Bill's motivation was purely intellectual. Sadly, the teaching of Greek in the prep schools, and in secondary schools, bit the dust even before Latin became a partial victim.

New appointments

Early in the new era, Dr Brangan retired and DR MICHAEL O'CONNELL was appointed to the position of School Doctor. It was a case of one devoted servant following another. Dr Michael's contribution to Headfort was immense. He subscribed to both tradition and modernity. He epitomized the virtues of the old-fashioned country doctor who travelled tirelessly to tend his flock; and, indeed, he had a collection of what might be called 'pet cures'. This does not mean that he encroached into the veterinary domain, but rather that he championed certain remedies on empirical, rather than purely scientific, grounds: quite simply, they worked. For two thousand years garlic has been known to counteract hypertension; so Dr Michael prescribed garlic to his hypertensive patients. He also managed to keep abreast of the morass of new medical literature and opinion. On one occasion he performed a service that lies so far beyond the bounds of duty of a school doctor as to almost defy belief today. A child became sufficiently ill to require a visit to hospital on an evening when the Headmaster was entertaining an official from the IAPS who had travelled from England to inspect the Irish prep schools. Of course, under the circumstances, it was the Headmaster's duty to drive the child to Dublin but, assuring him that the child's condition was not serious, Dr O'Connell insisted upon rendering this service himself, to allow the Headmaster to remain with his guest. Obviously the child was in the best possible hands, but it was a remarkable function for a school doctor to perform.

Juliet Long had asked to transfer from the position of Matron to that of Housekeeper, perhaps an even more demanding task. She served in this office gallantly for three further years before accepting a post as Matron at St Andrew's College in Dublin. Juliet showed tremendous loyalty and dedication to duty and was a tower of strength in all areas of School life.

Kells School Housekeeper's New Position

MISS Juliet Long, matron at Headfort School, Kells, for six years and housekeeper for three years, has left to take up an appointment as matron at St. Andrew's College, Booterstown Avenue, Dublin.

During her nine years at Headfort, Miss Long's innate kindness and efficiency won her the affection and esteem of the pupils and of the teaching staff. She was "mother" to from 90 to 100 boys for the six-year period, and they owe her a deep debt of gratitude.

BROWN OWL

Miss Long was Brown Owl to the 24-strong Primrose Pack in Kells where her unassuming and gentle disposition endeared her to young and old.

She attended the handcrafts class in the local vocational school where she proved herself an expert at the Carrickmacross lace level.

Before going to Headfort, she worked in the Children's Sunshine Home in Stillorgan and subsequently was appoint- ed assistant matron at Wesley College, Dundrum.

There are seventy boarders and 700 day pupils at St. Andrews.

Her friends in Kells wish Miss Long every happiness in her new and responsible post.

In the Headfort School summer newsheet, the headmaster paid this striking tribute to Miss Long: "For six years she was our matron until she requested the post of housekeeper upon Mrs. Pepper's retirement three years ago. Juliet has shown tremendous loyalty and dedication to duty and has been a tower of strength in all areas of school life, branching far beyond the usual scope of housekeeper. She will be sorely missed."

Untaxed Cars

James and Theresa Cassidy, Ballintlieve, Moynalty, were fined £10 each at Kells Court on Monday for driving untaxed cars at Carnaross, Kells.

Joining the staff on the same day as the new Headmaster was a remarkable lady, SIBÉAL ROONEY. Born in Sweden and escaping from Germany at the outset of war, 'Ma' Rooney was the most versatile musician imaginable. She studied music at Cork University under Professor Alois Fleischmann who taught her the Liszt piano technique, and imparted to her a wide knowledge of orchestration. She studied for a further two years in Heidelberg. Sibéal began her Headfort career as a junior mistress, teaching a range of subjects, conducting supervision duties and even playing in staff matches. Later she became Head of Music and taught, at different stages, piano, piano accordion, recorder, guitar, harmonica, drums, trumpet, saxophone, violin, viola and 'cello. She remained at the School, full-time or part-time, for thirty-two years until 2005 and was very much a Common Room character. For some years she taught children to crochet and one would find boys and girls working on complex creations in their dormitories of an evening.

Sibéal Rooney

LYNNE TILSON was appointed early in the new regime. She was a model Matron and devoted ten happy years of her life to Headfort. A vivacious person, she was adored by the children and it was a sad day for the School when in 1987, after enjoying a holiday in Morocco with the Headmaster and the riding teacher, she decided that she wanted to explore the world and embarked upon a two-year nomadic adventure with her two children and her sister.

KARIN OSTHUS, the mother of two boys in the School, helped to establish a new art room and taught the subject effectively for nine years until 1987.

Bill Stuart-Mills continued teaching until 1980. Despite failing health, he was a tower of strength till the end. He and Kate enjoyed several years of happy retirement during which they travelled widely. He died in 1985.

Mr. and Mrs. W. Stuart-Mills.

Farewell to legends

Kells Teaching Couple Retire

"I certainly do not exaggerate in saying that Bill is the finest schoolmaster I have known," declared Mr. Lingard Goulding, headmaster of Headfort Prep School, Kells, during a farewell party at Headfort in honour of Mr. William Stuart-Mills, second master, and his wife, Kate, music teacher, who have retired after 31 years' service.

JENNIFER FARRIS taught riding in 1974 and was replaced by BELINDA BATES, the niece of Sir Richard Musgrave, the following year. THE HON. ANGELA MARTYN-HEMPHILL also ran the equestrian department successfully for several years in the late 1970s. GERRY McLOUGHLIN taught mathematics and English in the junior forms from 1980 until 1982.

BART WEYAND and his wife TRISH were a breath of fresh air: 'alternative' would be an appropriate word to describe them. Bart was not known for his punctuality, but he lent a lateral dimension to his teaching of Latin. They lived in a staff house on the estate, quite close to the Sweetmans. Edith who was a keen gardener spoke enthusiastically in the Staff Room one day of the beautiful plants that were growing in the Weyands' garden. Little did she know that these plants were marijuana. The Weyands only stayed at Headfort for a couple of years before returning to their native United States, but they receive a favourable press from past pupils.

Two decades later the author found a young man of about twenty, wandering around the estate during the school holidays. In reply to an enquiry as to what he was doing there, the young man declared himself to be an American student who was 'back-packing' through Europe and, as with so many Americans, he was trying to trace his roots. He believed that he had been conceived at Headfort! He was, of course, the son of Bart and Trish. He had not spoken to his parents for a year or two and so the Headmaster brought him into the study and, despite the boy's reluctance, insisted upon telephoning a number in America and leaving father and son to talk for half an hour. It was a joyful occasion.

ROSEMARY BUTLER (née LALOR) worked with distinction at the School in the early 1980s, both in the capacity of riding mistress and then as

Housekeeper. Eventually she was 'kidnapped' by the landlord in 1989 to look after his horses. MICHAEL SMYTH has taught carpentry with enthusiasm, skill and patience since 1980. This is an especially popular activity in the two winter terms.

A valuable addition to the staffroom in 1979 was ROBIN SIMMONS who arrived to teach Latin. A scholarly man of great charm, he was a dedicated and conscientious teacher. It was a standing joke that the children's exercise books contained more of Mr Simmons's corrections than of their owners' original work. He was also a knowledgeable hockey coach. He retired in 1994 after fourteen years of devoted service.

NANCY REILLY was the backbone of the catering staff. She has a long association with Headfort, having done occasional jobs for Lady Headfort in previous times. She carries a host of stories about the estate, relating to years of yore, that she tells with charm and humour. A hugely hard-working person, Nancy is a fine traditional cook. She still works in the kitchen to this day. Her late husband, MICHAEL REILLY, worked on the estate for many years and latterly used to keep the topiary in shape.

The confessions of a rebel

Most schools have animated pupils who try to test the system. Here is a selection of the confessions of such a boy who was at Headfort in the late 1970s and early 1980s. I should mention that, contrary to what some of the staff thought at the time, he is now at the top of his profession, an award-winning sound recorder for film and television.

I arrived at Headfort aged eight years. Moving into boarding school was made easier by the Headmaster being my father's best friend. I never had any bullying or teasing and, having known Lingard all my life, I trusted the environment more readily.

The School itself was cold and beautiful. I never had my own skateboard or pony, but other pupils were quick to let me share theirs. Sports were seasonal and fiercely competitive. I played hockey, cricket, rugby and tennis. I was ever only really good at chess. Being on the chess team meant evening matches. Adults were much easier in the evening. We would go to Dublin for tournaments and visit Miss Long's house on the way back for supper. I did get some stick for being a 'chess poof', but the upside was that we toured in small numbers, so were more lavishly catered for. Lingard was a reasonable player, but I always allowed him to win our games: it would have been rude to win myself and unsettle the man's pride. [The cheek of the fellow! – author]

There were a thousand acres of forestry and farmland to roam, and roam I did. I never accepted authority and made things difficult for everyone, especially myself, as a result. I robbed food from the pantry, took mercury from the science lab and organized trips to the village shop. I didn't feel that I was as good at sports or in class as the other children, so decided to make my impression by being an outlaw. I discovered that there was a bell tower above the carpentry workshop and that, if I could connect a rope to the hammer, I could ring the bell remotely. I did this as my 'leaver's dare'.

Irish kids who lived far afield brought exotic exhibits to Headfort, such as sugar cane from Ghana and Christmas crackers from Aspreys. We smoked Russian fags and chased girls around the squash court in kiss-chase experiments. We made elaborate forts in the forest and established a complex social structure.

All this was a backdrop to a fantastic education. I learnt more in my four years at Headfort than in the next seven years of my formal education. Science, maths, English and art were taught with dedication and interest that stays with me today. There were fascinating characters at the School such as Bart Weyand and his wife – two American hippies. Bart taught us American football.

It was not all good. We had read the books about Colditz Castle, and Headfort looked a bit like Colditz. It was cold, really cold. We were often hungry, though I have to say the diet was good. I remember once rewiring a redundant 1950s electric heater that had been left in the dorm. I figured out how to use the switchboard to get juice into it and was a popular chap, before it started to sizzle and smell funny. My punishment was to sit at the top of the stairs for ages on a freezing evening, regretting that decision.

Mr de Raeymaeker invented a popular form of punishment: it was to deforest the estate and populate the stables with logs. For minor infringements we would spend Saturday afternoons carrying logs long distances. I didn't mind, because I got to see beautiful Golden Pheasants. The teachers were generally caring and sensitive people, especially Mrs Rooney who left me with an understanding and love of sound and music from which I earn my living today.

Outside of my family life, my time at Headfort has been the single biggest influence on my life.

Strikes

In 1978 there were extended postal and telephone strikes – a total communications breakdown. School reports had to be completed hastily one term and planted by Matron in the children's suitcases, rather than written at leisure and posted a week later. At Easter 1979 there was a petrol shortage, and numerous pipes burst inside the house – trials and tribulations to keep the new Headmaster on his toes.

Public Schools & IAPS

That year the Headmaster visited fourteen public schools in England over eight days during the Half Term break in May: the schools that he visited were either ones to which Headfort had recently sent pupils, or to which pupils were about to go. He repeated this exercise on a number of occasions in subsequent years in order to meet Headmasters, Headmistresses and, perhaps more importantly for past Headfort pupils, Housemasters and Housemistresses. It was valuable to establish contact with these people in order to make pupils' transition to secondary school as seamless as possible.

In his capacity as Chairman of the Irish Branch of IAPS – a role that alternated amongst the heads of Irish schools in membership – the Headmaster served two three-year stints on Council, from 1984 until 1986 and from 1990 until 1992. This necessitated attending Council Meetings five times a year in England during his first term of office; in his second term, Council Meetings had been reduced to three annually. Some of these meetings were held at the IAPS headquarters, initially in London and latterly at Leamington Spa, while at least two each year were hosted by one of the major public schools.

The IAPS Annual Conference was an important event held towards the end of the summer holidays – latterly, early in the Christmas Term. Originally, Conference alternated annually between Oxford and Cambridge, but later shifted to other university cities. Being geographically remote, it was useful for Headfort to keep abreast of the educational philosophy and developments of the British schools in membership.

8. WE ARE SQUATTERS

A crisis – Another unusual evening – Lord Headfort departs – Early computing
– Curtains – Teaching for the future – Communications – Summer nostalgia –
More appointments

A crisis

The years from 1979 until 1982 were stressful. Lord Headfort had put the estate on the market and would not grant the School a new lease. In effect, the School was a squatter for three years. This fact was widely known and, in consequence, enrolment dwindled. The situation became so acute that serious thought was given to amalgamation with Brook House that was also struggling. Meetings were held between the respective Board members and Headmasters as to the practicality of forming a new entity, to be known as Headfort Brook, on a fine site that had come onto the market. It would have been sad to leave the estate – it was this factor that eventually led the project to be abandoned – but the financial situation was bleak. Fortunately the School emerged unscathed, indeed strengthened, from the crisis, as will be related shortly. The Headmaster visited Spain on two occasions during the Easter holidays in 1985 and 1986 and initiated a flow of Spanish children to Headfort that has perpetuated to this day.

Another unusual evening

Lord Headfort enjoyed firearms. One winter's evening in the late 1970s the Headmaster was entertaining the Chairman of IAPS and other guests to dinner, when the serenity of the scene was pierced by a series of shots that rang out just beyond the window of the office that was being used as a dining room. The Chairman, Head of a school in Bristol, looked uneasy and, after a second volley was discharged, the Headmaster hastened to the front door to investigate. The wind was howling and rain was cascading down, but this did not deter the gunman from dissolving into cacophonous peals of laughter; another shot was fired into the night air before footsteps could be heard running towards Headfort Court where Lord Headfort lived.

The guests composed themselves once more and dinner resumed. By the time that pudding was served, however, more shots were fired. The Matron, Lynne Tilson, knocked on the door to report that many of the children had awoken and were thoroughly frightened. This time the Headmaster had no choice but to track the nuisance back to source. Once more there was frenzied giggling as the Marquis scuttled through the starless night towards his home. The Headmaster followed; reaching the front door, he rang the bell, but was left dripping on the doorstep for several minutes. Eventually the door was opened by one of Lady Headfort's Filipino servants. The Marquis was convulsed in laughter; he proudly displayed the pair of Holland and Holland guns that he had bought in Scotland the previous week and threatened to demonstrate them further. The Headmaster tried to balance his anger with a degree of conciliation in an attempt to calm the befuddled landlord.

Dinner was completed in peace, but the Chairman of IAPS dined out upon this Headfort story for a long time. Possibly he thought that such behaviour was commonplace amongst Irish schools.

Lord Headfort departs

A few bizarre incidents from those years come to mind. On one occasion Lord Headfort wrote to the Headmaster from Hong Kong, informing him that a Commonwealth Conference would be held at Headfort, and instructing him to acquire tents from the government, such that the children might sleep on the games field to vacate the dormitories for the use of our Commonwealth brethren. This was at a time of maximum hostilities in Ireland – it was perhaps optimistic to expect Mrs Thatcher, among others, to confer some forty miles within the Republic. And in those days, the standard of accommodation at Headfort fell far short of five-star status. Lord Headfort had acquired an early telex machine with which he would communicate with many of the world's prominent politicians and heads of state, offering them the benefit of his advice upon international affairs. It was consequent upon his probably unilateral respondence with Mr Ian Smith of Rhodesia that the notion of Headfort's Commonwealth Conference was born.

On the morning that Pope John Paul II arrived in Ireland for his visit in 1979, Lord Headfort summoned the Headmaster to the roof of the house just before ten o'clock in the morning. Also present were three or four of the estate workers, carrying hoes, shovels and picks. His Lordship held to his ear a small transistor wireless that was reporting the Papal flight's progress towards Ireland; as the plane touched down at Dublin Airport, Lord Headfort commanded, 'Headmaster, hoist the flag!' With some embarrassment, the Headmaster edged towards a Heath Robinson contraption that had been attached to one of the chimneys; he hauled upon a string that actuated a lever that dragged the family flag aloft. His Lordship then delivered a lengthy homily, ostensibly welcoming His Holiness to Headfort. Throughout this performance the labourers, and indeed the Headmaster, stared at their boots in total disbelief at the surreal situation in which they found themselves, perched precariously on the roof of the four-storey mansion, listening to our peerless peer's megalomania. After the homily, the purpose of the exercise became manifest when His Lordship opened a giant leathern casket; out poured all manner of alcoholic beverages. The Headmaster excused himself to go and teach, but the others remained on the roof, toasting the Pope copiously until a quarter to one, when they descended from the roof to the ground floor, bouncing unsteadily between the walls and the banisters.

By 1971 the School had started to use the secondary avenue past the Stable yard. Lord Headfort installed a series of steep ramps with signs reading, 'Beware of pheasants, horses, children' (the order was significant). Some parents tried to sidestep the ramps by driving on the grass alongside, in order to protect their cars; so Lord Headfort lodged ten-foot-long planks, from which six-inch nails protruded, on either side of the drive where the ramps were situated, with the intention of puncturing the tyres of offending parents' cars. David Wild was livid: he envisaged children becoming impaled upon these nails and he enlisted a posse of pupils to help him remove the planks.

Lord Headfort was a renowned and accomplished aviator. He was the authorized Chief Flying Instructor of the Meath Flying Group and launched the commercial career of a future Aer Lingus pilot, the author's brother, by giving him his first flight in his Auster in 1967. The Group charged £3 17s 6d for an hour's instruction, about half the cost of lessons at Dublin Airport.

Frank Biggar was the Group's principal instructor; he lived in a cottage on the estate. As well as giving instruction, Biggar carried out maintenance on both the Auster and His Lordship's Lake Amphibian. At one time Michael Headfort was the agent for the Lake craft that was built in Maine, USA; he owned one of these planes himself and used to land it on the lake at Virginia. He also held the agency for a crop-spraying aeroplane in the Congo. There was always an aeroplane in his hangar. He used to hold rallies at Headfort to which eminent international aviators and aviatrices were invited. The Meath Flying Group, later referred to as the Headfort Flying Club, had its headquarters in the basement of Headfort Court where those magnificent men in their flying machines would convene of an evening.

> Two French planes are going about everywhere. The two pilots are friends of Lord Headfort. There is going to be an air display soon. The colour of the planes are blue. They cost about £2000 pounds, and the do thirty miles to the gallon. Miss Fisher has a horse called Stag's head.

The future Aer Lingus pilot recalls that to share the tiny Auster cockpit with Lord Headfort, a very large man, was a claustrophobic experience. The aircraft had a control-stick that rose vertically out of the floor and its side-to-side movement guided the banking of the plane. With the Marquis at the helm, the rolling ability of the aircraft was limited to about half its normal range because the stick came rapidly into contact with his enormous thighs. It made landing in a crosswind virtually impossible – knowledge that was disconcerting to the student pilot.

Lord Headfort was notorious for 'buzzing' the cricket pitch while opposition teams were batting. He crash-landed one of his planes in the airfield, an occasion that is etched deep in the memories of the pupils who were in the School at the time. Kate Stuart-Mills was in the garden of Green Bungalow that day and had the terrifying experience of watching the plane head directly towards her house. Fortunately, it completed its crazy course some yards short.

One of Lord Headfort's two Austers, built in 1950

Lord Headfort's pupil's 2010 BRM Aero NG4

His departure from the estate marked the end of an era. Life at the School thereafter was less entertaining, but far simpler. He was sorely missed by his friends and by his employees. Michael Headfort was one of the world's truly colourful characters. The tales about him are legion, some more credible than others. For some years he suffered from alcoholism. On one occasion his second wife, Virginia Nable (Nena), gleefully told the Headmaster that Michael was no longer drinking; however, the Headmaster knew full well that a lemonade bottle full of whiskey was secreted behind the pendulum in the grandfather clock.

Lady Headfort was a close friend of the Marcos family. In March 1973 Mrs Imelda Marcos (she of the shoes), wife of President Fernando Marcos, came to stay with the Headforts at Headfort Court and she presented a magnificent cabinet of Philippine shells for the science laboratory.

Lord Headfort was an avid snuff taker: he would produce an elegant, Georgian, silver snuff box, and offer it to everybody present. There were generally few takers; he would sprinkle a liberal portion of the pulverized tobacco leaf onto the top of each hand and insufflate copiously through the left nostril, snort through the right, before calling into service one of the forty voluminous red-and-white spotted handkerchiefs that he kept for mopping up operations.

After he had sold Headfort Estate, he lived the last twenty-five years of his life with Nena at her home on Lubang Island in the Philippines. He acquired the title, 'Commodore of Coastguards', using his yacht, 'Kenlis', for the purpose. He performed philanthropic works there, including presenting a library and an X-ray machine to the community.

One of the School's early past pupils used to visit Michael Headfort on Lubang. He recalls that, on the day of arrival on his first visit, his host greeted him with, 'Paddy, you must come to the funeral. There are only two Lords on the island and one of them is dead.' After they had planted the second Lord, they went to a target shooting range. Michael wanted to hone his firing skills in order to protect his 'Kenlis' against pirates.

During the final twenty years he drank no alcohol.

Early computing

1980 saw the acquisition of the School's first computer, an Apple 2. Headfort was the first preparatory school in Ireland to embrace the new technology. In 1984 Headfort held a Computer Seminar for teachers of the subject in Irish IAPS schools. In those days teachers were feeling their way with these new devices; very few of them had any formal training. Headfort was ahead of the field. Indeed, one session of the seminar was devoted to three of Headfort's knowledgeable pupils demonstrating their expertise to their seniors by showing what they had been able to achieve in the new world of bits and bytes (four bits = one nybble: two nybbles = one byte).

Curtains

The dormitories sported curtains for the first time that year as the result of a generous gift from parents whose son had won a major scholarship to Downside. The presence of curtains enhanced the children's chances of sleep in the long summer evenings. A past pupil tells the tale of swallows chattering in the gutters just above the curtainless windows in the 1950s. When another boy visited the lavatory after 'lights out', an unfortunate swallow

'I am not a swallow!'

would be manhandled out of its safe gutter and implanted in the absent one's bed. Bats would sometimes enter Trojans and The Dean's Room because, as a past pupil remembers, 'the Headmaster insisted upon opening the windows'. Quite right! The boys would try to snare the bats with fishing nets, while the girls would scream at high volume until the Headmaster hastened from the Study to expel the unwanted guests.

Teaching for the future

It is a paradox of the profession that teachers seek to prepare children for life in an age in which they themselves will not be present. As Khalil Gibran expresses it,

> For their souls dwell in the house of tomorrow,
> Which you cannot visit, not even in your dreams.

The Summer Term Newsletter of 1980 viewed the problem as follows:

> Those who now go forth from Headfort will be in their early thirties by the end of the millennium. What will their world be like? It profits little to teach them for the present (let alone the past, if I may preempt the cynic), for they will not live their lives in the present. Surely it behoves us to attempt the exercise of mental topology – that Gibran denies us – and peer deeply through the nebulous temporal dimension in the hope of extrapolating at least an outline from the other side.
>
> A few pointers should yield to mental elasticity. Firstly, the Computer Age is already with us and today's children must surely learn its technology and also the philosophy that is concomitant with it. Secondly, we must recognise that there will be less work, more play. So far, I hear no complaint from the children; but, as any schoolmaster will tell you, too much playtime poses its problems: boredom develops and behaviour becomes less social. We must therefore educate for leisure, as well as for labour.
>
> Another pointer. Our generation has been so profligate in its use of raw materials that there will be precious little left for our children to inherit. We have not provided for their energy requirements and, as you know, children have copious energy requirements. 'Let them pull in their belts and do without,' I hear some say. Yes, they must, but 'tis a bitter pill to swallow. We must educate therefore for a lifestyle that precludes 7-litre V8s and other toys that lavishly consume precious stocks of energy-giving raw materials.
>
> There will be a further levelling among groups: between rich and poor, manager and worker, black man and white man; even between the roles of man and woman. Never before will the power of communication have assumed such importance. We must educate therefore for communication; and to communicate, one must learn to understand the other fellow, to respect his cultural distinctions, even when one disagrees heartily with his thesis. To communicate successfully demands a high standard of literacy to impart precision of meaning, especially to those of unfamiliar culture.
>
> None of the pointers that I have cited – education for leisure, education independent of materialism and education for communication – is new; indeed, they were all inculcated by the Greeks through the traditional subjects that we still teach today. What is peculiar to our time is the urgency with which the new thinking must be implemented and advanced.

Those same pupils are now in their mid-forties. Some of the issues that that newsletter addressed more than thirty years ago have been revealed. There has of course been an exponential increase in the areas of our lives that are controlled by computers; communication has been undertaken by new media (although the standard of literacy has not risen); jobs are scarce and many people must eke out their time in leisure pursuits; and the stock of fossil fuels is so low that at last people are beginning to take measures to conserve power by developing smaller cars, some driven partially by electricity, and by heating their houses with solar power.

That term, one of the pupils in the Upper Sixth produced a remarkable project, based upon his concern about nuclear disaster, a topic that has resurfaced alarmingly today, thirty-two years later. It was entitled Project PENCIL (Protection of Earth against Nuclear Catastrophy, Inhibiting Life), incorporating 'Nifty Sausage' (Nuclear Fall-out Shelter for Survival of Earth) and filled several exercise books.

Communications

In his delightful, period detective novel, *Oscar Wilde and the Ring of Death*, Gyles Brandreth has his hero pronounce,

'Soon, I'm told, we shall all be linked by telephone – the length and breadth of the land. The telephone is about to revolutionize both the art of conversation and the science of detection. I am thinking of having one installed in Tite Street.'

'Do you know how to use a telephone, Oscar?' enquired Robert Sherard.

'Not yet, but I have children, Robert. They will teach me.'

And so it is with all new technology: if you cannot operate your latest piece of electronic equipment, seek the advice of somebody who is under the age of twenty.

It was much the same in Ireland until the end of the 1970s. Before then Headfort's telephone number, proudly embossed upon the School's writing paper, was Kells 65. When the town secured an automatic exchange in 1981, the number became 40065; later it swelled to 04640065 and eventually 0469240065 – internationally, 00353469240065 – fourteen digits, sufficient to identify one trillion customers; which is strange, considering that the world's population is seven billion.

That same year Headfort acquired a 'cordless' telephone; thus it became possible for parents sometimes to establish contact with the School. Previously, unless the Headmaster happened to be in his study, a member of the downstairs staff would have to embark upon the lengthy journey from the kitchen to the study on the next landing to answer a call, by which time the caller had generally rung off.

Summer nostalgia

The Summer Term Newsletter in 1981 bore the following passage under the heading 'Nostalgic end of term' that could have been written at any time:

> During the closing weeks of the Summer Term, amidst the myriad activities and functions that take place, the older boys and girls form incredibly close relationships with each other, as they come to realize that one chapter of their personal histories is drawing to a close. They share their likes and dislikes, discuss their aspirations and anxieties, and pledge to remain in contact when, as young fledglings, they fly the Headfort nest. On the penultimate day, with all sportswear packed, little groups walk wistfully over well-loved spots, each child trying to savour, in anticipation, the sense of severance from that umbilicus that has nurtured him through five years of mind-splitting development, from the day of his arrival as a grubby eight-year-old, exhibiting instant response to unconditional stimuli:

> … at his feet, some little plan or chart,
> Some fragment from his dream of human life,
> Shaped by himself with newly-learnéd art."

> until now, the day of departure as a fast-maturing young person, equipped with a broad portfolio of embryonic skills and knowledge,

> Shades of the prison-house begin to close
> Upon the growing boy [or girl].

> Wordsworth had in mind the closure of the age of innocence and the advent of the burden of responsibility. During the formative years the child sheds his absolute self-centredness, wherein the world and all its inhabitants are seen as satellites dancing to his every whim, and begins to find that he himself is but one, unexceptional, albeit unique, unit of the cosmos. He is discovering also that the world is not entirely a beautiful place; that adults are fallible (a shocking discovery, this), that riots, murders and suicides occur, that love is potentially unstable, and that henceforth he must apply his own criteria of right and wrong to protect himself against the snares that the world has set.

The boarding experience helps the neonate gently to slough his illusory skin and to assume a more realistic, tougher hide, but this realisation can be a lonely and very frightening experience.

1982 brought forth another harsh winter: heavy snow fell throughout the land in the New Year, thirty-seven pipes burst within the walls of the house and the boiler exploded. Many roads were completely impassable. The start of the Easter Term had to be postponed by six days.

More appointments

A key Headfort figure arrived that year. Sir Richard Musgrave recommended PEGGIE BALL for the position of Headmaster's secretary. Peggie, who had previously worked in the Estate office, became an influential figure in the life of the School for the next twenty-two years until her retirement in 2008. She was the Headmaster's 'Girl Friday': he often stated that he could not have survived without her supreme efficiency, her local knowledge and her encouragement when times were hard. A person of high intelligence, she has an analytical mind that enabled her to view problems from a fresh perspective.

Peggie Ball & the Headmaster at a children's party

When Peggie Ball retired as secretary ten years later (after an interval she returned in the role of Bursar), RENEE RYAN became the Headmaster's secretary. She too rendered loyal service and dealt with the quirks and foibles of her Headmaster for many years. Under the next regime, she moved away from the office and began to work in the matroning department where she may be found to this day.

One day the Headmaster telephoned David Gibbs, the Warden of St Columba's College, to enquire whether he had a suitable candidate for what is today called a 'gap' student. The Warden thought for a moment and then replied, 'Ah, I have one who is pure gold.' He perhaps understated the metal: MICHAEL BOLTON should have been described as platinum. He arrived at Headfort in 1981, originally for one year, and is still here thirty-one years later. His roles are almost infinite: he taught geography for many years; now he teaches science. He coaches rugby football enthusiastically and skilfully; creates breathtaking stage-craft for Headfort's drama and now directs drama himself; he has encouraged gardening and photography; has designed a nature trail and outward bound course. Today he is the Boarding Housemaster and also master in charge of ceremonies and 'events'. A behind-the-scenes man, he is a member of the Dig it and Dung it Society and has written the definitive history, 'Headfort House'.

DONNA WOODS was a successful teacher for several years. She managed to make the Irish language popular. MARIAN BUCKLEY joined the staff in 1989 and taught mathematics, computing and Irish with enthusiasm.

MARY MAHER assumed the riding mantle in 1989. She knows every detail concerning horses and most details concerning children. A hugely vital and attractive person, she has been one of Headfort's great riding teachers. During her time, a twenty-nine-jump hunter trial course was built, a large arena was erected and a set of professional jumps installed. Her influence at Headfort expanded even further in Headfort Today.

ROSEMARIE SHIELDS (née DOLAN) came to teach piano and direct the school choir. She subsequently became Head of Music and, in the next regime, widened her horizons, as will be revealed. Soon after Rosemarie's arrival, the Headmaster initiated, at IAPS level, the notion of an annual Choral Evening; the idea was that, while much of the member schools' inter-action involved competition, this event was to be one of cultural cooperation. Each year the schools would foregather once or twice for rehearsals and then present a concert. The first Irish IAPS Choral Evening was held in the Ball-room at Headfort in 1991 and subsequent concerts have alternated between the several schools. Rosemarie Shields has helped to design the programmes and trained the Headfort choirs.

First arriving on the scene in the 1980s, DECLAN DONNELLAN has been a popular tennis coach to several generations of pupils. He takes the same trouble over the totally uncoordinated racket wielder as he does with Headfort's budding Wimbledon stars of the future.

1980 was the year in which a young gap student called Dermot Dix returned to his old Alma Mater for a year. He maintains that the Headmaster paid him just enough to keep the tank of his Mini Minor sufficiently full to convey him to the Railway Bar after work.

When did MARY WILKINSON first work at Headfort, and in what capacity? This multi-faceted lady had already produced three sons for Head-fort, one of whom is a current teacher at the School; she has since served as Matron, Housekeeper, chauffeuse and wardrobe mistress extraordinaire. It was during Mary's term as Housekeeper that one of the domestic staff, a dear, simple soul who had worked conscientiously for several years in the kitchen and dining room region, and probably did not know what a man was, approached her one morning and stammered the astonishing news that the doctor had informed her that she was pregnant. Mary tried to hide her surprise and muttered something along the lines of, 'and who is the fortunate young man?' The reply startled her somewhat: 'Ah, sure, I didn't ask him his name.' It could only happen at Headfort.

Mary's sister, CAROLE BARRY, is another past Headfort parent who has worked at the School in many capacities, including Matron and Housekeeper. Since she retired in 1999 after five years' service, she is still one of the first people to whom successive Headmasters have recourse in times of crisis.

HELEN LANGAN, home from Rhodesia, was a colourful Housekeeper who joined the staff in 1980 for a number of years; she possessed a ripe vocabulary. She was replaced by Mary Wilkinson who rendered wonderful service until 1998. ELEANOR DE EYTO is another who worked with great loyalty in this fiercely demanding position.

Two past pupils each taught science for a couple of years when Peter Bamford retired: JOHNNY SPICER, one of six siblings all at Headfort, and subsequently step-father to one pupil and father of another; and SELENA MCKENZIE (née KINDERSLEY), sister to one past pupil. Both of them did excellent work in the laboratory and also contributed widely outside it. Headmasters like to have past pupils on the staff because they know how the place works.

Another past pupil, EVA FILGATE, worked effectively for two years at the end of the millennium as Assistant Matron, as well as teaching junior geography and science.

9. A LEASE IS SIGNED

Hallelujah! – Upstairs–downstairs – North–South relations – Swimming pool
'Bubble' – Boy soprano – Bank of Headfort cheque books – 1984 & Newspeak
– A sporting achievement – Duvets – Cigarettes – An academic landmark –
Reevaluation on transition – Changing society – Computing comes of age

Hallelujah!

1983 was a golden year for Headfort. The School had been squatters for almost three years, but now the estate was finally sold to B.J. (BILL) KRUGER, a Canadian paper magnate, and at last a new lease was signed. Confidence soared and enrolment rose rapidly once more. Most importantly the School became a Charitable Trust. In the past, it had traded as a Limited Company, always running within very tight margins, generally making either a surplus or a deficit in the order of two or three thousand pounds each year. However in years when the School managed to accrue a small profit, company tax had to be paid and the earnings could not be ploughed back into the business.

Charitable status and the signing of the new lease meant that, for the first time, the Headmaster was empowered to appoint a new Board of Directors, men and women with multifarious skills upon whom he could lean for advice. This was an enormous boon to him, after five years struggling in the wilderness on his own. Dick Musgrave accepted the position of Chairman, and GEORGE FÄSENFELD, RAYMOND GILMORE, GABRIELLE LAND-SEER, PETER LYONS and past pupil NOEL McMULLAN joined the Board at this time; they were all of immense value to the School in negotiating the lease, and continued to offer wise council in the years ahead. Raymond and George, in particular, sought to convert the Headmaster into a more commercial animal. Other people who rendered valuable service on the Board for periods of time during the Middle Years include DENNY WARDELL,

SEAN GALVIN, ANDY COX, LIZ SPICER, MICHAEL STAFFORD, DAVID SHILLINGTON, MARY WILLIAMS, RADINE HAMILTON, CAROLINE PRESTON, PHILIP MYERSCOUGH, MONICA FLOOD, BILL KRUGER, ANN MARSHALL and DERMOT MULVIHILL. Michael Stafford and Philip Myerscough, in collaboration with Peggie Ball who had become Lady Captain of Headfort Golf Club, organized a couple of highly successful golf classics in aid of the School.

Headfort golfers

For several years Bill Kruger had adopted the pattern of flying to Ireland from Canada every fortnight during the shooting season to 'bag' pheasants and duck. He would shoot at Dunsany Castle, the home of Lord and Lady Dunsany, on Saturdays and at Headfort on Sundays, before flying home. He rented Headfort Court on these occasions. Eventually, as he grew older, he decided to buy Headfort Estate and make it his permanent home. Although initially lukewarm towards it, Mr Kruger gradually grew fond of the little School that he found on his doorstep. He used to enjoy talking to the children during his morning walk as they played on the lawn; they were invariably polite and charming to the benign old gentleman. He awarded two entrance scholarships for a five-year period. Later he joined the Board of Directors. Many years afterwards, in 1990, having enormously enjoyed Headfort's production of Alan Bennett's *Forty Years On,* he threw a wonderful party in Headfort Court for the entire cast.

Upstairs–downstairs

After six years of playing the Fire Officer on a line, drastic action became unavoidable. In the early hours of 14 February 1981 a terrible inferno enveloped the Stardust Ballroom in Artane, County Dublin. 841 revellers were enjoying a discotheque that night when an electrical fault in the roof caused a conflagration. Forty-eight people were burned to death and a further 214 were injured. In the aftermath, it was revealed that there were bars to the windows in the lavatories, such that people could not escape; the ceilings were lined with flammable, carcinogenic material; some of the emergency doors were bolted with padlocks.

Understandably, there was nationwide concern about fire safety; Fire Officers became especially vigilant.

At Headfort the decision was taken completely to reorganize the house, such that the children would sleep on the ground floor in the west wing, and learn withup. The Headmaster summoned the staff to the study one break and told them that there was no alternative but to convert the dormitories into classrooms and vice versa. Each person was given a ground plan of the four stories of the house and invited to lend thought as to how to reconstitute the School. A fortnight later the staff reconvened to exchange their ideas; from these deliberations the house was effectively turned upside down.

The 'upstairs–downstairs' operation was one of the biggest upheavals in the School's history, and one of the most successful. On the final day of the Easter Term the children were given the instruction, 'take up your bed and walk', and so they carried their beds downstairs and passed the final night of the term camping on a mattress on the floor; this was regarded as a wizard wheeze. During the Easter holidays a majority of the staff, and even a few noble pupils, spent many hours thwacking nails and sploshing paint, as the top two storeys of the house were converted from dormitories into classrooms and the lower two were transmogrified in the opposite direction. It was a massive operation that had a great unifying effect upon the staff – what today would be called 'bonding'.

One of the principal benefits of the reorganization of the house was that the laundry was moved from the stable yard, whence an acreage of clothing had to be carried to the top of the house to be stored in the 'sewing room', to a utility room at the back of the kitchen. The drying room is nearby and clothes are now kept in an adjacent room.

Those Easter holidays were frenetic for the staff as, together with our friendly professional builder, Paddy O'Reilly, they strove to have the new-look School shipshape in time for the start of the Summer Term. The versatile and artistic Victor de Raeymaeker was the chief decorator, and remained so for many more years. A couple of days before term opened, the Headmaster suddenly realized that the new dormitories had no names. They were hastily christened Hypnos, Morpheus, Utopia, Elysium, Paradise, for the boys, and Isis, Vesta, Selene and, later, Artemis, for the girls, thus replacing the former Romans, Normans, Vikings, Celts, Picts, The Zoo, Spartans, et cetera. Initially the boys had to travel up two flights of stairs for their morning and evening ablutions, which was an inconvenience, but over the next few years more bathrooms were built; nowadays, many of the dormitories are en suite.

To help to finance this upheaval, a stylish Ball was held. Tickets were expensive, £200 per double ticket – in 1983! There was tremendous enthusiasm for the upstairs–downstairs operation, and parents subscribed generously to ensure that the Ball was the social event of the year. The gowns that the ladies wore that evening still live in the memories of those who attended.

That term's newsletter bore the following introduction, entitled 'The Mock Phoenix':

> The Phoenix, fabulous Arabian bird, redolent in gold and red plumage, worshipped by the ancient Egyptians, would immolate itself every 500 years or so and arise, rejuvenated, from its own ashes.
>
> What an ennobling sacrament! Purification and perpetuity attained through reincarnation. Necessity urges desperate measures. If a Fire Officer calls for change, then, *mutatis mutandis*, a new organism springs from the loins of the previous.
>
> The *Mock* Phoenix is the most apposite symbol of the New Headfort because re-birth came about through pyrophobia, although no conflagration raged (nor was likely to).

North–South relations

1983 was the year in which Headfort began travelling to Northern Ireland for sporting and cultural events for the first time since the outbreak of 'the troubles'. The Headmaster sought written permission from parents of the children who were selected to embark upon that first venture. Two families withheld permission, but their children never permitted them to do so again.

One boy who was a member of all of the sporting teams in those days suffered from severe kinetosis. The author's heart went out to the poor little man for whom these journeys must have been excruciating. He had the uncanny knack of alerting the driver as to exactly when he should stop the minibus. Unlike certain others, never once did he fail to give sufficient notice, and yet his timing was within nanoseconds of necessity. Curiously, he never suffered on the way home: his affliction was presumably a nervous reaction to the encounter ahead.

Swimming Pool 'bubble'

Also in 1983 a polythene 'bubble' was erected over the swimming pool. This remained in place until the end of the Middle Years. It may not have been a thing of beauty but, by retaining solar heat, it enabled the pool to be used far more widely for many years, despite the vagaries of the Irish summer.

Boy soprano

That year the finest boy soprano who has been at the School completed his Headfort career. In his final term a video recording was made to immortalize his talent. Accompanied in the grandeur of the Ballroom by Sibéal Rooney, he sang three pieces, including Mendelssohn's haunting 'On Wings of Song', as his fitting, yet demanding, swansong. The video panned across the estate, identifying rhododendrons and hydrangeas of multifarious hue, and capturing shots of carefree children going about their diurnal course. For one so young, our songbird injected a surprising intensity of emotion into his singing, drawing deep into his reserves, to give his audience a joyous experience. As the result of his work, he was awarded the principal boy soprano's role in a national production of *The King and I* during the holidays and, in the Gala Performance on opening night, he sung and acted before the President of Ireland.

Bank of Headfort cheque books

In 1984 Bank of Headfort cheque books were issued to each child with which to learn to manage his pocket money. It became a tradition that a packet of Rolos be given to a pupil at the end of term if his cheque book reconciled with the record of the Headmaster's secretary.

1984 & Newspeak

Naturally, George Orwell's dystopian novel, *1984*, was studied in the Upper Sixth that year. Arthur Koestler defined education as 'catalysing the mind'. This contrasts with the Concise Oxford Dictionary's definition, 'train (persons) … train (animals)', with its Pavlovian overtones. Koestler's ideal educator would trigger a reaction in his pupil without being involved in the product; he should not be a conditioning agent, for to influence is to intrude.

Orwell's 'Ingsoc' (English Socialism) is antithetical to Koestler's catalytic view of education. Fundamental to Ingsoc is the language Newspeak. Newspeak is less a means of communication than a medium for the expression of orthodox, Ingsoc thoughts. It was the intention that, when Oldspeak had been finally superceded by Newspeak, an heretical (i.e. anti-Ingsoc) thought would be literally unthinkable, because no word could correspond to it. The vocabulary of the language was being continually reduced, and the scope of words narrowed, in order to diminish the range of thought. The word 'free' still existed in Newspeak, but it could only be used in the sense, 'this child is free from lice'; since political and intellectual freedom no longer existed, even as concepts, there was naturally no word for it. It was hoped that eventually the vocabulary of Newspeak would reduce to zero, such that no thought involving the higher brain centre would be possible. Then articulate, but thought-free, communication would be reduced to a form of laryngeal spasm. Big Brother would hold full control over his flock.

The Newspeak word for such utterance is 'duckspeak' which is defined as quacking like a duck, without thinking. Many a time that term a member of the Upper Sixth was addressed as a 'doubleplusungood duckspeaker' as a term of abuse. But, how mistaken! What could indicate a higher level of Ingsoc orthodoxy than the ability to duckspeak? A marvellously Zen idea!

A sporting achievement

Headfort had an especially strong hockey team in 1984 and for the first, and so far only, time in its history reached the final of the Leinster Hockey Union Under Thirteen Cup.

Cup finalists in 1984

Although hockey is one of the School's three principal games for both girls and boys and holds sway in the Easter Term, Headfort suffers a severe disadvantage in this sport in that it does not own any form of artificial surface, let alone a fancy 'astroturf' that many of the Dublin schools possess; and of course a grass pitch, although delightful to play upon, is an unreliable surface in the Irish winter.

Despite this handicap, Headfort reached the final of the competition that year. The entire School was conveyed by minibus, and staff and parents' cars, to Three Rock Rovers Hockey Club in Dublin to challenge Brook House, a team that was expertly coached by their Headmaster, Chris Macdonald, before he was lured to Headfort. Brook House was also strong, but Headfort had beaten them narrowly, both at home and away, during the term and so entered the final with a degree of confidence.

Headfort had never played on an astroturf surface before. Neither had Brook House; however, Chris Macdonald had craftily hired the pitch the day before the match and his team developed a sophisticated method of taking short corners – one that would not have worked on grass. This was to prove crucial in the final. At half-time, the Headfort myrmidons held a 1–0 lead; however, in the first ten minutes of the second half, Brook House executed two superb short corners to put them in front, and they finally won an exciting game 3–2.

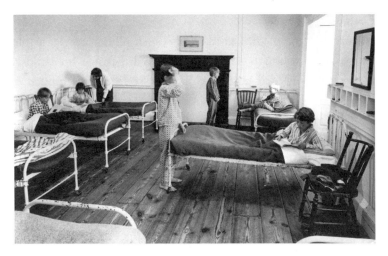

Edith Sweetman tucks up a child in a mid-1970s, pre-duvet dormitory

Duvets

In 1985 duvets replaced sheets and blankets in the dormitories. The original intention was that duvet covers should be of a uniform colour for each dormitory, but the children outlawed that idea; in consequence, duvets extolled the glories of Marilyn Monroe, Elvis Presley, Manchester United and other lurid images. In the same year children were permitted to invite visitors home at the weekend for the first time.

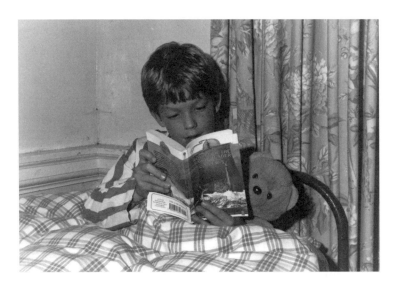

'Me & my Bear' in the duvet era

Cigarettes

As in much of the rest of the world, cigarette smoking was rife at Headfort. I refer to the staff, although it was not wholly unknown for children, who follow the example of their elders, to have the odd drag behind the squash court. The upstairs staffroom used to be suffused with smoke, which of course radiated into the children's corridors and classrooms.

Just as in Irish cinemas and aeroplanes in the 1960s, Headfort's downstairs staffroom was a suffocating environment. Those who did not smoke found the atmosphere barely capable of sustaining human life. Sometime in the middle of the 1980s the Headmaster had the temerity to request staff not to smoke during staff meetings, to which they graciously acceded. Of course, years later it became illegal to smoke at all in public places.

An academic landmark

1986 was the first time that Headfort had sent children to each of the 'big three', Eton, Harrow and Winchester, all in the one term. At the same time pupils advanced to other famous secondary schools: Ampleforth, Campbell College, Downe House, Downside, Glenstal, St Columba's, St Mary's Shaftesbury and Uppingham.

Reevaluation on transition

It was a time of reevaluation within the independent school sector. In England a Working Party was established by the Independent Schools Joint Council (ISJC), comprising bodies from all types of independent schools under the chairmanship of Ian Beer, Headmaster of Harrow, to investigate aspects of transfer from preparatory to senior school. These deliberations held relevance to Headfort because eleven out of the thirteen members of the Upper Sixth that year were destined for HMC schools.

It was clear that greater emphasis would be placed upon oral and practical work and that some form of internal assessment would be introduced. It was Sir Keith Joseph's (the British Minister for Education) policy to issue by the end of the decade a certificate for all school leavers in the form of a record of achievement. This would be a dossier, recording all of what had been achieved

HEADFORT

GOVERNING BODY
The school is a Charitable Trust,
governed by a Board of Directors.

Sir Richard Musgrave Bt. (Chairman)
George J. J. Fäsenfeld
Raymond J. Gilmore
W. Lingard W. Goulding
The Most Hon. The Marquis of Headfort
Peter J. Lyons

Noel McMullan
Gabrielle Williams
Dr. Andrew Cox (alternate to Sir Richard Musgrave)
R. W. Newport F.C.A.
(Secretary and alternate to Lord Headfort)
 Auditors: Touche Ross & Co.

STAFF	Years of Service	Position	Subjects
J. E. Sweetman, M.A. (T.C.D.)	36	Senior Master	History, Geography
Mrs. E. Sweetman	27	House Mother	
J. A. Leyden, M.A. (Oxon)	16		English, Mathematics
Mrs. A. Leyden, Trained Teacher (University of London)	16	Remedial Teacher	English, Mathematics
C. P. Bamford	15		Science
V. De Raeymaeker, H.Dip.Ed.	14		French
W. L. W. Goulding, B.A. (T.C.D.), H.Dip.Ed.	12	Headmaster	Mathematics, English
Mrs. S. V. Rooney, Mus.Bach. (U.C.C.)	12		Music
Revd. Canon A. R. Olden, M.A. (T.C.D.)	9		Scripture
Mrs. L. Tilson	9	Matron	
Mrs. P. Ball	8	Headmaster's Secretary	
Mrs. K. Osthus	8		Art
R. G. H. Simmons, M.A. (Oxon)	7		Latin, Greek
Mrs. H. Langan	6	Housekeeper	
Monsignor J. Shortall, P.P., V.G.	5		Scripture
M. D. C. Bolton	5		Mathematics, English, History, Physical Educ.
J. Brunnock, B.A. (U.C.D.), H.Dip.Ed.	5		Irish
Revd. J. Conlon, C.C.	2		Scripture
Mrs. R. Butler	2	Riding Mistress	

School Doctors:
Dr. M. J. O'Connell, M.B., B.Ch., L.M., L.F.O.M., M.C.G.P.
Dr. J. M. J. O'Connell, M.B., B.Ch., D.Obs., D.C.H., F.P.C.

September, 1986

Headfort staff in 1986

at school, be it academic, practical or cultural. The document would be standardized in format and was intended to assist a prospective employer to form his assessment of an applicant.

What might be the effect of this upon prep schools? Well, there would almost certainly be less compulsory examination papers, but greater opportunity to offer evidence of accomplishment in newer fields of endeavour. At the heart of the recommendations was the idea of compiling 'subject profiles' that would show details of topics covered during the final two years at prep school, as assessed internally by the pupils' own teachers. Profiles could be prepared for such topics as craft–design–technology (CDT), electronics, computer studies, art, music, drama, as well as traditional subjects. Concomitant with subject profiles would be a 'general profile' that would give evidence of personal qualities and cultural and sporting accomplishments. The general profile seemed to be simply a standardized version of the character reference that the prep school Headmaster already wrote to his public school counterpart at the time of transition.

Much of this made sense. However, what caused a good deal of soul-searching at the time was how to introduce some form of machinery to safeguard against the traditional subjects from being downgraded and overall standards becoming eroded.

Chapter fifteen will reveal whether these predictions came to pass.

Changing society

The 1987 Newsletter contained the following:

> In my address at the Valedictory service, I alluded to a degree of change that was perceptible in children over the ten years of my tenure of office at Headfort. It is part of a continuing trend and not peculiar to the last decade, but it would appear to have run almost full-cycle. Due to the explicitness of media communications, modern children are no longer sheltered from any of life's truths, howsoever unpalatable, but are exposed from an early age to the salient issues of the day that are debated by their elders. Thus, unless they are deaf and blind to external influences – which they are not – your children cannot fail to be versed in the instruments of planetary destruction, for example, or in the existence of opiates and amphetamines, of deviant behaviour and unattractively-transmitted diseases.

Nothing wrong with knowledge, one might argue. Indeed. However, the introduction of this particular type of knowledge so early in the learning process can pose a problem; for children are being subjected to a barrage of seamy information before they possess the maturity to interpret it critically. They receive it hypothetically, in an experiential vacuum. Thus they are peculiarly susceptible to the glamorous presentation of any of these matters, which may assume obsessive importance in a young mind. In our weekly Current Affairs meetings, for which children gather and present items of news, it is rare these days if one or more of the following topics is not raised: nuclear warfare and disarmament, 'defence' missiles, murder, drug hauls, abortion, AIDS. One may regret the intrusion of these issues, but there is no point in trying to suppress them.

Computing comes of age

In 1988 the subject of computing was incorporated into the timetable for every child. They learnt how to interact with the new machines: how to type, to use software packages and to program in a high-level language. From early on, computer games that involved zapping aliens were frowned upon; indeed, they were outlawed, except at weekends. Otherwise children might only play games that they had designed and programmed themselves. Several children became adept at communicating with the computer and composed quite sophisticated games, considering the limited capacity of the 1980s machines. A generalization: it was normally the boys who became absorbed with computers; only one girl comes to mind as having shown special aptitude in those years. Around this time, the pupils' magazine, *Headfort Bizarre*, was generated by computer for the first time by a committee that was elected each term by the pupils themselves.

10. FORTY YEARS ON

Forty years on – A bumper year – Girl contralto – An abomination –
Political correctness – Staff and Board changes – Hard times – We win the Cup
– Public speaking – Drama 1

Forty years on

1989 was the fortieth year of Headfort's existence as a prep school. An Anniversary Garden Party was held on 1 July to celebrate the occasion. The highlight of the event was the presence of Mr and Mrs David Wild who travelled from Devon; it was the former Headmaster's first – and, sadly, only – return to Headfort after his retirement twelve years previously. Many of 'his' past pupils came from afar to greet him. The grounds looked magnificent: under Michael Bolton's creative eye, boys and girls had devoted hours of their leisure time to ensure that Headfort appeared at its most attractive for Mr and Mrs Wild. Every evening, children, clad in plastic bin liners, could be seen painting doors, windows and drainpipes in the stable yard; or shifting earth, clearing the moat, building a rockery. They resembled a swarm of ants, striving towards a common goal.

David and Barbara Wild stayed at Headfort for a week. It was a memorable occasion and many of their friends had the opportunity to renew their acquaintance.

A bumper year

1990 was a marvellous year for Headfort. The Upper Sixth was one of the strongest ever. The School was good at work, good at games, good at drama and there were several fine musicians. Four scholarships were won to secondary schools, both in Ireland and England. And the School population reached over one hundred pupils in the Summer Term – all boarding.

Headfort c 1990

And another boon … From the Easter 1990 Newsletter:

Water, water, everywhere. All our troubles now are ended – well, our aquatic troubles anyway. Throughout the School's history we have suffered from problems with the water supply. Water was pumped from the river by an antediluvian 'ram', transported through atherosclerotic pipework. The ram was prone to sit down on the job, especially at weekends, leaving us carrying buckets. The system was designed for a large household but, even in Headfort's squirearchical heydey with thirty-six gardeners and a plethora of underfootmen and ladies' maids, the demand for water cannot have been as great as for 100-odd children.

That was all in the past, however. During the term Mr Kruger connected the estate to the Mains supply, with the result that we now have a reliable flow of clean water to replace the brackish, semi-solid substance that used to cough and widdle its way through our taps. Just imagine, if you can, the joy of being able to see your toes in the bath for the first time. In the past, as with Bertrand Russell, we had to deduce their existence logically.

In celebration of our newfound aquafecundity I propose to install a sprinkling of showers in place of some of the baths. Next term your children may shower to their hearts' content and Headfort will boast the cleanest children this side of the black stump.

Girl contralto

Another memory from 1990 stems from the final gathering of the Summer Term when, before the entire School and parents, our wonderful young contralto gave a moving rendition of Orfeo's 'What is Life to me without thee?' from Wilhelm Gluck's *Orpheus and Eurydice*, a part immortalized by Kathleen Ferrier. It is rare to find such a mature contralto voice in a girl so young.

An abomination

For some years the Headmaster had felt embarrassed by the primitive nature of the dormitories while showing prospective parents around the School. Sometimes he would try a limp phrase, such as:

'We merely use the dormitories for the function of sleeping, don't you know? The children actually live in their classrooms.'

'Quite,' says Mrs Prospective, wrapping her coat tightly about her neck. An icicle forms under her husband's nose.

And so a plan was formed to introduce an element of comfort to the dormitories and, in Stage Two, dare it be mentioned ... a calorie or two of warmth?

A startling event took place in 1991 when radiators were installed in the dormitories. Past pupils could be heard gasping in horror:

'My God! Heating in the dormitories?'

'Shiver me whiskers!'

'Goulding's gone doolally!'

'Totally senile.'

'When I was at Headfort, we had to cut the stalactites from the side of our beds in order to get up in the mornings.'

'It was at least ten degrees minus.'

'Colder, my dear fellow, much colder.'

'Yes. Those were the days.'

Political Correctness

From the Christmas Newsletter:

It is a strange world for which we are preparing your children. In Brent, the Looney Left have proscribed reference to teddy-bears, because they are 'Eurocentric' and 'bourgeois'. An employer must ensure that he offers equal opportunity when advertising a position. He must avoid any suspicion of sexism, ageism, racism; perhaps if he makes his appointment on the criterion of aptitude for the job, he may stand guilty of 'aptism'. The Dutch have recently reduced the age of consent to twelve. In contrast, Don Marquis suggests that, if a child proves himself incorrigible, he should be decently and quietly beheaded at the age of twelve – a critical age, evidently.

Dennis Silk, the distinguished Warden of Radley, speaking at the IAPS Conference in Manchester recently, opined that the principal problems of education in the 1990s are 'greed' and 'softness'. Modern children, he contended, will do most things for a handful of silver – but they prefer gold. Many Headfort children received an inoculation against influenza this term; would that they might have had a second jab to protect them against materialism – it is more contagious and debilitating. The average Adrian Mole and his Pandora bring back to Headfort far more valuable possessions than did their elders, and a few of them talk very big when they discuss pocket money. No harm, one might argue, unless the attachment to these possessions grows too strong. Materialism is prevalent however, and although we try to inculcate counterbalancing values, Headfort is not immune to it.

Following along the same lines, here is an excerpt from the Easter 1994 Newsletter, under the heading 'Educational Modernity':

I read recently about the English headmistress who disallowed her pupils to attend a performance of Shakespeare's Romeo and Juliet because it portrayed love that was exclusively heterosexual. I could draw either of two conclusions: one – the reflex – was that the lady had flipped; and the other, more disturbing, was that, in experiencing shock, I myself was approaching gagadom. In the arrogant belief that I still held retention of at least some of my marbles, I tried to view the issue from her point of view: there must be Yin and Yang in everything; every shade, creed, proclivity must receive equal emphasis. Sounds reasonable, but …

Consider Shakespeare, or Sean O'Casey. To approve the love between Romeo and Juliet – or Jack and Nora – is not to impugn that between David and Jonathan.

Yet, even if I quietly mock the more extreme manifestations of educational modernity, there is no doubt that we at Headfort have also moved on in our thinking. Twenty years ago our production team would have been feign to present on stage Rosie Redmond, a young lady somewhat 'lapsed', in our production of The Plough and the Stars.

Certain things have always been permissible within Irish society: drunkenness, no problem. Fluther Good could have been as fluthered as bedamned fifty years ago, and nobody would have fluttered an eyelid.

Staff and Board changes

In 1992 PETER LYONS succeeded Sir Richard Musgrave, who was spending more time abroad, as Chairman of the Board. Sir Richard was appointed Patron of Headfort in recognition of the manifold services that he had rendered to the School over many years.

At the end of 1992 Jack and Edith Sweetman retired after forty-one years (slightly less in Edith's case) of magnificent service. They had been instrumental in structuring the School, almost from the beginning.

For the academic year 1992–3 CHRIS MACDONALD was appointed Assistant Headmaster and JEAN MACDONALD Housemother. Chris had been Headmaster of St Paul's Junior School in Darjeeling from 1964 until 1978, and came to Ireland in 1978 to work at Brook House, assuming the Headmastership there in its final years from 1982 until 1990, when the proprietors closed its doors. His appointment as Assistant Headmaster was a great boon to the Headmaster for the final decade of his tenure and also for the first five years of Dermot Dix's. Chris Macdonald was a wonderful schoolmaster. He was calm and rational. He was good with all categories of personnel: children, staff and parents; he had the knack of pouring oil upon troubled waters. He taught history and assumed from the Headmaster the role of coaching Top Game hockey. He was also instrumental in the structuring of Sports Day, working alongside John Leyden. Jean Macdonald was a caring Housemother to the girls, and subsequently taught art to the entire school. She introduced basketball to the School, especially for the girls.

John Leyden was appointed Senior Master at this time and he developed several new procedures, relating to timetabling and the scheduling of extracurricular activities.

BRENDAN MUNSTER taught clarinet, flute and saxophone in the early 1990s.

PHILIPPA COLLIER has given cookery lessons with devotion for many years. Not surprisingly, this is a favourite afternoon activity, especially among the less fanatical games players. They swell with pride when their enticing concoctions appear on the table at teatime.

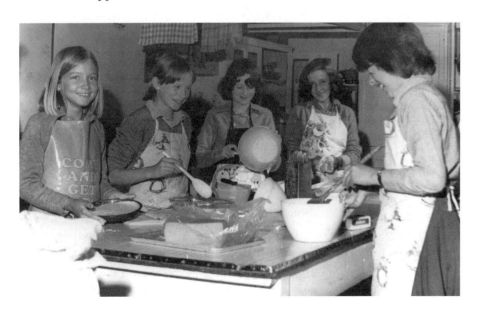

PAT SWINEY replaced Lynne Tilson as Matron in 1987. She was a reliable person in whom the Headmaster, parents and children had confidence. Latterly she asked to transfer to the kitchen region where she donned her chef's hat for another few years of excellent service.

A key appointment was made in 1993 with the arrival of past pupil NEVILLE WILKINSON to teach English and mathematics; a wonderful games player and knowledgeable archivist, he has became one of Headfort's indispensable members of staff. He continues to serve in all areas of School life in Headfort Today.

The Summer Term of 1993 saw the departure of two irreplaceable treasures, Peter Bamford and Victor de Raeymaeker; Peter had reached retirement age and Victor accepted a post in his native Bruges.

Peter Bamford   *Victor de Raeymaeker*

A year later the Headmaster received a virtual prose-poem from Victor in which he spoke of the grass being not necessarily greener on the other side. He was teaching French through the medium of Dutch and admitted to occasionally being lost, mid-sentence, for a Dutch word and receiving help from the pupils, 'just as happened twenty-one years ago when sniggering Headfort brats delighted in explaining to me the difference between "third" and "turd."' He was admiring his beloved Flemish primitive painters in the beautiful city of Bruges where he lived and enjoying the high culinary tradition of Belgian household cooking. On Christmas Eve he performed in a medieval Christmas play in which he took the part of a soldier who boasted of how many innocent children he had slaughtered.

The following summer Dr Michael O'Connell retired. His replacement was readily achieved by the substitution of his son, DR JOHN O'CONNELL, who had worked with his father for several years and knew Headfort inside out. Dr John who trained at Temple Street Children's Hospital also had a marvellous manner with children: they never knew whether he was joking or being serious: while they were trying to work out which, he had injected an entire needle's worth of serum into them. Dr John served loyally until the end of the Middle Years and beyond.

Hard times

In 1993, following the illness and subsequent death of Bill Kruger, the estate was once more put on the market. This again gave rise to rumours of uncertainty as to the School's future and over the next couple of years numbers dropped. However, on 25 March a new fifteen-year lease, renewable at five-yearly intervals, was signed. Parents and prospective parents were told that they might breed children afresh, secure in the knowledge that Headfort would be there to educate their progeny. It took time for the world to be reassured.

1993 First XI

We win the Cup

In 1993 Headfort began to participate in the Leinster Cricket Union Under Thirteen Cup. That year the School reached the final, but was defeated by Belvedere College. In 1995 Headfort won the Cup for the first time, beating the highly favoured Wesley team in an exciting, low-scoring final on a saturated wicket. When Headfort had slumped to fifty-eight for nine in its twenty-five overs (the only time in that season of sixteen games that it had lost more than two wickets for less than 100 runs), the captain told his men that he had only rehearsed a victory speech and would be tongue-tied if they lost. His bowlers dismissed Wesley for eighteen.

*Mr David Pigot (Ireland & Phoenix C.C.) presents the Leinster
Cricket Union Under Thirteen Cup to the Headfort captain in 1995*

During a successful tour of England that season, Headfort ran up a score of 245 for four against The Oratory and dismissed them for 198.

Guard of honour for a centurion

From 1993 until 2004 (with the exceptions of 1996 and 2002) the exploits of Headfort's cricketers were commemorated in an annual production bearing the generic title, *The Cicada* (a cicada being an homopterous insect, akin to a grasshopper – hence, a cricket) that became known as the 'Headfort Wisden'. The last few versions were *Cicadacide* in 2001, *The Posthumous Cicada* in 2002, *Not really a Cicada* in 2003 and *The Cicada's Final Incarnation* in 2004.

Public Speaking

The Headfort Ballroom is a large room with a high ceiling. It is not easy for young people to make themselves heard clearly by an audience.

The Kilroy Cup (1986) and the Potts Cup (1988) are public speaking competitions, for seniors and juniors respectively, that are contested each year towards the end of the Christmas Term. Children choose a passage to read from a given list; then they are presented with an unseen piece to deliver in front of the whole school and, generally, a visiting adjudicator. It is quite a daunting experience, but valuable in teaching them to enunciate clearly.

Oracy, an ugly word, is surely a discipline that should be encouraged in the young: to beware the habit-formed tone of voice, punctuated betimes with ridiculous emphases and somnolent monotony. One should speak half as much and twice as well.

Of course, there is nothing new in this; it is just a re-emphasis of an old notion. In 393 BC Isocrates opened a school in Athens, near Aristotle's subsequent Lyceum, whereat he inculcated rhetoric, essentially for the training of orators. He taught astronomy and geometry as a 'gymnastic of the mind', and dialectic, the art of debate, as a practical technique. For Isocrates, rhetoric was a culture, not some smart-aleck facility for scoring offensive points off another person, as became the custom in some of the later Roman schools. Seneca wrote, 'Non vitae, sed scholae discimus' (we teach, not for life, but for the classroom). Rhetoric subsists in the content as well as the expression of thought. The aim at Headfort is to develop children who are orate.

David Wild used to conduct 'Current Affairs' in the old library on Saturday afternoons. In the Middle Years, when children started to go home at weekends, Current Affairs moved to Tuesdays after lunch. The top four forms attended in the Ballroom. Each week one child was required to prepare and deliver information on Irish affairs, one on British affairs, a third on

European and a fourth on World affairs. Other children could contribute from the floor. They were encouraged to read the newspapers and to seek information from any source. This exercise also taught children to project their voices in a large auditorium.

Drama 1

From the earliest times there had been some form of drama at Headfort, including concerts, recitals, pageants and revues. Bill and Kate Stuart-Mills produced twenty-three Christmas Carol Concerts; in 1966 David Gamble and Peter Armstrong produced plays for a few years, one called *Have You Anything To Declare?* and another, *The Sport of Kings*; then in the mid-1970s John and Amanda Leyden produced more Christmas concerts, a Christmas Passion play in the Ballroom in 1974 and a series of short, home-written plays in the old Playroom that were enjoyed. One year John directed an abridged version of Nikolai Gogol's *The Government Inspector*. The former Matron, Eileen Armstrong, and SHEILA LYNCH assisted Mary Leftwich with the costumes.

A past pupil from the 1950s recalls a visit from Micheál Mac Liammóir, Hilton Edwards and Anew McMaster, three of Dublin's finest actors, who performed several short pieces at the School. This pupil still treasures their autographs.

In the 1980s the School began to tackle more challenging, full-length plays, performed in the spectacular setting of the Robert Adam Ballroom. This was enabled by the skills, firstly of Mary Leftwich, then of Mary Wilkinson, wardrobe mistresses of consummate imagination and flair, and Michael Bolton whose stage sets were of nigh professional standard.

St Patrick's Day became a red-letter day in the life of the School. Beginning with a General Knowledge test in the morning, there followed the Parents' Hockey match in the afternoon, and then the final performance of the play in the evening. The Ballroom was packed to the rafters, such that the youngest children had to sit on rugs on the floor at the front.

Appendix B shows a list of these productions. The theory was that, if children were offered something trite, the result would not be memorable; whereas, if they were given a challenge that was truly demanding, then it was astonishing what they could achieve. It became a matter of pride that, by the beginning of the run, every word could be heard distinctly from the back of the Ballroom. This followed weeks of rehearsal at which a miserable critic in the back row would constantly call, 'Can't hear!'

Memories of the productions remain vivid for those who acted in them and those who watched. *Under Milk Wood* in 1981 was not really a School play: it was a form play, performed solely by the Upper Sixth that contained six pupils, all boys. The mighty six enacted thirty-three characters from amongst the quixotic citizenry of Llareggub, necessitating lightning changes of costume. Mary Leftwich dressed some of the actors in three sets of clothes at the outset, such that one layer could be peeled off rapidly, instantly to convert The Rev. Eli Jenkins into the 'fallen' Rosie Probert, and thence into the haberdasher, Mr Mog Edwards, for example.

In 1986 the Upper Sixth produced William Trevor's *The Old Boys*, the story of a handful of septuagenarians who live in the past and vie for the honour of becoming President of the Old Boys' Association of their former school. Many of these old fellows live at the Rimini Hotel and I fear that a few of them are beginning to lose their marbles: General Sanctuary's delusional psychosis, for instance, leads him to believe that he is still living in the regimental mess. The Manageress, Miss Burdock, holds awful sway at the Rimini – chaps say that she even keeps a cane! She was the sole actress in the cast – Mrs Jaraby is insistent of the fact, but doesn't Mrs J. knit beautifully?

Amadeus in 1988 was one of Headfort's most beautiful productions. Peter Schaffer's script required a modest touch of expurgation to render it suitable for the prep school stage. However, the hero retained a degree of 'sauciness', although the Headfort production team presented him as less cretinous, more sublime, than the original portrayal. Apart from Wolfgang Amadeus himself, a wonderful performance was given by the aging Antonio Salieri, the self-styled 'Patron Saint of Mediocrity', who, I'm sorry to say, cut his throat rather gruesomely towards the end – it wasn't pretty. Throughout that Easter Term Mozart's glorious music resonated throughout the Ballroom every evening. By the end of term, even those who were not especially musical might be heard humming arias as they traversed the corridors between classes. One scene did not go quite as planned. At the end of the play Mozart lay dying, with his wife, Constanze, and young son, Karl, by his bedside. He was composing the haunting 'Lacrimosa' from his *Requiem* that could be heard pulsating in the background, when the baton dropped from his hand and his life ebbed away. Four dignified servants entered the room and reverently draped a white sheet over the body. They bore him on a stretcher and gently lowered him into a paupers' grave

Under Milk Wood

Dai Bread, the baker.

1st. Voice..

Mr. & Mrs. Cherry Owen.

The Old Boys

Mr. & Mrs. Jaraby.

Sir George Ponders and Mr. Nox.

The Committee Meeting.

Under Milk Wood *and* The Old Boys *from the early 1980s*

off the back of the stage, before shovelling 'lime' upon the body (while the actor, rapidly restored to life, scuttled hastily away under the stage to avoid being doused in flour). The production team expected that this most solemn and poignant moment of the evening might extrude the odd tear from the audience; instead, a liberal sprinkling of mirth could be detected, as our sublime Wolfgang was tipped over the edge of the stage, landing safely on the high jump mat that had been placed strategically underneath. Audiences are invariably fickle.

In 1989 Headfort drama tackled a full-length Shakespearean play for the first time. *Julia Caesar* was performed to a packed audience on the Ides of March and again on St Patrick's Day. The bard's title for the play was modified slightly to register the fact that a girl played the role of Caesar. Great care had to be taken over the assassination scene during the dress rehearsal and the first performance, because Mary Leftwich was growing paranoid lest her magnificent costumes be destroyed by the copious quantities of 'blood' that the conspirators wished to discharge. The final night was truly gory. Cinna the Poet won the audience's heart with his inane laughter, and you will never have witnessed a more blood-curdling scene than the death of Brutus: transfixed most gorily on Strato's sword, he managed to gurgle his serene final message, 'Caesar, now be still; I kill'd not thee with half so good a will', with the death rattle clearly audible from his punctured lungs.

> Forty years on, when afar and asunder
> Parted are those who are singing today,
> When you look back, and forgetfully wonder
> What you were like in your work and your play...
>
> Forty years on, growing older and older;
> Shorter in wind as in memory long,
> Feeble of foot and rheumatic of shoulder,
> What will it help you that once you were strong?

Peculiarly amongst institutions, schools possess the power to induce nostalgia. When, with the passage of time, we grow just a little less agile, a little less virile; when we come to appreciate that our achievements have not been quite as meteoric as we had expected, that our aspirations will probably never be realized; then, it revitalizes the waning confidence to reflect, perhaps with a smidgeon of hyperbole, upon our halcyon days – those days when the world was at our fingertips and we felt in full control of our destinies. It is easeful to regurgitate, as it were, our moments of glory (we discard, of course, those of ignominy – memory is tastefully selective).

Alan Bennett's *Forty Years On* was presented one year after Headfort's fortieth anniversary. The playwright defined his play as, 'a life-support system for the preservation of bad jokes.' We rather relish bad jokes at Headfort: they are the stuff of childhood humour – not just 'nudge-nudge, wink-winkery', but also the honest-to-goodness, ghastly pun. When an audience groans under the force of a painful pun-ch (aw!), it is because they wish that they had thought of it first, or at least seen it coming in time to duck.

Forty Years On was the most complicated play that the School has undertaken. The recursive theme of a play within a play within a play, and even a school play within a school play, required considerable acting ability and stagecraft to render it intelligible to an audience. Fortunately, as has already been suggested, that year's Upper Sixth was the cleverest of all those in the Middle Years – it was peopled with boys and girls of great academic ability, musical talent and zany imagination – and there were exciting performances from pupils in the lower forms as well. Two special memories: the Headmaster (of the school within the school) addressed the audience before the start of the school play. He was in his final term at the school and was holding a cup of tea in his hand as he launched into a prayer, as was his wont at every opportunity: 'Oh Lord, take this cup from me', he intoned, whereupon a little boy, whose name chanced to be Lord, stepped forward and removed the cup. 'Oh, thank you, Lord', said the Headmaster, looking down in some surprise.

Bennett's Lady Sybilline Quarrell caricatures the 'Bloomsbury Set' society hostess, Lady Ottoline Morrell, who was a cousin of Britain's Queen Elizabeth, the Queen Mother. Lady Ottoline was a strikingly attractive woman with blazing copper-red hair and turquoise eyes. She had affairs with Bertrand Russell and Augustus John among others. But it was her extreme height that the Headfort production team chose to focus upon. Hence two actors were employed to represent her, one sitting upon the shoulders of the other, the combination swathed in a magnificent flowing gown. In rehearsal for the school play (within the school play), she (they) was (were) behaving in a disgracefully flirtatious manner with Bertrand Russell when the straight-laced Headmaster (of the school within the school) appeared. He roundly upbraided Lady Ottoline for unseemly behaviour and, when he recognized that two boys were involved in her representation, he ordered them to separate at once. He addressed Tupper, an especially cheeky schoolboy,

'Tupper, I knew that you would be at the bottom of this.' With a grin, Tupper replied,

'No, Sir, I was on the top.'

Rosemarie Shields produced a romantic version of *The Sound of Music* in 1991. The choir was in fine voice and there was some superb solo singing.

Victor de Raeymaeker's impression of Judge Taylor at Maycomb County Court

The Empress of Blandings was presented in 1992. It was an amalgam of excerpts from five of P.G. Wodehouse's novels that related to the loony Earl of Emsworth and his gross, prize-winning porker. Our Earl was splendidly dotty and there was also a special performance from Dame Daphne Winkworth. After leaving School, the Earl became an avid collector of Wodehouse's work and owned several first editions.

To Kill a Mockingbird was a thought-provoking production in 1993 that saw Michael Bolton's stagecraft soar to new heights. In the critical court scene, the black people were confined to a balcony, whereas the whites sat below. The balcony had a decidedly vertiginous effect upon a few of the actors.

Atticus Finch takes aim at a mad dog. Heck Tate, the Sheriff, and Jem Finch, watch anxiously. Miss Stephanie Crawford and Miss Maudie Atkinson cannot bear to look

As with Shakespeare, very little amendment was required to the script of Sean O'Casey's *The Plough and the Stars*. There were memorable performances from Jack and Nora Clitheroe, the quirky Uncle Peter who hadn't missed a pilgrimage to Bodenstown these twenty-five years, The Young Covey, Mrs Jinnie Gogan and her consumptive daughter Mollser, Mrs Bessie Burgess, the boozy carpenter Fluther Good and the 'fri'fly refeened Lady from Rarthmeenes'.

Headfort's adaptation of Baroness Orczy's *The Scarlet Pimpernel* revealed Mary Wilkinson's costume skills at their zenith. The haute couture at Lord Grenville's ball was spectacular. The interpretation of Sir Percy Blakeney saw one of Headfort's outstanding acting performances, and there were numerous charming cameos as well.

The Prioress & Sisters of the Convent of St Hermine les Vignes

The programme notes contained the following:

> We seek him here; we seek him there;
> Those Frenchies seek him everywhere.
> Is he in heaven? Is he in hell?
> That demned, elusive Pimpernel.

Liberté, Égalité, Fraternité.

The glistening blade cascades downwards in a rasping crescendo of sound.

Splat! A moment of indefinable, stomach-churning horror as steel penetrates the victim's neck, searing effortlessly through epidermis, subcutaneous tissue, muscle and bone. The total severance releases an arterial Niagara of oxygenated blood that bespatters the faces and clothes of the baying, hysterical mob. The aristocratic head – eyes distended in a primal fix of terror – disgorges the sinewy contents of its cranial cage as it tumbles into the putrescent, wicker basket among other ci-devant Counts, Marquises and parasitical clergy.

Daily – indeed hourly – the hideous instrument of death claimed its myriad victims: old men, young women, even small children, until one day it would demand the head of a King and his beautiful young Queen.

There was but one cloud on Citizen Chauvelin's horizon. Recently a number of aristos had succeeded in fleeing from France and arriving in England. It was said that a band of meddlesome Englishmen were snatching lawful victims from under the very nose of Madame la Guillotine. Their leader had assumed almost supernatural qualities in the eyes of the French.

Tonight, Ladies and Gentlemen, we shall see which of those two giants of intrigue, M. Chauvelin or the Scarlet Pimpernel, will triumph in their ultimate joust.

Monsieur Chauvelin & Lady Blakeney

II. ANNUS MIRABILIS

Headfort's 'annus mirabilis' – Effects of the sale of the estate – The arrival of day pupils – Personnel – Bad language – Runaways – Headfort's worst day

Headfort's 'annus mirabilis'

1996 was a monumental year in Headfort's history.

Firstly, Headfort bought Headfort! Throughout the first forty-seven years of its existence the School had been a tenant of the landlord. Now the School – or, rather, the Trust, whose sole rationale is to promote education – owned its property and possessed collateral that would prove vitally important in the years ahead.

To describe this event is the appropriate time to pay tribute to the then Chairman of the School Board, Peter Lyons. Mr Lyons had already been prominent in negotiating the School's favourable lease with Bill Kruger's company back in 1983, and at this critical moment he was magnificent. Hippocrates had a simple theory of dreams: during the day the soul receives images; during the night it produces them. It may be that, whilst receiving images, the Headmaster muttered to Peter Lyons how jolly it would be if Headfort were to acquire ownership of its property. This was a far-fetched notion indeed, considering that the School's only assets were a few old desks. However the School did hold a valid lease. The vendor's agent had even asked the Headmaster whether he would care to move the School elsewhere. He would not – unless many millions of pounds were forthcoming with which to start afresh in an equally magnificent demesne. The initial asking price for the estate had been unrealistic and there was little demand in the first couple of years.

At this point Peter Lyons wrought his magic: he began to investigate the apparently remote feasibility of purchasing the property. Negotiations were complex and protracted – far too much so for a mere Headmaster to comprehend – but what Peter Lyons achieved in that period has kept this School secure into the foreseeable future. Eventually Headfort Trust would front a consortium, comprising a farmer, a forester–prospector and itself, that divided the 900-odd acres according to each party's requirements. Four noble, anonymous benefactors were found to lend Headfort's portion of the required purchase price on extremely generous terms. In consequence, the Trust now owns Headfort House and some forty acres of playing fields – a very generous allotment for a mere one hundred children.

Effects of the sale of the Estate

The purchase by the Trust of the School's portion of the Estate, granted the School an enormous boost in confidence that was rapidly translated into an increase in pupil numbers, as parents realized that Headfort was there to stay. Had the School remained a tenant, rather than becoming a property owner against which it could borrow capital, it is doubtful whether it would have survived the crisis that was to occur six years into the future.

There were inevitably minor disadvantages. Whereas previously the School had had the use of approximately nine hundred acres, it was now slightly restricted. The only real sufferer was the equestrian fraternity – who else needs all that space? Formerly the riders had the run of most of the estate in which to roam freely on horseback: they could ride the Long Wood Walk, canter through the Windmill Field and lead the ponies into the river, although naturally they could not encroach upon the agricultural land. Now their scope is somewhat reduced. Nevertheless, a generous parent funded a hunter trial course through the woods that contains twenty-nine fences; and other parents presented a fenced paddock where professional jumps have been installed. A six-acre paddock beyond the games field was exchanged for some woodland on the east side of the house to provide more space for equestrian purposes, so the Headfort riders are remarkably fortunate. No other Irish prep school has anything approaching the amount of land that Headfort possesses.

Sixty-seven houses were built on the north side of the avenue. They have been tastefully constructed and the new amenity blends attractively into the landscape. The Main Courtyard where Lord Headfort used to stable his horses now contains handsome, small houses. Below, at the bottom of the avenue, is the Lower Courtyard; and above is a region called The Orchard that contains slightly larger houses. Finally, just outside the School's boundary, stands Blackarch Wood where five, fine, two-storey houses lie in seclusion.

Bicycling became a less desirable activity. Prefects and Dormitory Captains had always been permitted to bring their bikes to school and, especially in the summer evenings, they could traverse the estate in pairs at their will. BMX bikes were ideally suited to Headfort's undulating, cross-country terrain. Now, with the increase in traffic, the avenue is less safe and the ambit is restricted. Gradually the number of children's bicycles on the estate fell away and they have now disappeared altogether.

The large and small islands where children would sometimes go for picnics, and which contain the graves of members of the Headfort family, are now part of the new eighteen-hole golf course, designed by Christy O'Connor Junior, and are consequently out of bounds to the children. In former times, David Wild used to supervise 'The Island Game', a military-style form of hide and seek. On one occasion a boy fell from a coniferous fir in which he was hiding. He had been startled by an owl that was sharing his hiding place.

Despite the mild limitations imposed by the trilateral distribution of the Estate, Headfort children retain plenty of space and a wonderful ambience in which to grow up.

The arrival of day pupils

The second momentous event of 1996 was that the School threw its doors open to day pupils and five-day boarding. Until September of that year Headfort had been one of just seven out of the 514 IAPS schools (and the only one within the thirty-two counties of Ireland) that catered exclusively for boarders. All of the others accepted day pupils, either exclusively or predominantly. Headfort's uniqueness meant that those Irish parents who wanted such a service necessarily had to choose this School; however, towards the end of the century the concept of boarding was beginning to veer away from what many modern parents sought. Headfort now broke rank with tradition. Initially, three local girls and three local boys arrived on a day basis. Today, sixteen years later, day pupils constitute more than a third of the School's population.

The decision to discontinue Saturday morning school was a necessary concomitant to accepting day pupils. Local parents wanted to keep their weekends sacrosanct for family time. It did pose problems though. The abolition of five classes every Saturday aggregated to some three weeks of teaching time over the course of a year, and so it was necessary to contract the remainder of the week somewhat: reduce a few minutes from the children's 'constitutional' after breakfast; prune a few minutes off break; reduce 'rest', after lunch; even games time was marginally curtailed; an extra afternoon class was squeezed in; and school holidays had to be pared back by a few days each year. Not ideal from the logistical point of view, but 'the customer is always right' and even traditional institutions must adjust to changing circumstances.

John Leyden, in his capacity as Senior Master, contributed valuable input into the restructuring of the daily timetable.

10th February, 1996

Headfort Opens Its Gates To Day Pupils After 47 Years

HEADFORT, Ireland's leading preparatory school is to open its gates to day pupils, aged from seven to 13, from next September.

Founded in 1949 in Kells, Headfort today is a co-educational, non-denominational school that prepares children for a wide range of secondary schools in Ireland and abroad. Speaking about the decision, headmaster Lingard Goulding said: "The decision to take day pupils is based on demand due to the change of emphasis in family life."

Mr. Goulding stressed: "Headfort will remain committed to the boarding ethos but day pupils will spend a full working day at the school and avail of the entire range of academic and recreational activities that Headfort offers. Senior day pupils will remain at school to do supervised 'prep', together with boarders, after tea."

The classes at Headfort are small. They average less than 12 and do not exceed 16. The range of subjects taught at Headfort is much wider than at most primary schools. A qualified remedial teacher is also available to give private tuition to students with learning difficulties.

The core curriculum subjects will be confined within the five weekdays; Saturday mornings will be devoted to a range of activities which will include archery, canoeing, chess, bridge and photography. Day pupils may attend Saturday morning activities if they wish.

Day pupils arrive

Personnel

1998 saw the arrival on the staff of PIERS LANDSEER. Educated at Head-fort, St Columba's and Trinity College, Dublin, and a fluent Spanish speaker, Piers's special brief was to communicate with the Spanish pupils and teach them English while others were learning Latin or Irish. He also taught junior mathematics and, being a fine sportsman himself, took an enthusiastic Second Game rugby, as well as being instrumental in the resurgence of interest in squash and chess. He was a valuable addition to the ranks.

KARINE MAZET was only at Headfort for a couple of years towards the end of the century, but she taught French well. Another short-term teacher who was successful was BRENDAN O'HARA in the science laboratory.

Bad language

Here is an excerpt from the Easter Newsletter of 1997:

> There has been an excess of bad language in the School recently. Doubtless, children have always used bad language among themselves, but today's breed takes less trouble to conceal it.
>
> Of course, Headfort holds no monopoly over bad language. There has been rampant inflation in its usage throughout society. The media must assume some responsibility – the so-called 'nine o'clock watershed' is merely a fob to the sensitivity of puritans. And of course many words that were formerly deemed to be entirely beyond the pale are now quite kosher.
>
> Am I being insufferably stuffy even to address the issue? I think not. Am I using double standards? Perhaps. Many of us may utter a discreet indelicacy from time to time. Time and place are significant: such utterances should never occur when they might offend. Of course, most modern children are, by the age of ten or twelve, well versed in the terminology of the gutter, but it is inelegant to hear a child roar an expletive at another.
>
> Bad language comes in three parts of speech: the verb, the adjective and the noun. Let us consider each in turn.
>
> The verbal form, delivered with vehemence in the imperative mood, and frequently qualified by the adverb 'off', is an invitation to the offendee to go away: 'depart hence' might perhaps be a more acceptable style.
>
> The adjectival form is really a case of stunted vocabulary. It employs the present participle of the appropriate – I should say inappropriate – verb. The

verb generally relates to a function that is not habitually discussed in the withdrawing-room.

The substantival form of bad language at least offers scope for imagination, in that it is based upon metaphor. 'You are a .....', where the missing sobriquet is a synonym for the offendee. Unfortunately, there is a fearful sameness in the choice of synonym: it tends to be anatomical or scatological. In most cases the analogy is inaccurate.

Is bad language a fearful crime? Objectively speaking, no. However, any word or phrase that is hurled at another person with intent to cause hurt is language badly used.

Runaways

From the earliest times there have been rare instances of children running away from Headfort. Sometimes this has been due to genuine unhappiness or desperation: more often it was an act of bravado. Our fugitives have generally not been at large for long and were content to be repatriated. Nevertheless such incidents are an enormous anxiety to the Headmaster and staff who are responsible for the children's safety.

Two dramatic instances come to mind, each of which has borne the sobriquet, 'The Great Escape' in Headfort folklore. The first took place in 1974. It happened that David Wild was in England at an Old Cheltonian Dinner at the time, leaving Jack Sweetman in charge of the School. Three boys, aged eleven or twelve, resolved to bicycle towards Dublin in the middle of the night. They stocked themselves with provisions from the kitchen, 'borrowed' three of the Prefects' bicycles and headed off into the cold night air sometime before midnight when it might be assumed that Matron and the house staff were asleep. History does not relate whether the bicycles had any form of lighting – it seems improbable.

The first that the School heard of the escapees was when the Matron, Juliet Long, received a telephone call from the Navan police at half past seven the following morning with the news that they had apprehended the three boys who were now safely detained in the cells. Jack Sweetman drove off to retrieve the lost sheep.

The second instance took place in 1989 when Lingard Goulding was Headmaster. It was the year in which a Friday Exeat weekend was incorporated into each term. This escapade, that occurred towards the end of the Summer Term, made a mockery of the Headmaster's control system for weekend Exeats. In those days children simply had to notify the Secretary that they were going out with their parents and to nominate any guests whom they might take.

On this occasion four highly intelligent twelve-year-old boys – Polo, Rab, Tambo and Timon – carefully planned an unsupervised weekend's camping in the fields at nearby Carlanstown. Their preparation was meticulous: during a previous weekend they had spirited a gas cooker into the School and stowed it in a secret sanctuary. In true criminal style, they held a 'dry run' and 'enjoyed' an unappetizing al fresco meal of lukewarm baked beans in the woods.

As Timon explains:

> Our major deception was to inform Peggie Ball that we were going home for the weekend, and our parents that we were staying in. We felt that we were merely exploiting an obvious loophole in the system and we were tremendously excited at the prospect of running away to spend a weekend on our own.

Giving the duty master a wide berth, Rab and Polo set out with their cooker early on the Saturday afternoon to conduct reconnaissance. However, Timon and Tambo were engaged in a cricket match at Brook House and did not return in the School minibus until the evening. They then calmly walked out from Headfort with a dilapidated suitcase containing several blankets, a couple of bath towels and a small amount of food, the staff assuming that they had been collected by their parents. They travelled across Lord Headfort's airfield and the several meadows of crops, eventually reaching Carlanstown some four miles distant where they met the advance guard. They thought that they might have been spotted by Sibéal Rooney who drove past them on the road near her house. One can imagine the courage that it must have taken to venture forth alone at night into the silent fields and minor roads. They did not have a tent and would have to sleep rough, with just a blanket or two to cover them.

> We found that Rab and Polo had already met some local boys and we joined in an impromptu GAA match for an hour or so. We were regarded with a mixture of curiosity and a degree of suspicion by these villagers. There was also a sinister element – one chap invited us to stay in a tent in his garden but we then found him stealing food from our bags. We sensed it was time to withdraw.
>
> We retired to spend the night a little way up the road and bedded down with some towels in a hedgerow. This was not before time, as we spotted a group of local lads striding up the road, looking for us. Who knows what their

intentions were? It was less than five-star accommodation, but mercifully the weather was pleasant. I remember sleeping quite badly due to the discomfort, and being plagued by insects. It was light by about 4:30 am and Rab managed to cook a few sausages on the stove.

After 'breakfast' we cut down a small tree with a Gurkha knife and stripped its branches. We slung our luggage along it and set off down the road, with one person on either end, and the gear swinging freely in the middle of the thoroughfare. We decided to move to a more secure spot and, as we wandered down the road, we came across a house with a tent in the garden. In our hypo-manic, semi-wild, vengeful state, we concluded that this must be the house of the chap who'd stolen our food the night before. We jumped over the wall and quietly took it apart (but did not damage it), thus achieving what we felt was a sense of cosmic justice.

The boys had never considered how they would spend their weekend of liberty, and so on the Sunday morning they found themselves ensconced in the woods with no plan of action. They were cold, dirty, hungry and insect bitten, and were beginning to question the wisdom of their bravado, and what the consequences might be. Timon, nowadays an eminent psychiatrist, recalls that, after the initial euphoria, harmony began to unravel and their behaviour degenerated towards that of the boys in William Golding's *Lord of the Flies*, but happily without such a tragic outcome.

Unfortunately, with our increasing hunger levels, we started to become tetchy with each other and it wasn't long before anarchy was amongst us. We decided to split up, Tambo and I going to Kells to buy some food, and Rab and Polo staying put.

Timon and Tambo walked all the way to Kells and back, some three miles in each direction, pausing to dive into a ditch when they spotted John Leyden's car travelling to Mass. They composed maledictory epigrams, perhaps some of them in Latin, with which to assault their erstwhile colleagues. They returned to the campsite to find that the other two boys had strewn their belongings ubiquitously, that the remaining food was gone and that Polo, despite being a technological geek, had burned himself on the gas stove.

As may be seen, collective morale was low and they sensed that they had had enough of the adventure. Timon and Tambo separated from Rab and Polo again, heading back across the fields to the School, concocting a flimsy alibi to explain their early return in the middle of Sunday afternoon;

meanwhile, Rab and Polo took the road to Kells to buy more food. Mastication sharpens the intellect, they thought. Not far from the gates of the School they were apprehended by a member of staff and the game was up. With a little more care they might have escaped detection but, as Timon suggests today, it would have been difficult to confine their adventure to themselves: small boys are notoriously indiscreet.

That afternoon the Headmaster had taken another bunch of older girls and boys on a bicycling trip to Trim and Bective Abbey and, upon returning home at about nine o'clock, he received the news of the adventurers. They were summoned from their beds and, although the Headmaster could not help privately admiring their courage and initiative, they received the dressing-down of their lives. Feeling guilty about the inefficacy of his Exeat procedure, the Headmaster sheepishly informed their parents of what had happened. One of them wrote back that he should have given the boys a hearty thrashing.

One shudders – the Headmaster shuddered – to think of what might have happened to four young boys, alone in the open countryside for an entire weekend. Thereafter, documentary evidence was required before children might leave the School at weekends.

Headfort's worst day

Headfort's worst day occurred in 1980 and it also began with a pupil running away, but this was a different type of event to those recorded above. The pupil in this case was truly suffering from anhedonia, the state of not being able to enjoy things that are normally pleasurable. His was no mere prank, no *fol-de-rol*.

It was on a Saturday in the Easter Term and the Headmaster was due to drive the First XI to Aravon in Bray that afternoon for a hockey match.

Shortly after breakfast it was noticed that one young gentleman was no longer present. Investigation revealed that he had had an altercation with a member of staff over a trivial issue and, in consequence, had elected to absent himself from the premises.

Search parties of senior children were despatched to scour the grounds: staff cars patrolled the local roads, but there was no sign of our runagate and everyone became gradually more anxious. The situation was especially awkward because, although the boy was an Irish citizen, his parents chanced to be living in Asia; naturally the Headmaster did not wish to alarm them by sending a telegram, unless it became absolutely necessary. Eventually he notified the boy's uncle and aunt who lived in Ireland and, when there was still no sign of him by mid-morning, he contacted the police.

While such a drama was being enacted, the Headmaster could not of course travel to Aravon; instead, another member of staff, Robin Simmons, drove the team in the School minibus.

The day wore on and there was still no news of the missing pupil. Lunch came and went – none of the staff was inclined to eat much. Eventually in mid-afternoon the tension was broken: the police telephoned to report that they had picked up the errant boy a couple of miles down the Mullingar road. He had apparently proposed to walk to County Offaly. He was returned to School where he was treated with sympathy.

Crisis averted. The Headmaster relaxed for the first time that day… but not for long. An hour or two later he received a second telephone call, this one reporting that the Headfort minibus had crashed on its way home from Aravon and that children had been injured.

Here was the worst nightmare for any Headmaster. He leapt into his car and, with a shocking disregard for the national speed limits, betook himself to Loughlinstown, just south of Dublin, where the accident had occurred. Our minibus had been steaming down the dual carriageway on the main Bray to Dublin road, when a car emerged from Cherrywood Road, a small satellite lane, and rammed the Headfort craft amidships. Our driver was in no wise culpable.

The impact had been of only moderate force but, since minibuses were not equipped with seatbelts in those days, the occupants were tossed about like bombarding atoms in a nuclear accelerator and several of them incurred minor injuries. The lady who drove the other car was naturally shocked, but otherwise unhurt. Robin Simmons acted in a most professional manner throughout the ordeal and arranged for the wounded to be transferred to Loughlinstown Hospital that was conveniently only a few hundred yards from the scene of the accident. A local Good Samaritan took all those who were uninjured into her house and plied them with Elastoplast, sweet tea and cakes, as a mother cat applies her tongue.

When the Headmaster arrived at the hospital, he found to his massive relief that none of the injuries was serious. One boy was detained overnight with concussion, and a couple of others received needlework for cuts and gashes. Most managed to sport some form of battle scar.

The Headmaster of Castle Park, Palmer Carter, had heard tidings of the accident on the RTE News at six o'clock and had driven to the scene to offer assistance. He very kindly lent the author his minibus with which to transport the by now rather hyperactive children back to County Meath, the Headfort vehicle being hors de combat.

There followed a series of calming telephone calls to parents, and all the other procedures that must be undertaken, following an accident. It had been an horrific day and, of course, one could not help conjecturing how much more terrible it might have been.

The following morning's Sunday letters home yielded some thrilling literature. For once there was a variation on the old theme,

> Dear Mumy 'n Dady,
>   I hope you are well. On Wensday we plaid St Grovel's.
>   They were rubish. We were brillant. We one 10-nil.
>   Lots of luv from yor famous son,
>   Murgatroyd x x x x x

On this occasion, the drama of the previous day's events had stimulated the young writers' creative powers – both those who were, and those who were not, on board the ill-fated bus. The member of staff on duty had to moderate some of the more lurid embellishments of the accident – bucket-loads of blood, hundreds of stitches, limbs pointing in sundry directions – in order to deter a flock of worried parents from launching themselves post-haste towards the School in the expectation that they would discover their sons and daughters on Death's doorstep.

The following Wednesday, feeling rather like Manchester United survivors after Munich, the First XI travelled to Brook House without six of their warriors who were still on the injured list.

On such a day there are surely better jobs than being a Headmaster.

12. A HALF-CENTURY COMPLETED

Celebrations – More modern nonsense – Rise in numbers – Board members –
The Habitaunce – Sorrow – More appointments – Death of Sir Richard Musgrave
– Drama 2 – Sundry sports – The Northern Tour – Intimations of mortality –
Headfort in Africa – Moon controls education – Foot & mouth disease –
Last things

Celebrations

Headfort completed its first half-century in the academic year 1998–9 with a spectacular range of celebratory events throughout the three terms: an Evening of Jazz with the Ian Shaw Trio & saxophonist Mornington Locket; the Headfort Celebration of Food & Wine; an Antiques Valuation Day & Fine Arts Fair; an Open Day with which to commence Kells Heritage Week; the Headfort Fiftieth Anniversary Ball; and, as the culmination of the year's celebrations, the Headfort Fiftieth Anniversary Concert at the National Concert Hall in Dublin.

The Celebration of Food & Wine also included a display of Headfort merchandise. The wonderful Zucchi rondels in the Robert Adam Ballroom were reproduced as circular place mats and coasters. There were wine glasses

HEADFORT ANNIVERSARY WINES
THE HEADMASTER'S ASSESSMENT

"My favourite pub crawl is the beat from Dijon to Mâcon, the source of these four fine wines, imported for Headfort directly from Burgundy. Our flagship hails from St Aubin, near Beaune; it bears a pedagogic quality: erudite, upstanding, full-bodied, the possessor of a rich colour and noble bouquet. This is a wine of gravitas that presents a straight bat at the dinner table. Friends of Headfort will enjoy equally the classical, acacia-honey nose and dry, scholarly flavour of the white Headfort Pouilly-Vinzelles. L.G

bearing the Headfort crest, hampers of food and wine, silverware, Christmas cards and other items. Upon the over-burdened Headmaster fell the onerous chore of tasting and selecting The Headmaster's Choice of Headfort claret and Headfort white Burgundy, cheeky little beverages that sold out very rapidly. Michael Stafford had kindly arranged the warehousing.

The Headfort Fiftieth Anniversary Ball took place in the Summer Term. The day began with an Old Boys' Cricket match. In the evening a champagne reception presaged the most elegant event of its generation. The ladies' gowns were sumptuous and, because of the 'black and gold theme', even the gentlemen could disport themselves like peacocks.

The year of celebration concluded with a gala evening of music at the National Concert Hall in Dublin with the Irish Chamber Orchestra and Mícheál Ó Súilleabháin. Headfort parent Olivia Cahill negotiated this marvellous event. The entire School was seated in the Choir Balcony and the 'Headfort family' managed to sell 1200 tickets to individuals and corporate entities.

Headfort School's
50th Anniversary Concert
With the Irish Chamber Orchestra &
Mícheál O' Súilleabháin

requests the pleasure of

..Company.
At The National Concert Hall, Dublin
On Thursday 21st October at 8.00 pm
and afterwards to a Black Tie reception in
The Carolan Room

Very many parents, both past and present, lent skill, imagination and dedication to coordinate all of these events. The principal organizers of the Anniversary Year were Radine Hamilton (chairman), Pam McDowell and Michael Bolton.

More modern nonsense

In 1998 the Headmaster wanted to advertise for a matron in the national newspapers, but was disallowed to do so because the term 'matron' is gender-specific. Well, really! It was decreed that the word 'matron' might only be used in the advertisement if accompanied by the sentence, 'this is an equal job opportunity', an unattractive piece of gobbledegook that would have been flagrantly untrue. One might contend that a male person could fill the role of a school matron: he could wash and sew, administer medicines and kindness; yet it would require a further shift in society's mores before Headfort parents would be content for a man to supervise their daughters' bathing.

It had become unfashionable to differentiate between characteristics that are essentially male and those that are female. Why must one emasculate on the one hand and defeminize on the other?

The Headmaster wrote a letter to the Irish Times, expressing his objection to such political correctness. The letter concluded,

> Sir, it is a very great nonsense that I may not advertise for a female matron. Perhaps, in future, parents' parting words to their sons and daughters as they bid them farewell on the school steps will be, 'Don't forget to ask Patron for your cough-mixture.'

Rise in numbers

It was apparent that Headfort Trust's purchase of the house and its portion of the grounds had enhanced confidence in the School and numbers began to rise again, to the extent that a seventh class was opened in September 1999.

Board members

In 1998 Peter Lyons retired as Chairman of Headfort School, but retained the Chairmanship of Headfort Trust, the body that owns the property and rents the house to the School. LYNN TEMPLE, past pupil himself and father of three Headfort pupils, assumed the reins of the School company. At this time Peggie Ball became the company secretary. Noel McMullan retired from the Board at the end of the Middle Years. He had rendered innumerable services to the School over a long period of time.

In 1999 Peter Lyons retired from Headfort Trust. His value to the School had been beyond measure. He handed the chairmanship to DICK BLAKISTON HOUSTON. Dick's immense contribution to the Trust really falls under the next period, Headfort Today. Denny Wardell had been a supremely active member of the Trust Board, but now retired. Nick Nicholson, Anne McFarland and Lingard Goulding became directors of the Trust and they remain in office in 2012. Nick's knowledge of houses and Anne's financial wizardry proved invaluable over the years.

The Habitaunce

Before he retired as Chairman of the School Board, Peter Lyons was the prime mover of an act of tremendous generosity towards the Headmaster. In the 1996 trifurcation of the estate, the School had acquired a suite of rooms beyond the Ballroom, leading to Headfort Court. The following year the Board of Directors presented this apartment to the Headmaster for life. The Board made this gesture in the knowledge that the recipient was approaching the end of his tenure. The apartment, which the Headmaster christened 'The Habitaunce' (a Spencerian term, meaning a dwelling place), was attractively decorated and he was able to furnish it to his taste. Having spent the previous couple of decades living in a bedroom and bathroom on the first floor of the house, in the midst of the School quarters, and working in the study (an inspiring room certainly, with its curved, olive bookcases and south-facing aspect), it was a life-changing delight to have a 'home' into which to retreat after work each evening, and to look forward to such a congenial abode in which to pass the years of retirement.

A spectacular party thrown by Peter & Alison Lyons for past & present Directors of the School on the occasion of Lingard Goulding's retirement in 2001

Sorrow

During the two World Wars, Headmasters frequently had to endure the agony of announcing to the school that a boy whom they had recently nurtured and grown to love had been killed in action. Fortunately, the modern Headmaster is spared this experience. Nevertheless, in a reign of almost a quarter of a century, tragedies are bound to occur. Four Headfort parents – two mothers and two fathers – took their own lives during the Middle Years, and several other parents died while their children were in the School. Even more distressing for the staff were the rare occasions when our past pupils died at an early age. The letter printed here was written, when he was about ten, by a courageous young man who succumbed to illness in the bloom of life.

Saturday, 26th March,

Dear Mr. Goulding

Thank you ever so much for sending my teddy and track-shoes, I missed my teddy quite alot the nights I did not have him. I got the package today. Thank you very much for sending my track-shoes, now I can practice my athletics, which is good. I got some new track-shoes the other day, they were hard ones, they would be good for cricket, squash and tennis.

I went to hospital last Friday to see about my stumonick. I have to go again to get may kidneys and things checked. ▮ is coming back to-day at tea-time which will

-2-

be nice and ▮ is coming on Monday. I hope all the matters are well. Looking forward to next term. Thanks again for sending my teddy and shoes. love

From

▮

P.S. Will you thank Miss. Ball for sending the package.

In Wordsworth's words:

> The good die first,
> And those whose hearts are dry as summer dust
> Burn to the socket.

More appointments

Out of doors, JERRY McGOVERN served well as groundsman for several years, following the departure of Johnny Grimes in 1992. When he left in 2000, PETER SHERIDAN was appointed. Peter is a giant of a man: as strong as an ox, he can lift enormous pieces of machinery single-handedly. He keeps the estate in shape.

JULIAN GIRDHAM joined the Board in 2001. It was felt that another educationalist was required and Mr Girdham, the sub-Warden of St Columba's College, was the ideal person. He was of immense value during the closing period of this dynasty, although his principal influence lay in the future. Another highly valued 'transition' Board member was LUCINDA BLAKISTON HOUSTON, mother of six Headfort pupils and wife of the Chairman of Headfort Trust.

BETTY BRITTAIN succeeded Carole Barry in 1999 and worked capably until 2002, both in a housekeeping capacity, as well as in the office. She had a sensitive approach both to the children and to colleagues.

CATHERINE CUNNINGHAM taught Science and Irish successfully for several years, beginning in 1998, before heading overseas to widen her experience. EILEEN SUGRUE gave excellent service as Laundress in the 1990s.

THE REV. WILLIAM RITCHIE and FATHER JOHN CONLAN looked after the School's spiritual needs for a decade or so during the 1990s. William used to take the Protestant scripture classes and John assisted John Leyden with the Roman Catholics, as well as attending the School for confession and to say Mass. These two gentlemen gave devoted support to Headfort, frequently attending Carol Services and Valedictory Services. Earlier, MONSIGNOR JOHN SHORTALL, an intellectual man with a wide range of interests, had also shown kindness towards the School.

PATRICIA CASEY was an efficient, hard-working member of staff who could turn her hand to virtually any department. She stepped into the breach as Matron, Cook and Laundress. Extremely versatile, she gave worthy service for several years. Past pupil JOANNA SPICER, member of a famous Headfort family, returned in 1997 for two years to teach Irish and act as Assistant Matron.

It was of course an advantage to have a native speaker to teach the French language. M. Prudor was the first Frenchman at Headfort; then the School had been fortunate to retain the Belgian, Victor de Raeymaeker, for twenty years. Three other French people served subsequently for a few years each: CHRISTOPHE CHENNAUX from 1994, followed by Karine Mazet from 1998, and JEAN MANCHON in the mid-2000s.

FIONNUALA GREENING was Matron for a short period and MARY KENNEDY stepped into the breach when Fionnuala became ill.

Death of Sir Richard Musgrave

On 2 December 2000 Sir Richard Musgrave died on Syros, the Greek island where he and Lady Musgrave lived for much of his final years. Dick was one of the stalwarts of Headfort history. He had an overwhelming love for this little School and its children and he served it in innumerable capacities down the years. He gave limitless support both to David Wild and to Lingard Goulding.

Dick Musgrave's expertise in game keeping was such that he was head-hunted in both the United States and Canada to manage large pheasant shoots. It was in Virginia that he encountered a spot of bother with the authorities when the odd hawk, a protected species, found its way into the hunters' bag. Until his dying day, the author will recall the occasion when the familiar, gravelly voice slowly infiltrated his insomniac consciousness over the World Service at three am one morning with the words, 'I am the first criminal member of my family since King Charles I.'

Drama 2

In 1996 Neville Wilkinson combined with Michael Bolton to form the renowned international production team of Notlob and Nosnikliw. They offered an enchanting version of Richmal Crompton's *Just William*. The eternally scruffy William Brown, together with his henchmen, Ginger, Henry and Douglas, collectively known as the Outlaws, met at the Old Barn to devise delicious strategies against their enemies. Poor William had to tolerate the company of Violet Elizabeth Bott, the spoilt, lisping daughter of local nouveau-riche millionaire, in order to prevent her from carrying out her threat to 'thcream and thcream till I'm thick'.

In 1954 the author had watched the incomparable Siobhan McKenna play George Bernard Shaw's masterpiece, *Saint Joan,* at the Gate Theatre in Dublin. Micheál Mac Liammóir who, together with his partner Hilton Edwards, had founded the Gate in 1928, played a simpering Dauphin in that production. For several years it had been the author's wish to present this work at Headfort; he was waiting until he found a girl to fit the part; she would have to be highly intelligent, a sufficiently strong actress and have the striking looks of a Joan. Such a girl became available in 1997 and no further bidding was required. St Joan is a demanding play, full of ecclesiastical quiddities, as well as plenty of violence. Our Joan carried it off superbly, as did her Dauphin and a large supporting cast.

St Joan

It is rare to stumble upon a musical masterpiece before its composer's birth. That evening the audience experienced a relativistic phenomenon when, after the Coronation of King Charles VII at Rheims Cathedral in 1430, the choir mysteriously sung the beautiful Hallelujah motet that Mozart was to write some three and a half centuries later. Remarkable, really.

Toad of Toad Hall revealed another of Headfort's finest actors in the title role in 1998. Given the part only five weeks before the dress rehearsal, this quirky animal managed to maintain his endearing boastfulness throughout the play, despite being unable to conserve a clean driving licence. Together with his colleagues, Mr Rat, Mr Badger and Mr Mole, Toad waged perennial warfare against the Wild Wooders – riff-raff such as stoats and badgers.

Mr Toad and his associates, Mr Badger, Mr Mole and Mr Rat

'The Scottish Play' was chosen to celebrate Headfort's half-century. Once again, a special actor was required to tackle the leading role. Our *Macbeth* had over four hundred lines to learn – a considerable quota for a thirteen-year-old boy with academic and other demands upon his time – and his Lady Macbeth had more than half that number. They were splendid, as were many of their courtiers.

Macbeth & Lady Macbeth

The three witches

Leave it to Psmith, another entertaining dabble into P.G. Wodehouse's inimitable nonsense, was presented in 2000. The plot is a typical Wodehouse romance: Psmith (the 'P' is silent, as in 'psychosis'), retired fishmonger, inveigles himself into the Earl of Middlewick's idyllic castle, where there is the usual crop of girls to woo, crooks to foil, imposters to unmask, haughty aunts to baffle and valuable necklaces to steal. Apart from the admirable Psmith, there were sterling performances from the Earl and Countess of Middlewick and The Hon. Freddie Bosham, their vacuous son.

Finding a new biography of Rudyard Kipling in an Exeter bookshop, your author discovered, from a letter written to his wife – Kipling's wife – that Kipling had originally intended to write *The Jungle Book* as a play. In 1901 he produced a scene and a half that was published in the biography, and then stopped. Here was the opportunity for the author to complete the task of writing *The Jungle Play* and for Headfort to present the 'World Première' in 1991. Once again Mary Wilkinson, together with her team of Carole Barry and Vivienne Potterton, had to display all of their imaginative genius to dress our man cub, Mowgli (that part was easy: he wore virtually nothing), plus Akela the wolf, Bagheera the panther, Baloo the bear, Hathi the elephant, Tabaqui the cheeky jackal, Shere Khan the Royal Bengal tiger and a zoo-full of other animals.

Akela, Mowgli and Shere Khan

Sundry sports

Certain activities have come and gone over the years. In the Early Years boxing was taught, and also target shooting, before reaction to the IRA campaign rendered it illegal to use guns; children were taught formal gymnastics, conducted for a while by David Wild during break in the Summer Term. The Middle Years saw groups of children set off on their bicycles of a Sunday, laden with picnic lunches, and embark upon the forty mile round trip through back roads to Trim and Bective Abbey. Before they were permitted to embark upon this tortuous ride, the adventurers had to prove themselves to be physically fit, and their machinery had to pass the Ministry of Headfort Transport (MOHT) certificate of roadworthiness. This did not prevent Micky Studd's bicycle from developing four punctures on one ride; eventually the tour leader (your author) had to carry the miserable *vélo* on his shoulders, plus child on the crossbar, to the nearest pub, where he left the children, giving strict instructions to the publican; he then rode rapidly back to School and returned with the minibus to rescue the marooned party. Others, principally the non-cricketers, would take to the river in kayaks, shooting the 'rapids' between Navan and Slane. From time to time a fencing instructor would visit the School.

For more than a decade Michael Bolton took a team of six Headfort boys and girls to Scotland to contest the hugely popular 'Gordonstoun Challenge'. This is a splendid event, designed to attract prep school pupils to Gordonstoun.

The Gordonstoun Challenge

It involves a series of practical examinations in all manner of disciplines, culminating in a 'special project', an imaginative, outward-bound-style challenge – for which Gordonstoun is renowned – that calls for initiative, teamwork and leadership.

For many years cross-country running was in vogue; the (in)famous 1.9-mile 'Slow Cows' course was traversed a couple of times a week by the senior pupils in the Easter Term, and each child tried to achieve his personal best (PB) time. The run was so named after an unpunctuated traffic sign that read, 'Slow Cows Crossing', situated at the corner where the runners left the Kells road and headed back into the estate. The record for the undulating course, held jointly by two boys, but some four years distant in time (1991 and 1995), was left at ten minutes eighteen seconds. Only a handful of boys over the years ever ran it in under eleven minutes. The girls' record was eleven minutes fourteen seconds. In the final week of term, when everybody was very fit, the Carlanstown Grand Prix was tackled; this was a five-and-three-quarter-mile (nine km) course through fields and country lanes; it was taxing stuff, but afforded a sense of satisfaction to those who completed it. For a few years the School's cross-country runners took part in a schools' hill-running competition held over St Columba's gruelling mountain course.

The Northern Tour

Every March all of the Irish prep schools would convene at Rockport in County Down to race over their scenic course on a Saturday morning. The Northern Tour was a highlight of the Easter Term for a dozen years. It involved an overnight stay at one of the Northern schools and, apart from the race at Rockport, it included an Irish IAPS hockey tournament, generally held at Cabin Hill or a neighbouring hockey club, on the Friday afternoon. Often more than twenty Headfort children travelled – the First XI hockey players, plus boy runners and girl runners. On the Saturday afternoon the party used to visit an ice-skating rink in Belfast and on many occasions kind Northern parents would entertain the entire party to a gargantuan feast, before the minibus, plus a car or two, would wend its way southwards with a bunch of happily weary small people falling asleep in the back seats.

In Headfort Today the equestrian contingent has been taught to play polo, and throughout the years ballet, ballroom dancing and modern dance have been introduced to the extracurricular menu from time to time; the Terpsichorean muse has risen and fallen in its popularity.

Chris and Jean Macdonald used to run camps for the senior girls in their garden towards the end of the Summer Term. The girls would pitch tent during daylight hours and then feast in the Macdonalds' garden before settling down for the night. This was a hugely popular activity.

Intimations of mortality

May 1999 saw a fin-de-siècle event: Lingard Goulding announced that he would retire at the end of the Summer Term in 2001. This left almost seven terms in which to troll for a replacement. The Chairman appointed a sub-committee for this purpose, which he led himself; the Headmaster was also a member. Given all that time, they could not get it wrong. Could they?

Headfort in Africa

The year 2000 was notable for Headfort's cricket tour to South Africa. Fourteen boys and several parents flew to Durban where they were royally entertained by generous parents, Sheelagh and Robert Davis-Goff, who owned a

Headfort touring party in KwaZulu-Natal, 2000

farm at Balgowan, between Howick and Mooi River. Four rondavels, small, circular, thatched houses were to be the Headfort cricketers' homes for the next ten days. In front of the rondavels rippled an inviting swimming pool. A minibus transported the team to their several games against school and club sides in KwaZulu-Natal, all within about an hour and a half of base. Headfort won three of their four games and lost the other by just two wickets – a fifth game, against the KwaZulu Under 13 provincial side at Kingsmead in Durban, was cancelled because of thirty-six hours of continuous rain. As the party drove into the Drakensberg mountains for one game, a Headfort cricketer intoned,

Headfort batting in South Africa, 2000

Headfort batsmen display their range of strokes. Note the swimming pool 'bubble' behind the batsman who is playing the back-foot cut stroke

'I will lift up mine eyes unto the hills from whence cometh my help'. He was rebuked by his coach, on the grounds that this ancient quotation from the King James Bible is tautologous, because the word 'whence' means 'from where'.

After the cricket was finished, the party drove northwards to the Hluhluwe (pronounce it as you will) game reserve in Zululand. The wet weather in the southern half of the African continent that year was such that the big cats had the wisdom to stay at home, but numerous inyala, impala, wildebeest, buffalo, wild buck, warthogs and zebras presented themselves, plus the occasional cheetah. The prize exhibit was an enormous white rhinoceros, grazing only a few yards away. It looked thoroughly docile and amiable from the relative safety of the jeep. The following day the party took a boat trip up the St Lucia estuary where numerous hippopotamuses (or hippopotami) were seen, and the more observant boys spotted a couple of crocodiles patrolling threateningly just beneath the surface. The School's cricketers had played in England and the Isle of Man before, and rugby teams tour Scotland on a biennial basis; but this was the first time that a Headfort party had ventured into another continent.

Tea between innings in Africa

Domestically, Headfort's cricket team was very strong at the turn of the century. In 1999 they won fifteen games, but lost the final of the Leinster Under Thirteen Cup to Belvedere, having to bat in desperately wet conditions. Remarkably, nine batsmen played an innings of thirty or more runs for Headfort that season. Again in 2000 the School reached the final of the Cup, this time narrowly losing off the antepenultimate ball of the match to an even stronger C.U.S. team, led by Eoin Morgan, a future England Test player. The team also toured England that year and attended the opening day of the first Test Match against the West Indies at Edgbaston. Perhaps the best cricketer that the School has produced scored a remarkable 768 runs and captured exactly fifty wickets during the season. The scorecard of a game against The King's Hospital demonstrates the School's batting strength.

The perfect bowling action

Tuesday 9th May - at Headfort

HEADFORT

C. Cahill	not out		120
H. Goff	c Aylmer	b Johnston	62
W. Norris	not out		39
	Extras		16
		for 1 wkt.	**237**

Did not bat: T. Morton, J. Brunton, B. Dunne, L. Roe, A. Hamilton, E. Shackleton, J. Blakiston Houston, E. Callow

Fall of wicket: 1/137

BOWLER	OVERS	MAIDENS	RUNS	WICKETS
Johnson	7	-	69	1
Harris	5	-	42	
Aylmer	4	-	49	-
Donovan	4	-	27	-
Green	1	-	7	-
Sale	1	-	5	-
Headley	2	-	18	-
Telford	1	-	15	-

Scoring rate: 25 overs: 9.5 runs / over

KING'S HOSPITAL

O. Harris	st Brunton	b Norris	6
C. Aylmer	lbw	b Cahill	4
R. Headley		b Shackleton	0
G. Telford	c &	b Shackleton	0
P. Donovan		b Shackleton	4
S. Johnston	not out		1
J. Mills		b Norris	0
P. Parkhill	st Brunton	b Norris	0
C. Greene		b Callow	0
A. Laraggy		b Rauscher	2
J. Robinson	run out		0
	Extras		12
			29

Fall of wickets: 1/7, 2/8, 3/8, 4/17, 5/19, 6/20, 7/20, 8/20, 9/27

BOWLER	OVERS	MAIDENS	RUNS	WICKETS
Cahill	2	-	11	1
Shackleton	2	-	7	3
Norris	1	-	1	3
B Houston	1	1	-	-
Callow	1	1	-	1
Rauscher	1.5	-	3	1
Dunne	1	-	5	-

Scoring rate: 9.5 overs: 3.1 runs / over

RESULT: HEADFORT WON BY 208 RUNS

A big victory for Headfort in 2000

Moon controls Education

It had long been a source of irritation to the Headmaster that the schedule for the education of the nation's children should be determined to a significant degree by the lunatic Christian calendar. Why, in God's name, His followers should choose to celebrate the alleged resurrection of His son on 'the first Sunday after the full moon following the northern hemisphere's vernal equinox' is their own business. But what is irksome and inexcusable is that the Department of Education should determine the start of children's Summer Terms in accordance with this haphazard event.

Easter fell upon 23 April in 2000, the first time it had fallen so late since The Easter Rising of 1916 – it will be 2079 before it happens again; consequently the secondary schools did not start their term until early May; they finished at the end of May, allowing them a bare four-week Summer Term leading to the Leaving Certificate. How ridiculous!

On this occasion, the Headmaster, with just one further year to run before his retirement, decided to 'kick against the pricks' in the Department. He reconvened the School for ten days' work before Easter, gave the children a long weekend and then resumed the term. Thus Headfort, uniquely amongst Irish schools, enjoyed a normal Summer Term. A majority of families expressed themselves content with Headfort's decision but, of course, it cannot have been especially convenient for parents who had children at other schools as well.

Foot & mouth disease

During late 2000 and the early months of 2001 Foot and Mouth Disease struck the United Kingdom. The Irish government went to great lengths to keep it out of this country, which they managed to do… for a while. Citizens were asked to avoid foregathering in groups. Sporting fixtures were cancelled and Fine Gael cancelled its *Ard Fheis*.

The effect upon Headfort was that the hockey season was more than decimated – only three games were played with other schools – and the Northern Tour, the highlight of the Easter Term for many children, was cancelled. One felt sorry for them, especially those in their final year.

Of course, the government's tactics were totally illogical, because people still attended churches and pubs. Surely the risk of a group of children spreading the disease by playing a game of hockey in the open air was infinitely less than that of citizens, comprising farmers and others alike, congregating compactly in churches on Sunday or in stuffy and smoky public houses, as they were in 2001, at eventide.

Last things

Lingard Goulding retired as Headmaster at the end of the Summer Term 2001. It had been a good year: numbers were high and the joint Captains of the School had each achieved something special for themselves and for the School: the head girl won an exhibition to her secondary school, and the head boy led the First XI through an unbeaten cricket season of thirteen matches, including winning the Leinster Under Thirteen Cup for the second time in the School's history, by defeating St Michael's in a one-sided final.

All was set, one thought, for a successful transition of authority.

The retiring Headmaster on the Front Steps

PART THREE

Headfort Today
2001 into the future

13. THE MODERN ERA BEGINS

*A swingeing year – Resurrection – White smoke – The new philosophy –
Manifestations of the new philosophy*

A swingeing year

The academic year 2001–2 was a swingeing time in Headfort's history.

CATHAL McCOSKER, the newly appointed Headmaster, had taught at
Eton College and Cothill House preparatory school before he came to Headfort. He worked here for two terms under his predecessor, before assuming
office.

The opening of a Montessori department was a significant innovation.

Entrance to the Montessori School

A pre-prep class

The appointment of MARY KELLY was excellent: a fine teacher of mathematics and geography, she has a winning manner with children. Ten years on, she is a highly valued member of the teaching staff.

The geography lesson

Cathal McCosker also appointed CHARLES O'TOOLE who gave several years of dedicated service.

MARGUERITE MORGAN joined the secretarial department in the role of Bursar. Hailing from Zimbabwe, she is well versed in the use of commercial software packages and she keeps her finger on the School's purse strings.

That summer the Headmaster took a party of girls to Eton College and to St George's School, Ascot to play tennis.

There was a large increase in the number of both teaching and administrative staff that stretched the School's finances to the limit. Cathal McCosker left Headfort at the end of the School year.

Otherwise, let us draw a line under that year. Here it is:

―――――――――――――――――――line―――――――――――――――――――

Resurrection

Michael Bolton was appointed Acting Headmaster for the first two terms of the 2002–3 academic year. It was probably not a role that he relished, since it cramped his style and restricted the time that he could devote to his myriad strengths; nevertheless, he began the task of rebuilding the School and restoring the ethos and structures that had been established in the Early Years, nurtured in the Middle Years, but which had been considerably unravelled during the previous twelve months. One innovation that he introduced was to serve lunch on a canteen basis, rather than planting the children at long tables with a teacher at the end to dispense food, as had been the practice from the beginning. The canteen system offered a wider choice of food and, despite what some people had feared, the majority of the children managed to convey their plates to the table without bequeathing too much of their content to the floor.

Michael Bolton appointed MARIAN CAROLAN as Head Matron. Her extensive medical knowledge has been of inestimable value. She has also shown special kindness to the foreign students, frequently taking a group home for the weekend.

White smoke

Meanwhile the selection procedure was in progress once more. DERMOT DIX, who had not applied in the first round, was eventually appointed Headmaster to lead the School into the new millennium. A past pupil of Headfort (where he was taught by the Headmasters of both the Early Years and the Middle Years), Dermot Dix won a scholarship to St Columba's College. After school, he spent a year as a gap student at Headfort, before graduating in history at Dublin University and taking his MA at Cambridge. He taught in New York for sixteen years, during which time he married Dr Chandana Mathur. The couple have one son.

This time the selection panel had chosen wisely. Today the School is led by a man of high intelligence, with wide experience and one who is sensitive to the feelings of the entire Headfort body. Apart from his comprehensive headmagisterial duties, Dermot Dix teaches history and religion, and he coaches both the School's First XI and the Girls' XI at hockey, as well as assisting with the cricket.

The new philosophy

Dermot Dix spent his last six years in New York teaching at The Dalton School (motto: 'Go Forth Unafraid') in Manhattan. Dalton was founded in 1919 by Helen Parkhurst, an associate of Maria Montessori, and is a 'progressive' school. It is strongly child-centred. In most schools, the teacher speaks and the children listen. At Dalton the teacher constantly elicits the pupils' input. Regular debate and discussion are the keystones of the learning process. Students are encouraged to entertain each other's opinions, as well as the teacher's, and to follow their own individual paths and interests. The process is akin to Socratic dialogue, except that the teacher, the modern Socrates, does not supply the answers to all of the questions that he poses: these are found through collective exploration.

The Headmaster at work

Some might think that 'progressive education' is woolly and too politically correct, and that standards would inevitably fall. This is not the case. Dalton has one of the best records in the USA for placing students in top-ranked colleges and universities.

Let us hear it from the horse's mouth:

Teaching at Dalton made a profound impact on me, though I had already planted myself firmly in the 'progressive' camp before working there. I had already begun a pedagogic journey whereby I was increasingly less committed to sheer coverage of material in my history courses, preferring instead to spend more time teasing out with students the implications of what we were studying together. In short, I had come to entertain serious doubts about how much my (and other teachers') lectures could possibly be retained by students; in an earlier phase of my career I might have patted myself on the back after a class in which I felt I had transmitted a good amount of knowledge about a given time period – without having spent enough time and energy in discussion with the students, discussion which would allow me to gauge the level of their assimilation of the facts and themes I thought important. Now in my classes, twenty-five years after my teaching career started in earnest in New York, I spend far less time covering the facts and much more time in open discussion.

I still prefer the seminar-style layout of a classroom, with desks or tables in a U shape around the room – making it easier for students to engage with each other as well as with the teacher. The more conventional arrangement of a room into rows makes this kind of student-student interaction much less feasible. Occasionally other Headfort teachers have used the seminar layout, though rows are preferred in general – and indeed rows make perhaps more sense for the younger students in the primary-school cycle in that they render classroom management more straightforward (not all student-student interaction is likely to be aimed at improving the stock of knowledge of the group!).

When I took up my job at Headfort in 2003 I was aware that I was moving back into a more 'traditional' teaching zone than I had been used to in New York. Yet, I said to myself, Headfort had always shown itself to incorporate much that might be deemed 'progressive', despite its more traditional appearance. Teachers at Headfort have always valued 'individuation' (though I am sure they would hate that word!), have always encouraged their pupils to chart their own courses rather than merely following the herd. This was the case when I was a pupil in the 1970s, in the last few years of David Wild's tenure; and certainly Lingard Goulding has done much to move the school in a progressive direction, while retaining a great deal of the carefully established routine of his predecessor. I had kept in touch with the school and its people during my years in New York, and I knew this to be the case. The careers of John and Amanda Leyden, hugely important teachers to successive generations of pupils at Headfort (they have just completed their 42nd year at the school and have thus broken Jack and Edith Sweetman's previous record of service), have also done much to encourage the progressive approach of which I write.

After nine years at the helm at Headfort, I have a strong sense that one of the school's great strengths lies in its combination of the best of 'traditional' and 'progressive' approaches. We use a truly rigorous curriculum, and are proud of our record of preparing our pupils for entry into the most demanding of secondary-school environments both in Ireland and the UK. Yet the school has an increasingly softer, kinder atmosphere – a process that started with David Wild's introduction of girls and proceeded with Lingard Goulding's introduction, among other changes, of day pupils and the weekly boarding option – whereby its children are seen as partners, albeit junior ones, in their own process of education.

Manifestations of the new philosophy

When challenged, Dermot Dix declares that the alterations that he has introduced to the School have been mundane. This observer does not concur with that view.

The Headmaster of the Middle Years had done so much teaching, and held such a disdain for political correctness, that he had perhaps allowed certain clerical areas to slip. Under Dermot Dix's leadership, the School has assumed a more professional profile. All of the staff are properly qualified for the work that they perform. Headfort Today complies with the expectations of modern parents who are more demanding than those of yesteryear.

Both in terms of educational philosophy and in the manner in which the building is employed, there have been far-reaching improvements.

Educationally first: in the Early Years the Headmaster would publicly announce the marks attained by every boy in the school at an end-of-term ceremony called Mark Reading that was held in the Ballroom, thus: 'Peasbody, four thousand two hundred and seventy-four; Anstruther-Gough-Fortescue, three thousand eight hundred and ninety-six; Fotheringay-Thomas, three thousand one hundred and three...; Clotworthy, nineteen...' Little Lord Peasbody would crow: the gormless Clotworthy would cringe. The Headmaster of the Middle Years was not quite as explicit, but he nevertheless used to post in each classroom the end-of-term ranking of every child in the class. The present Headmaster believes that children's grades (let alone their marks) should not be published; he sees these as being the business of the child, the teacher and the parents. Children are no longer ranked in their school reports. In the Head's report he indicates whether a child is in the top, middle or lower third of the class. Grades are assigned such that the parent has an idea of the child's absolute ranking, rather than how he or she compares with his peers. Each term's Form List is posted in alphabetical order, rather than in academic standing, as had previously been the case.

HEADFORT

Report for month ending _2nd Dec, 1961_

Form _3_   Number in Form _13_

Name _____

Subject	Top Boy's Marks	My Marks	My Place
Latin	1338	458	3
Greek			
French	110	64	7
English	306	184	4
History	49	30	8
Geography	62	24	12
Scripture	70	53	8
Mathematics	812	429	4

Monthly Orders

The original ethos of the School was geared towards boarders. In 1996 the first day pupils arrived and every effort was made to accommodate them happily. Dermot Dix has taken further steps to fit day pupils more seamlessly into the life of the School. For instance, day pupils and boarders now do their 'prep' together (originally, day pupils did 'homework', partly during rest and partly after they had left school, whereas the boarders did their prep under supervision late in the evenings). Today prep is done in two sections: half an hour before break in the mornings and half an hour before high tea in the evenings. All work is now finished for the day by six o'clock.

Girls' sports are more carefully structured. The girls' hockey team, for example, is as active and busy in terms of matches as is that of the boys. The girls follow a three-sport year (hockey–basketball–softball/rounders) to correlate with the boys' hockey–cricket–rugby.

Recent years have seen numerous sporting tours. In 2004, and again in 2009, the cricket team visited Shrewsbury and played several matches. In 2005 the Headmaster took a girls' hockey team to Cambridge. The rugby team travels extensively: as well as their biennial tour to Scotland to play Lathallan, a seven-a-side squad competed in a tournament at Mowden Hall

A try!   2009 First XI

The coach offers advice at half-time

in Northumberland in 2010 where they acquitted themselves with credit. Also that year the Headmaster took the girls' hockey team to North Wales where they played three games.

Headfort seven-a-side squad in Newcastle, 2010   *Headfort on the charge*

Rugby squad, 2005   *A well-organized scrum*

The Girls' hockey team on tour in Wales, 2010

Headfort has moved even further down the œcumenical route. All children, be they Roman Catholic, Protestant, Hindu, Muslim, Jew, agnostic (a term coined by Professor Thomas Huxley, 'Darwin's Bulldog') or atheist attend religious classes together. Instruction is comparative, rather than doctrinal.

The Montessori department has evolved unrecognizably. Smartly located above the stables, it is a delightful little centre of learning-through-play for Headfort's 'small fry'. In 2004 the gulf between Montessori and prep school was bridged by the introduction of a pre-prep class for five- and six-year-olds.

The music department increased in the first years of the new regime; Rosemarie Shields remains Head of Music, teaching piano and also training the choir, but several instrumental specialists joined the department on a part-time basis. At the time of writing, these are KIERAN HOLT who teaches woodwind and piano, KIERAN McDONNELL, guitar, and JOHN McQUILLAN, percussion. Rosemarie Shields has shown her versatility in other fields. She began to teach the Irish language and helped to give it the status of other subjects. She also assumed the role of part-time Housekeeper, acting as manager to the cleaning and kitchen staff.

Somebody forgot to remove his reed cap!

Traditionally, boarding schools were Dickensian institutions: 'toughen the little blighters up' was the cry. Today we live in a more caring – some would say softer – society. In Headfort Today the appearance of the School is more civilized and attractive than formerly. There were movements in this direction in each of the previous regimes, but the living conditions of today's School are more in keeping with the expectations of twenty-first-century parents. Firstly, the dormitories have been attractively embellished: there is more of a family appearance to them. Other improvements include the establishment of a sports arena in what used to be Lord Headfort's hangar; a Common Room for the boarders; a more salubrious carpentry shop; and – a strange metamorphosis this – the conversion of the former outdoor lavatories into a 'dive' whence a small troupe of rock musicians, under John Leyden's expert tutelage, emit plangent, feral sounds into the night air that challenge the eardrums of those who pass by.

The standard of food has improved during these years. It lies high in the Headmaster's priorities, perhaps due to his own Headfort experience. A Head Chef and increased kitchen staff have been hired to ensure that fresh food is cooked from source material. The menu is based on a three- or four-weekly rota, such that Monday's lunch, for example, is not tediously predictable. LIZ CHARLES was the first Head Chef; she set a high standard and has been followed with equal dedication by SUSAN CASEY.

A past pupil from the Middle Years who is now a restaurateur and food critic writes as follows:

Christmas dinner

I remember the truly awful food, the liver and bacon being the stand-out winner for worst. I remember the skin that used to form on the cocoa. I remember the freezing dorms, the scratchy blankets, your insistence upon lots of fresh air; also no duvets or tights were allowed [later, my dear] and having to march through ploughed fields as part of our fitness routine. I remember being part of a group of bolshie girls who managed to convince you that holding a school disco would be a great thing. It was – for us – and so, emboldened by our success, we asked for another to be held. You quite rightly turned us down flat! As someone who had recently arrived from the Bahamas, I found Headfort pretty unbearable for the first term, but settled in very well after that. Beside the dreadful grub and freezing cold, I remember a school full of tradition, the wonder of those formal rooms and the rush you'd feel descending the stairs and trespassing into those sacred rooms we were all banned from entering (but often did). I remember wonderful teachers and an excellent education.

The Headmaster of the Middle Years feels uncomfortable about this pupil's perception of the grub in those days, but of course she is a professional in the field and therefore difficult to please. Mark Twain writes of his boarding school, 'We didn't starve, but nobody ate chicken unless they were ill, or the chicken was.'

Another change introduced by the new Headmaster was to alter the nomenclature of the school year. Henceforth, instead of the 'Christmas' and 'Easter' terms, the secular expressions 'Autumn' and 'Spring' are used.

14. CHANGE, YET CONTINUITY

The classroom – Board & staff matters – A sporting success – A dip in numbers – Change in structure of the School year – Drama 3 – Change of personnel in Headfort drama – Drama 4 – Athletics & Sports Day

The classroom

Throughout the Early Years and the Middle Years each child made his class-room his island; he kept all of his personal possessions either in his desk or in his private case on the surrounding shelves, and he knew that none other would use his desk. The staff used to visit the several classrooms for lessons. During 2001–2 this routine was reversed; henceforth, each member of the teaching staff was given his or her own classroom and the children would move to the appropriate room. However, they still kept their belongings in one particular classroom. This system had some advantages, particularly for the staff. It was convenient for a teacher to have all the tools of his trade in his own room. Indeed, when the new Headmaster had been appointed, he considered reverting to the old system with which he had been familiar as a boy, but members of staff were reluctant to be relieved of their newly acquired empires and so the new system prevailed.

However there were disadvantages to the innovation, as was brought home to the author when he was asked to teach English for a fortnight in the Summer Term of 2007 to replace a colleague who was absent. One day the class was interrupted on several occasions after the start of the lesson by children appearing at the door, seeking to collect books from their desk that they had forgotten to take to their next class. After several such interruptions, a pupil was declaiming *Sohrab and Rustum* in dramatic style:

Then Rustum raised his head; his dreadful eyes
Glared, and he shook on high his menacing spear,
And shouted, RUSTUM! Sohrab heard that shout,
And shrank amazed: back he recoiled one step,
And scanned with blinking eyes the advancing form:
And then he stood bewildered; and he dropped
His covering shield, and the spear pierced his side.
He reeled, and staggering back, sank to the ground.
And then the gloom dispersed, and the wind fell,
And the bright sun broke forth, and melted all
The cloud; and the two armies saw the pair;
Saw Rustum standing, safe upon his feet,
And Sohrab, wounded, on the bloody sand.

At this critical juncture came another knock on the door.

'Please, Sir, may I collect my French book?' But this time the former Headmaster had reached his limit of tolerance: his uncharitable response was,

'No, you're too late. It is ten minutes past the start of class. Off you go, and I hope that Monsieur de Sade will eat you!'

This rebuke met with the approval of one little chap in the front row who was clearly enjoying his Matthew Arnold: he piped up,

'That's the spirit, Sir!'

Board & staff matters

Lynn Temple retired from the Board in 2003, having given sterling service over a number of years, including steering the School valiantly through a fraught period. JOHN MORTON, father of four pupils, succeeded him; he was a generous benefactor to the School and assisted the new Headmaster to embark upon the modern era.

BENNY SHERIDAN was a hard-working Board member who served from 2004 until 2011 and POLLY ROWAN HAMILTON has offered her skills since 2008. Johnny Spicer rendered loyal service, as did ROBERTA DUNN. Successive Headmasters have been deeply grateful to these people who give their time freely in the midst of busy lives for their love of the School.

Stalwart employees who have served recently in the important domestic region include DOREEN MEEHAN, PATRICIA GAVIN, MARIE WHITTY and TINA O'CALLAGHAN. PADDY COLDRICK, a skilful craftsman and meticulous worker, arrived to help Peter Sheridan to keep the grounds, and especially the fabric, in order.

EMMA FINNEGAN has worked capably in the administrative department since 2002; computer literate, she runs the office efficiently. After Peggie Ball retired, Mary Maher joined Emma in the office where she has demonstrated her entrepreneurial and marketing skills, promoting equestrian events and lending valuable counsel on the Public Relations committee. Another fine horsewoman, LIZ ROZARIO, shared the riding duties with Mary from 2007 until 2011.

Lingard Goulding returned to teach mathematics and English for a further three years, both under Michael Bolton and Dermot Dix. He also taught clarinet and saxophone to a few eager girls and boys until 2005, and continues to look after Headfort's cricket.

A practice game in 2006, a year in which we had a female wicket-keeper

A sporting success

That year, 2003, Headfort defeated C.U.S. at Malahide in a tense final of the Leinster Cricket Union Under Thirteen Cup, taking the trophy home to the Royal County for the third time.

2003 Cup winning team at Malahide

A dip in numbers

2004 saw a minor crisis when numbers dipped once more. For the second time consideration was given to merging with another school, on this occasion with a local secondary college, and accepting pupils higher up the age range. This would have yielded increased revenue, but would have incurred significant capital expenditure in building the extra facilities that would be required to educate older children. As ever, Headfort managed to haul itself out of its difficulties without the need for such a drastic upheaval. Of course, since 1996 the School owns its property and so has collateral against which to survive a lean year.

Change in structure of the School year

Over the years the School has had to adapt to the changing calendar of Irish education in general. In his prospectus of 1949, Romney Coles declares the approximate term dates to be as follows:

Easter Term: 20th January to 7th April
Summer Term: 8th May to 28th July
Christmas Term: 16th September to 18th December

Later, the Easter Term became a briefer affair, terminating about a week after St Patrick's Day, although it started rather earlier in January; and, even into the mid-1980s, the Summer Term still ran into the middle of July.

Nowadays, though, driven largely by the secondary teachers' desire to escape as soon as the earlier-and-earlier public examinations have finished, the Summer Term is disastrously foreshortened. Even towards the end of the Middle Years, it had been clipped back to the beginning of July, principally to facilitate the Pony Club Camps that many pupils attended, and since then it has reverted even further. In compensation for the short Summer Term, the Autumn Term is now a very lengthy affair that begins early in September – indeed, some secondary schools actually start their Autumn Term in August. Admittedly it is alleviated by a half-term break.

Drama 3

Alice in Wonderland was the 2003 dramatic offering. Our Alice held the audience spellbound. The White Rabbit, the Cheshire Cat, the Duchess, the Mad Hatter's tea party, the March Hare, the Dormouse, the Gryphon and the Mock Turtle all featured in Lewis Carroll's delightful anthropomorphic allegory.

David Copperfield was the first production of Dermot Dix's era. It was adapted into dramatic form for St Patrick's Day 2004. The programme notes end as follows:

ALICE IN WONDERLAND
by
Lewis Carroll

HEADFORT

MARCH, 2003

I beg of you, submit yourselves on a cloud of fancy this evening. Be indulgent of our shortcomings and mingle with our heroes and heroines as they transport you back through a century and a half to a coarser, but more decorous, age. You will, I fear, witness dastardly actions, turpitude and a veritable Heep of infamy, but you will also behold true beauty. You will watch an appealing little boy (represented by three actors as he grows older) develop in moral rectitude, eschewing all baseness, treating all men with equal honour. In the fullness of time he becomes infatuated with the enticingly gorgeous, yet shallow, Dora; and, when Dora dies tragically young, he grows to realise, with a little help from his adoring Aunt Betsy, that his childhood sweetheart, Agnes, has ever been the true object of his affections. Can there remain a dry eye in the house when David, radiant and handsome, gazes into the alluring eyes of his beloved and breathes to her the immortal, sweet-nothing words,

'Oh Agnes, Oh my soul, so may thy face be by me when I close my life; so may I, when realities are melting from me like the shadows which I now dismiss, still find thee near me.'?

Aunt Betsy & David Copperfield   *Mrs Steerforth & Rosa Dartle*

Uriah Heep   *A sailor*

After a thirteen-year interval, *The Empress of Blandings* was reprised in 2005, and once more the audience enjoyed the wacky occurrences at Clarence, Ninth Earl of Emsworth's Castle. This time the two-person porker danced a wild cancan to the accompaniment of the sensual notes of a soprano saxophone. Amongst a host of plausible performers, His Lordship, his sister Lady Constance Keeble and Dame Daphne Winkforth, his former flame ('Little Winky'), played the principal comic roles.

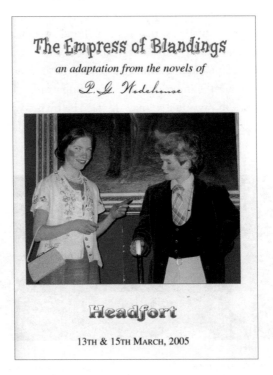

The Empress of Blandings

an adaptation from the novels of

P. G. Wodehouse

Headfort

13TH & 15TH MARCH, 2005

Clarence, Earl of Emsworth & Dame Daphne Winkworth

Change of personnel in Headfort drama

After 2005 there was a change of personnel within the world of Headfort drama. The author who had adapted plays, conducted auditions of the cast and directed the nightly rehearsals since the 1980s would no longer be in Ireland during the Spring Term. His role of Director fell into the capable hands of Michael Bolton, his assistant down the years. Mr Bolton has received valuable help with adaptations from his mother, Mrs Poppy Bolton, who is a distinguished writer. Robert Pelant has become a master craftsman in the field of stage construction and he specializes in operating the highly complex and sophisticated system of lighting and sound production that the School now possesses.

In recent years Geraldine Colley has produced delightful junior plays in the Summer Term. Rosemarie Shields assists her with the music.

The costume powerhouse, comprising Mary Wilkinson, Carole Barry and Vivienne Potterton, marches on, undiminished, into the future.

Drama 4

Another of the Headmaster's important innovations was the conversion of the former gymnasium into a purpose-built theatre for Headfort drama, made necessary by the restoration of the Ballroom. This building in the stable yard was no longer required for its original purpose, following the development of the hangar into a sports hall. Henceforth there would be a permanent stage, and the complex set of lighting apparatus could be housed in a fixed location, rather than having to be erected and removed each dramatic season.

2006 saw a new slant on a previous theme, entitled *Not Quite William*, adapted by the notorious duo of Notlob and Nosnikliw.

Alan Parker's *Bugsy Malone* was 2007's colourful, and very high-tech, production. Copious use was made of the video camera to display background images on a giant screen.

In 2008 a handful of fairy tales by Hans Christian Anderson and the Grimm brothers under the title *A Grim Night for Hans Christian Anderson* was based upon the competition between these two camps for the title of best writer of fairy tales.

Sue Townsend's *The Queen and I* was 2009's offering. This featured exceptional performances from Queen Elizabeth II (or, rather, her alias) and Adrian Mole, the latterday Holden Caulfield, who had somehow crept into the script. The actress who played the part of the Queen had showed her prowess on stage over several years. The thirteen-and-three-quarter-year-old Master Mole had also shone in the previous year's play. This was the first production to be held in Headfort's new bespoke theatre.

Geoffrey Chaucer's *Canterbury Tales* was a suitably cultural theme for 2010. This was one of Mrs Poppy Bolton's brilliant adaptations and was apparently quite delightful.

In 2011 and 2012 the School presented a series of form plays, in which every child in the top few forms of the School had an involvement.

A new development is that JOHN GRANT, the Kells pantomime king, now teaches drama in the Montessori school.

The author much regrets that he has been twelve thousand miles away and hence unable to watch most of the recent plays.

The production of a play is the ultimate team experience. Each actor depends upon the skill and timing of his fellow actors, the lighting technician, the sound technician, his personal property manager and the stagehands whose job it is to ensure the correct location of the general properties on the set for each scene. The prompter's role demands massive concentration; he or she is a principal contributor during the long evenings of rehearsal, guiding all the actors as they gradually learn their lines, but it is a source of pride that he generally has no business at all by the time of a Headfort dress rehearsal. Most years the School will have a few naturally talented actors, but by the end of the run the supporting cast has usually reached a level of competence that will sustain the leading players and be able to convince an audience. In a school production, aesthete and athlete, academic and mechanical, blend together in the common weal. It creates at least as strong a bonding as any team sport.

Athletics & Sports Day

Headfort has never lent special emphasis to athletics. In the middle of the Summer Term a ten-day interlude occurs when there is reduced concentration upon cricket and tennis and children suddenly start running and lepping of an  evening. Out come the high jump apparatus and the landing mats (until halfway through the Middle Years Headfort's high jumpers landed in a pit of hard sand that was not beneficial to the skeleton), and in every free moment there is a cascade of young people, of all shapes and sizes, soaring over the bar and crashing onto the mats in an unending procession. They seem to derive a sense of physical pleasure from launching themselves into parabolic flight.

Sports Days today are much as they have always been, except that two of the original events are no longer contested. The discontinuation of one of these events is a blessing to those who had to watch it: The Throwing of the Cricket Ball was a deadly activity that took an inordinate length of time and was far from spectacular to behold. The other event that has ceased, the hurdles, is regrettable. However, the wooden structures were of fixed height, whether they be traversed by eight-year-old mini-folk or long-legged thirteen-year-olds, and in the course of time they broke and were not replaced. The author took a drink at Abu Dhabi airport in October 2011 with a past pupil who, some thirty-two years previously had crashed to the ground when he mistimed his take-off on a damp track and broke both his wrist and a hurdle.

John Leyden starts a race on Sports Day

Chris Macdonald introduced a splendid new event to Sports Day: the House relay race. The School is divided into two houses, Bective and Kenlis, both Headfort family titles, for the purpose of sporting competition. In the relay race, half of the members of each house are aligned at each end of the 100-metre track and every pupil in the School runs a length. It is a comical sight to watch children of different sizes and gaits competing together; the race engenders fierce partisanship and the cacophonous roar of support remains thunderous throughout the event.

Sports Day is a typical prep school show-off occasion. The School is rendered immaculate in the preceding days and everybody is on his best behaviour. It concludes with a huge tea on the lawn, whereat the Headmaster delivers a traditional speech and presents hardware to the senior and junior Victores and Victrices Ludorum.

All that is missing is P.G. Wodehouse's Gussie Finknottle.

David Wild at home in happy retirement

15. HEADFORT IN THE NEW MILLENNIUM

Chairman of the Board – More appointments – A trend – The curriculum today – Subject teaching – Renovation of the Ballroom

Chairman of the Board

In 2005 JAMES JACKSON, a Headfort father, became Chairman of Headfort School, succeeding John Morton. James gave generously of his time and expertise until 2012. Whether it be to his credit or his debit, he is the instigator of this book.

More appointments

Important recent appointments to the staff include ROBERT PELANT, LIZ PRATT–JARVIS and HENRY CLESHAM.

Robert Pelant hails from the Czech Republic. He is an ideal prep school master, being an excellent teacher and having a positive rapport with the children who respond warmly towards him. Liz teaches art, and has introduced Design to the School's timetable: computers are now used with more sophistication than previously as children learn the principles of composition. For this purpose the Headmaster created new, well-equipped rooms for both Art and Design. Some remarkable work is produced in both of these areas.

Work in the Art room

Henry Clesham is a past pupil of the School; he returned to his old Alma Mater in the role of Development Officer, having acquired many years of experience, working in senior roles at prominent English prep schools. He also teaches English to the Upper Sixth, assists with the rugby and organizes skiing trips. He is a lateral thinker and feeds the Headmaster challenging ideas.

GERALDINE COLLEY is an excellent teacher who joined the staff in 2008. She teaches all junior subjects as well as Irish; and, as has already been mentioned, she produces delightful junior plays. JOANNA JANCZYK (née STOINSKA) from Poland began work at Headfort as a cleaner and laundress in the nether regions of the building; however, she is a qualified teacher and now introduces mathematics and geography to the younger children with patience and enthusiasm, as well as taking games. She is a very sensitive person and she loves the children. ADRIAN PARKES taught general subjects and performed all supervision duties with enthusiasm for a few years from 2008. He had a particular penchant for computers.

A hugely important addition to the Board of Directors was TIM MACEY, former Headmaster of Newtown School and Warden of St Columba's College. With his experience in the field of private education, and his knowledge of Headfort in particular – he sent two daughters to the School in the Middle Years – he is of inestimable value to the Headmaster.

Around this time Neville Wilkinson assumed the complex role of assigning children to their various sporting activities each afternoon. This is not as simple as forming a Top Game, Second Game, Third Game and Fourth Game throughout the week, because there is a seemingly infinite range of exception conditions, such as riding, cookery, tennis lessons, swimming. Neville manages to fit the jigsaw together in such a way that the children are matched appropriately; also, every child knows what he is supposed to be doing and the teachers who are taking the games are aware of who is expected to be present. Neville also took over the task of running Sports Day, something that he does with quiet efficiency.

Neville Wilkinson takes a game of hockey

A trend

In the early days, nearly all of the teaching staff at Headfort, as at other similar schools, had been men, just as all of the pupils were boys. Nowadays there is a more even distribution of men and women among the teaching staff. This trend has been beneficial from almost every point of view. With a mixed pupil population – indeed, even without one – an equal presence of women and men in their lives cannot but be beneficial.

From a Headmaster's standpoint there are two difficulties inherent in this demographic change: firstly, many of the women teachers have children of their own and consequently cannot commit themselves to a full timetable that includes evening duties; and, secondly, fewer women than men are well versed in predominantly male games such as rugby football. Thus, a lesser proportion of the staff is competent to coach the School's principal games of rugby, hockey and cricket than formerly. It is a small price to pay.

The 'enemy' is down, under Michael Bolton's watchful eye

The curriculum today

Chapter nine revealed the British Minister for Education's proposal to issue by the end of the 1980s a standardized dossier for each pupil that would reveal all that had been achieved at school, be it academic, practical or cultural. This would lead to fewer compulsory examinations and the opportunity to offer evidence of accomplishment in newer fields of endeavour. Subject profiles would be prepared, and assessed internally, to reveal information on work done during the final two years of the prep school cycle and would include such topics as CDT, electronics, computer studies, art, music and drama.

The Headmaster maintains that little of the Minister's prediction has come to pass, at least at the preparatory stage. Despite this, the range of subjects has widened and the balance has changed somewhat. The core subjects, English, mathematics, science and French, still dominate the Headfort timetable, while history and geography retain their traditional positions. Computer studies and religion are taught once a week. Art and Design receive three classes a week at the junior end of the School and two at the senior end. Irish and Latin share a slot in the timetable. The author suggests that a strong case can be made to include Spanish alongside, or even instead of, French on the linguistic palette. The Headmaster is contemplating this option.

Audio-visual French class

There has of course been a shift in emphasis since the Early Years: science has reached the timetable and grown progressively in importance, and electronics was added to its domain in 1986; computers have been born; CDT has arrived; Irish is taught to some pupils. Inevitably, something had to give ground. The first subject to suffer was Latin – it is no longer studied by every student – but there is increased pressure upon all areas of the timetable. The Latin Common Entrance paper is now a shadow of its former self and there is no Latin Verse paper; mathematics is no longer divided into three discrete papers, arithmetic, geometry and algebra. Common Entrance mathematics has been subject to numerous changes over the years, as various topics were added to, and more were subtracted from, the syllabus. Where is topology today? And trigonometry, and matrices? Why, even Venn diagrams, a hugely important branch of modern mathematics that leads to the discovery of set theory, has been expunged from the syllabus.

At the secondary level, there is the widespread belief that GCE 'A' levels in England, and the Leaving Certificate in Ireland, are being 'dumbed down', as the unattractive neologism describes the process. The percentage of A grades seems to rise every year, despite the strenuous denial by the universities that the papers are easier.

Of course, one cannot believe them. With the considerable increase in the range of knowledge that modern students must glean, it is inevitable that less penetration is acquired in each subject. But it is a shame that the standard of the examinations is not maintained, even if expectations in each are slightly lowered. The overall effect is that modern students follow a broader syllabus, but in less depth, than those who went before. If one proposes to become a nuclear physicist, there is probably merit in specializing early; however for the majority of students, a more general, rounded education may be desirable. The classical education of their grandparents is certainly a thing of the past.

Subject teaching

One of the principal advantages that Headfort – indeed, most traditional prep schools – holds over national schools is that each child is taught by a range of different subject teachers, rather than spending the entire working day with a single form teacher. It must be challenging, to say the least, for both child and teacher, to be closeted in the same room with the same people all day long. At Headfort the children are exposed to different faces, teaching separate subjects, which is surely more stimulating, howsoever good a form teacher may be. In the juniormost form, however, there remains a degree of form teaching, although even these children receive visits from other teachers.

Renovation of the Ballroom

One of the most dramatic events so far in the modern era has been the spectacular restoration of the Ballroom to its former glory. Under the skilful management of Headfort Trust Chairman, Dick Blakiston Houston, ably assisted by Ann McFarland, Nick Nicholson and the Williams family, the Ballroom is now surely the finest room in Ireland.

Actually, the story goes back to the turn of the century when the trustees of Headfort Trust embarked upon a fundraising programme to restore firstly the exterior of the house and then the interior. The exterior work involved repairs to the roof and preventing the ingress of water from leaking chimney flashings and gutters which had wrought considerable damage to the east wall of the Ballroom in particular, as well as several of the portraits. Funding was scarce and work was laboured at first.

The turning point came in 2004 when, through the tenacity and skill of Dick Blakiston Houston, the trustees obtained for Headfort a nomination as one of the World Monuments Fund's (WMF) one hundred most endangered heritage buildings. The WMF is the leading independent organization dedicated to saving the world's treasured places. Based in New York, its experts have, since 1965, been racing against time, applying proven techniques to preserve important architectural and cultural heritage sites in more than ninety countries around the globe. Through partnerships with local communities, funders, and governments, WMF inspires an enduring commitment to stewardship for future generations. Headfort qualified for restoration due to its being the only original, surviving example in Ireland of the work of the Scottish architect, Robert Adam.

The nomination attracted wide publicity, and funders such as The Heritage Council, The Department of the Environment, Meath County Council and The Irish Georgian Society in America and in London were extremely generous. Together with numerous private trusts and individuals, they contributed approximately €1.1 million, and WMF gave €450,000. A balance of €0.25 million came from reserves in the Headfort Trust, totalling about €1.75 million.

Work on the Ballroom and The Diamond Hall was completed in 2010, following extensive research into the original paint used, by taking samples of the 1770 paintwork. This task was conducted by Richard Ireland who has lent his expertise to many important buildings in Ireland and England. Other work involved the complete rewiring of the house, including fire and smoke alarms, and computer network facilities; re-slating the West Wing, the School dormitory area; and connection of major services to the mains.

Skilled craftsmen renovate the Ballroom

The companies that contributed to this wonderful work deserve mention in a book about Headfort School, because it is the School that principally enjoys the fruits of their labour. The architects were Consarc Conservation, represented by Una Ni Mhearain. The decorators were Corlin from Castlederg, whose craftsmen spent 8000 man-hours over seven months, working on scaffolding for many hours each day in virtual silence, painting the delicate mouldings with meticulous care, using wafer-thin brushes. The main contractor for the remaining work was Rainey and Co., Dublin. The electrical contractor was Kells Electric, Ronnie McGrane's company. Ronnie has looked after Headfort's circuitry since 1975. He is ever available and now, thirty-seven years later, he is part of the furniture.

This colossal work will have secured the house in pristine condition for at least another generation. The Headmaster of the Middle Years feels rather guilty that he permitted the house to reach such a level of disrepair. In his defence, there was never sufficient funding to do more than 'keep the ship afloat'; it required somebody with the knowledge and drive of Dick Blakiston Houston to tap the necessary funding and mastermind the decade-long, on-going project.

16. SIXTY YEARS ON

Sixtieth anniversary

In 2009 Headfort celebrated its sixtieth anniversary. The event was marked
with a grand dinner in the Ballroom at which the Headmaster and his predecessor each spoke of the School's glories and of the minefields through which
it had swept.

Death of David Wild

David Wild died peacefully in November 2010 at the age of ninety-six. In
June 2011 a memorial service was held in his honour in the wonderfully refur-
bished Ballroom that David would have loved to see. Many of his old pupils
– middle-aged gentlemen now, plus one middle-aged lady – assembled for the
occasion, and it was a special delight to all those present that Barbara Wild
should have travelled across from their home in Devon for the service.

The Festival Weekend

A significant recent innovation is the concept of the Headfort Festival
Weekend. From time immemorial a surfeit of red-letter days has struggled for
prominence towards the close of the Summer Term. Since 2005 these events
have been grouped together in one weekend. This has the advantage that

At the Memorial Service for David Wild. Barbara Wild & Jack Sweetman are at centre front

parents, many of whom travel from far afield, only have to commit one weekend to their diaries, in which they will be able to watch their children perform in such varied events as Sports Day, the gymkhana, the Mothers' tennis match, the Fathers' cricket match and a musical concert; they may also dance the night away at the fancy-dress Headfort Party that has become an annual fixture. Michael Bolton, together with a committee of mothers, dreams up a specific theme each year, and he and Robert Pelant burn much midnight oil decorating the principal rooms accordingly. The 2012 theme is 'The Roaring Twenties – at home with Al Capone'.

Headfort fancy-dress party, 2006. The ten-month beard, dyed green for the occasion, was auctioned off the next day, realizing €700 for the School!

Valediction

As has already been seen, the principal act of valediction for Headfort's leavers during the Early Years was held in St Columba's Church of Ireland church in Kells. From the beginning of the Middle Years a valedictory ceremony has been held for all children in the Ballroom at the end of each Summer Term, whereat the Headmaster addresses children and parents, and speaks fondly of those who are about to depart, before presenting each one with his or her leaver's tie. It is a poignant moment for these young people as they emerge from the Ballroom into the Front Hall and thence out onto the front steps, proudly knotting their new neckwear, and preparing to leave Headfort as pupils for the last time. Nowadays, tears flow freely on these occasions and there is much hugging of dear friends from whom parting is such sweet sorrow. In the immediate post-war, all-male society, it would not have done at all to be seen to shed a tear or to hug a fellow pupil – Great Heavens, how soppy! However, the advent of girls in the School and a general softening of society's psychological attitudes, has released the necessity for the upper lip to remain constantly rigid, and rendered it acceptable – indeed, desirable – to express one's emotions.

The valedictory celebration is also the occasion for the award of prizes. Originally, these were given for random accomplishments, dependent upon a kind parent presenting a silver cup for a favoured activity. Many of these cups remain in circulation – although some, such as those for boxing, shooting and draughts, are no longer contended – but today there is more consistency in the award of prizes: at both the senior and junior end of the School, each mainstream academic subject is rewarded, as well as cultural and sporting pursuits. The principal award is The Headmaster's Prize that is presented for academic excellence; there is also a curious olive wreath, known as the Lougher-Goodey Cup that was donated in 1954 for 'the boy who has made the most progress, measured in terms of the effort involved.' Over time it tended to become an acknowledgement of a boy (sic) who had overcome some sort of handicap; more recently it may be described as a 'character' award and is presented to a pupil (one who has generally not won another major prize) whose overall contribution to the School in terms of behaviour (hence its unfortunate nickname, the Goody-Goody Cup) and involvement in a wide array of activities, has made him or her stand out in the eyes of the staff who frequently debate long and hard to nominate a winner from amongst a number of worthy candidates. Notable past winners include Dermot Dix and Neville Wilkinson.

Easter 2011

Easter fell on 24 April in 2011, even later than in 2000. This time Head-fort followed the lead of other Irish schools and did not begin its Summer Term until early May. The secondary schools had a three-and-a-half week term! Headfort managed to complete only five cricket matches. It will be 2095 before Easter falls on this date again, although in 2038 (and 2190) it will be even later, on the twenty-fifth.

Would that we might continue to date our years *ab urbe condita* (from the foundation of the city of Rome). However, in 45 BC (709 AUC), Julius Caesar immodestly added two extra months, Julius and Augustus, to the existing ten each year, and decreed that the time between vernal equinoxes be 365.25 days. The solar year is in fact eleven minutes shorter than that and, by the sixteenth century, the error had accumulated to approximately ten days. Since the spring equinox was tied to the celebration of Easter, and the Roman Catholic Church did not want that festival to drift towards summer, Pope Gregory XIII replaced the Julian calendar on 24 February 1582 in a papal bull that expunged the offending ten days from history.

However even the Gregorian calendar is fallible. After the year 4099 (in which year Easter will fall on 19 April) the calendar will have to be adjusted once more (more bull perhaps). From 5000 onwards it should be easier for Headfort to determine its Summer Term dates.

The Headfort riding team that won the Killossery Lodge Stud inter-schools league title in 2012

Recent sporting successes

Two of Headfort's best girl hockey players of the mid-2000s who are now senior pupils at their secondary schools in Scotland and England have been selected to represent Ireland in the National Ladies' Lacrosse team in 2012.

A team of four present Headfort riders won the Killossery Lodge Stud inter-schools league title for 2012, having triumphed over six legs of the series on Sunday mornings.

National Tree Week & the Headfort gardens

The School organized an open day on 4 March 2012 to coincide with National Tree Week under the auspices of the Tree Council of Ireland. That year's theme was 'Trees – our past, our present, our future'. A distinguished, local dendrologist (a past pupil, so I do not name him) conducted a guided tour to the public through some of the remote parts of the historic garden. Almost all aspects of horticultural history can be found at Headfort, from rolling parkland, walled garden, specific plant collections and woodland walks.

Headfort is renowned for its vast collections of rhododendrons and conifers that were laid down in the late-nineteenth and early-twentieth century. The rhododendrons, planted in soil that is naturally alkaline, are especially splendid. Their seed was collected directly from Yannan in China by the plant hunter George Forrest, rather in the manner of Frank Kingdon-Ward. Several of Forrest's expeditions were sponsored by Geoffrey, Fourth Marquis of Headfort (1878–1943). Indeed, there are even Headfort hybrids: *Hebe Headfortii*, a spreading evergreen shrub that was raised in about 1930 at Headfort, and *Chamaecyparis lawsoniana Headfortii*, a *cupressus* (cypress).

The Fourth Marquis, who was President of the Royal Horticultural Society from 1915 until his death in 1943, laid out a pinetum on the Great Island, a ten-acre island on the River Blackwater to the south side of the house. The Great Island is now part of the new eighteen-hole golf course.

The gardens have lapsed somewhat since the 1930s, but the American Garden has recently been restored by the aforementioned expert. In recent years the owners of Headfort Court, Peter and Pam McDowell, have developed their spacious garden magnificently: during summer it is a blaze of colour.

What was claimed to be the largest cherry tree in Ireland used to grow at Headfort. However, in 1953 a mighty storm felled it. The tree was acquired by Bun and Maureen Wilkinson of Moyfeigher Carvers and, some sixty years later, a pupil who was in the School at the time keeps a three-legged stool at home that was fashioned for him out of the old Headfort cherry tree.

A miscellany

'TUCK PLEASE!'

Returning from 'away' matches in the mid-1970s, the custom arose to stop at a large department store in Navan. With not a penny between them, the boys would harvest a mountain of sweets and present it at the counter, claiming that Fish's father owned the emporium. The bewildered salesperson, suspecting another scam, yet surprised by the conviction with which it was being perpetrated, would eventually be persuaded to make a telephone call – no mean feat in those days when there was only a party line – and the giant purchase would be ratified and charged to the generous parent.

ANTIDOTES

Up until the late 1970s cod liver oil tablets were supplied at every table in the dining room at teatime and each child was expected to swallow one. However, a past pupil recalls that, when surreptitiously slipped into a cup of hot tea, these gustatory horrors would burst open. He claims that he always drank his tea with circumspection, having checked to determine whether the telltale film of oil was floating on the surface.

Iodine and Gentian Violet were the acknowledged cures for cuts and abrasions in those days. Apparently these substances have returned to medical favour. Every morning Matron would dispense spoonfuls of Virol Malt. It was assumed that, in the early post-war years, the boys were suffering from inadequate nutrition. This may have been the case in England, but probably not in Ireland.

RAF BOMBER 'STRAFES' HEADFORT

A remarkable event took place one day in 1955. A group of boys were enjoying glorious summer weather with Bill Stuart-Mills on the games field, when an almighty roar was heard and a Royal Air Force Canberra bomber flew low over the School at tremendous speed. It circled and repeated the sweep before streaking back towards the border, a trip that would have taken four or five minutes. The past pupil who divulged this story maintains that Bill Stuart-Mills displayed a 'knowing look'.

The explanation is that the father of one of the pupils was an RAF pilot. He had taken an extraordinary risk to fly his plane over neutral territory and swoop over his son's school. Had he been apprehended, the consequence would surely have been dire. However, radar was fairly rudimentary in 1955 and the pilot avoided detection. Stuart-Mills who had been a navigator in the RAF was clearly privy to the lark. History does not relate whether David Wild was.

A ROYAL OCCASION

The nine Spanish pupils who were in the School attended a reception at their Embassy on 1 July 1986 to meet Their Majesties, King Juan Carlos and Queen Sophia during their state visit. All the protocol had been rehearsed ('Don't put your hands in your pockets when you are presented, Carlos.' 'Don't look at your feet when you curtsey, Carmencita'). Fernando presented the Queen with a bouquet of tiger lilies while Maria, the youngest, delivered a little speech of welcome to Ireland. Apparently the King and Queen made a special fuss over the children. When the Headmaster collected them after the Royal Couple had departed, he found several of them dancing the flamenco in a marquee.

THE RUBIK CUBE

For a short while in the early 1980s Professor Emo Rubik's famous cube was the universal toy at Headfort. There are some 4.3 x 10 to the power of 19 permutations for a Rubik cube – about forty-three quintillion. One clever girl developed an algorithm that enabled her to solve the problem in under a minute.

RAIDS ON THE KITCHEN GARDEN
A past pupil from the 1960s writes:

> While in Fifth Form a large number of us crept through the garden like locusts, seeking strawberries and raspberries. Jack Sweetman was apoplectic with rage and couldn't really decide on a decent punishment, beyond detention. Memorably though he called us all BFs which, even in its mildest derivation of 'bloody fool', was a shock from such a man. Threats of overnight transfer to Borstal were too implausible and never had much of an impact.

CENTENARY OF THE IAPS
1982 saw the centenary of the IAPS. The Headmaster attended the Day of Celebration that was held in London. There were functions at Westminster Abbey, the Banqueting House in Whitehall, a concert at the Barbican Centre and finally a grand banquet at the Guildhall in the evening. The pageantry at the Guildhall was splendid, but it was the concert at the Barbican that was truly inspirational. The IAPS orchestra included *Die Meistersinger von Nürnberg* by Wagner in its programme: the quality of musicianship in such young performers was astonishing.

GAP STUDENTS
Headmasters have always delighted to receive past pupils back at Headfort to serve as gap students, boys and girls who have just left secondary school and are awaiting the next stage of their lives – often going up to university. Their role at Headfort tends to be supervisory: to play with the children during their free time and lend support to the teaching staff. In the Early and Middle Years, although unqualified, they were actually let loose in the classroom.

From the point of view of the gap students themselves, theirs is a difficult brief, for they are neither fish nor fowl. They are semi-adults and thus aligned to authority, but they are also still children and naturally wish to associate with the pupils. Headfort has had some wonderful gap students over the years, boys and girls who have shown maturity beyond their years. Because they are past pupils and not full members of staff, they are not named here.

For some years Dermot Dix employed students, principally from New Zealand, through an international gap organization. These young people undergo training in London before they are released into schools around the world. At their best, they can be of immense value: at their worst, a disaster. Recently, Headfort has reverted to receiving more past pupils again.

A special gap student from the Middle Years who was not a past pupil of Headfort was Hugh Schofield. The author had taught Hugh at Brook House whence he won a scholarship to Clifton College. Hugh was the best classicist whom the author ever taught. Having sat his scholarship early in the Summer Term, he was set the task of translating the story of the boat race from the Second Book of Virgil's Aeneid from the Latin, then rendering it into English blank verse, to enable the teacher to concentrate upon the Common Entrance candidates. He was given five or ten minutes of the teacher's time at the end of each class. What he produced was remarkable. Does he still have a copy?

Nowadays Hugh works for the BBC in Paris. For many years the author has heard his former pupil expounding upon economic or political issues on the BBC World Service in the middle of the night, often from some of the most terrifying corners of the world.

Headfort School and Pegus Horse Feed jointly sponsored the 'Minimus' junior triathlon event in 2012. Tony McLean's picture of the wingèd horse Pegasus is seen in the Front Hall, proudly bearing Bellerophon and one of the Pegaside nymphs, possibly the huntress Artemis

17. 1949 TO 2012 — THE SAME OR DIFFERENT?

Modern children – Political correctness, again – The cotton wool syndrome, mad cows & statistics – Bullying – Homesickness – New Board members – Headfort Green – The sheer fun of Headfort – A past pupil's memories – Parents' memories – Summertime at Headfort – The future

Modern children

Watch the children lollygagging of an evening on the games field; observe the keen little faces striving to absorb a concept in the classroom; see them grazing eagerly in the dining room. These could be 2012 children, or equally 1949 children. Hairstyles may have changed a little and modern fashions and materials have updated their clothing, but they remain the same adorable, fun-loving micro-people, delving deep into every opportunity that a Headfort education has to offer them.

At the Adventure Centre in Carlingford

And yet there are differences. Today's crop of children is a slightly different breed of animal to that of yesteryear, and the Headfort programme has evolved somewhat too, as these pages have aimed to show.

Of course today's children are different, because they live in a different world: the world of information technology, materialism and instant gratification. Furthermore, those in society who care for children are no longer expected to say 'boo' to them when they transgress, lest their hyacinth sensibilities be damaged. What hogwash! 'Boo' needs to be uttered more frequently in society – nothing harsher is advocated – for children's psyches are more resilient than our namby-pamby psychologists are prepared to acknowledge. At Headfort the staff are not afraid to say 'boo' when necessary and the children's spirits are not broken: they may even be strengthened, and the girls and boys learn the lessons of social coexistence. Today the seedlings of emergent personality are permitted to peep above the soil, rather than being ploughed roughshod underground as in the past. Of course, sometimes these seedlings may grow wild and out of control. That is the price to pay for increased liberalism. Today's children are treated with greater respect and granted wider latitude than previously.

But they also tend to be overprotected. Yes, parents and teachers have a duty to offer every reasonable protection to the children under their charge; anybody who withholds, or fails to insist upon, such protection is culpable of neglect. However, the expression, 'every reasonable protection' should be regarded as a relative, rather than an absolute, phrase. Otherwise, children would be trapped in a cocoon and disallowed to grow up knowing excitement, tinged with a modicum of fear.

In 1986 the toothy British teleopsis presenter, Esther Rantzen, founded 'Childline' with the laudable aim of preventing abuse; however, this apparent universal panacea extended an open invitation to children nationwide to complain whenever they sensed a grievance. It was akin to parents who greet their child at the end of the school day with the question, 'And who was unkind to you today, dear?' The art of good parenting is to bequeath children the tools with which to resolve their own difficulties. Successive Headfort Headmasters have welcomed the prompt intervention of parents when a serious problem arises: only thus can they mobilize the wheels of remedial action. However the wise parent – the majority of Headfort parents down the years – puts his trust in the School's system of supervision and stands back from minor issues, permitting the child to develop his own technique for interacting with people whom he does not especially like, and for defending his corner.

Society has grown inherently lazy. It is too much trouble to open a door manually, so an electronic sensor detects our desire to enter a shop or an hotel and automatically opens the door for us. To carve a joint of meat is an intolerably physical task: an electric carving knife is employed instead. Modern man cannot be expected to actuate a toothbrush by hand in order to cleanse his teeth: he chooses a brush that vibrates electrically – what monstrous decadence!

All is a-twitter. Twenty-first century man, woman and child no longer breathe the balm of solitude: they must be twittering constantly, inconsequentially, to their friends. The mobile telephone is a double-edged sword; it is certainly an ingenious tool for inducing homesickness. Today Headfort pupils are allowed to bring mobile telephones to School, and use them at specific times, but those that contain a camera or internet connection are forbidden, in order to eliminate the risk of cyber bullying. Foreign students may send occasional e-mails home.

Oscar Wilde was right: the telephone, especially the mobile variety, has impacted heavily upon his domain of conversation, as have television and computers. Perhaps in consequence, the quality of debate in our parliament is frequently banal – not only Irish politicians are guilty, but equally their British and Australian counterparts whose vapid oratory the author also endures from time to time through the media of wireless and television.

Civilized conversation has to some extent been usurped by the ghastly phenomenon of the 'chat show'. The author was casually flicking through the channels on his television in Adelaide recently in search of a favoured programme, when he coincidentally spotted the sublime Dame Judi Dench, sitting vacuously in a chat show that was hosted by a creature called Graham Norton. Dame Judi, how could you so demean yourself? These performances consist of an unending flow of suggestive, innuendo-ridden vulgarities and depend upon an audience of sheep whose intelligence is low, even by the standard of that species, and who possess a mutant hyena gene; they guffaw at everything that is said, and reserve their loudest cackling for the unfunniest banalities. It is not prudery to dislike intensely the obviousness and unsubtlety of this hideous style of contrived humour.

Facebook and, of course, Twitter are modern examples of incessant twittering. Much of the drivel that appears on the 'wall' of many young people is hideously shallow and often unseemly. Why would they wish to advertise to the world their sexual exploits or aspirations and, worse still, their absolute desecration of the English language? (Apparently there is a Facebook application that enables one to transmit a message to the world immediately after one's death – how macabre).

Today's children are less dextrous than their predecessors. How sad it is that wonderful Meccano creations are no longer made – except in France and China. In the Early Years there used to be a room in the downstairs classroom corridor at Headfort that was devoted solely to the construction of model aircraft and boats. In the Middle Years a room on the first floor was assigned to the use of Lego builders. This constructive activity flourished for a few years and then lapsed in popularity and the room was absorbed for another purpose.

The computer occupies much of the time of many children, and adults. Certainly, much creative work is performed on computers and they command an increasingly pivotal role in education. At St Peter's College Adelaide virtually all of the learning material may be found 'on line' in 2012 – new textbooks are almost a thing of the past. Every boy brings his own Apple laptop to school each day. Notice boards have disappeared: to discover which sporting team a boy will represent at the weekend, which meetings he should attend, what cultural events are forthcoming, even what his daily homework is, he must refer to his computer – it is his constant interface with the life of the school. At Headfort Liz Pratt-Jarvis has taken the constructive use of computers to a new level. But computers are also used in society for purposes that are far from constructive and some that are positively harmful. Pornography – an 1850s word, deriving from the Greek *pornographos*, literally meaning 'the writing of harlots' – is rife on the World Wide Web. Nevertheless, the internet is among the greatest tools that has ever been invented: it is the fount of boundless knowledge to which modern students have immediate access. At no previous period in history has information been so readily available. Of course, traditional education is still necessary to teach children how to process and use this abundance of factual material. Albert Einstein maintained that knowledge in itself is limited: it is imagination that encircles the world. And in the fifth century BC, Socrates propounded the Zen concept that true knowledge exists in knowing that we know nothing.

Reading is now the pursuit of a minority. One past pupil from the 1950s recalls that by the age of eleven he had read the Brontës, much of Dickens, Trollope and Jane Austen, as well, of course, as Arthur Ransome, Biggles and The Famous Five. He attributes his lifelong love of reading to the encouragement that he received at Headfort. A boy who is now in his final year at Headfort always carries a book in his hands as he traverses the games field during his free time. He is extremely well read. Such children are rare nowadays. (Incidentally, his father, also well read, was an inveterate pencil cricketer and 'net game' player during his own years at the School in the 1970s).

Reading material in a school tends to be modal. There was a time when every child read Enid Blyton; *The Catcher in the Rye* became essential reading in the 1950s and '60s; then in the early 1980s came *The Secret Diary of Adrian Mole, Aged Thirteen-and-three-quarters* and its sequels. For several years no Headfort dormitory was without a dog-eared copy of an Adrian Mole story. They contained a blend of naïve sophistication, mild adolescent naughtiness and modern street-wisdom that proved irresistible to early teenagers. More recently the *Harry Potter* stories hold pride of place. In the Early Years the only comics that were permitted at Headfort were *The Eagle* and *The Boys' Own Paper*.

Political correctness – again

In July 2001 political correctness (whose issues need not be political and are rarely correct) was taken to a ridiculous extreme when the General Secretary of the National Association of Schoolmasters and Union of Women Teachers (NASUWT), speaking on Radio Four, recommended that, following a tragic accident in which a little girl had drowned while on a school trip to France, teachers should no longer take children on school outings, either locally or abroad. What arrant nonsense, what monstrous over-reaction! A competent staff – that generally includes a body of parents – should be even more capable than the average parent alone of ensuring children's safety, because they are experienced in supervising children and know what hazards to protect against. Indeed, many sad accidents befall children every year when they are in the sole care of their parents. It is this sort of negative advice, borne out of the litigious culture, that, had it been observed, would have denied countless children fulfilling and educational opportunities.

The cotton wool syndrome, mad cows & statistics

The following extract from the Easter 1996 Newsletter shows the then Headmaster's sceptical attitude towards certain modern values. He, your author, holds that attitude equally strongly today.

In Ireland we value human life highly. Terrorists may regard a cause – a united Ireland, for example, or membership of the United Kingdom – more highly than life (someone else's life), but the rest of us guard our lives and those of our children with jealousy.

I often marvel at how small children survive their early years – how they do not break their little necks or scald themselves or electrocute themselves. Some do, of course, but the majority don't. When we are young, we are rash and over-confident; as we mature, we grow cautious – strange, really, because one has so much more to lose when young. With only a fraction of our span to run, one might suppose we would be more profligate with it. Not so. When the end is nigh, we grasp desperately at what remains.

As we pollute the atmosphere copiously, we seek to render our environment ever safer and pay fortunes to comply with safety regulations. Dwellings become more fire-resistant, motoring cars sprout new safety features, protective clothing floods the market for workmen and sportsmen. But, we can never make our lives entirely safe and must take decisions based upon perceived statistical probabilities. Interest is heavily vested: it is excellent business for the manufacturer if we don a helmet when we ride our bicycle, and strap on knee-pads and elbow-pads and wrist-pads, when we go roller-blading.

Fatuous are the life-jackets and life-rafts that are stowed under our seats in aeroplanes. Before every flight, a hostess tells us in dulcet tones how we should fasten our jackets as the big ship plummets into the sea at several hundred mph. 'Lean forward and cradle your head in your hands' – that is most important; it can prevent you from suffering a stiff neck. The safety leaflet shows pictures of jolly little men and women with smiles on their matchstick faces, leaving the emergency exits on lovely slides as they slither happily to safety on the welcoming waves. My friends, in probability terms that is stuff and nonsense! If you wish to sail on the high seas, may I suggest that you choose a boat? If you go down in an airliner, you need not trouble with life-jackets and life-rafts and pretty little slides.

Our lives are of finite duration and an element of risk is ever present. I watch children roller-blading at horrific speeds and, whilst I quake with anxiety, I see in their eyes the look of exultation and I know that they are alive. We should not wrap our children in cotton wool by disallowing them to undertake any activity that contains an element of danger. Mankind thrives upon flirting with danger. Danger – or rather, the courage to overcome it – is the stuff of heroes and heroines. To eliminate all danger would emasculate our race.

Aeons ago, in my carnivorous days, I used to gorge upon the flesh of dead cattle. Presumably, since I am here to record the fact, those cows were relatively sane but, were I of the same disposition today, I should not hesitate to eat British beef. Forty people in a population of 60,000,000 contracted a disease that has not been shown to be caused by (but neither has it been proved <u>not</u> to be caused by) Bovine Spongiform Encephalopathy. A probability of less than one in a million is acceptable; I would feel safer eating the grilled fillet of a late cow of even middling intelligence than a traditional Irish, fried breakfast.

The foregoing critique of modern society of course identifies its author as being no spring chook. He recognizes the generality, however, that in compensation for inherent indulgence, today's children are more self-confident and discriminating than were their predecessors: they do not glibly accept what they are taught without question, but employ and express their critical faculties to a degree that would have earned them a hearty beating a few decades earlier. From the teacher's standpoint, they are more challenging, more alive to instruction. Generally they are sceptical, but not cynical.

Bullying

It is the unwise Headmaster who declares that there is no bullying in his school. Unfortunately, human nature is such that the herd is sometimes tempted to persecute either the weak or the one who is in some wise different. This tendency is not peculiar to children, but it is particularly distressing when it visits a defenceless girl or boy.

One reads of horrific treatment of younger by older boys in *Tom Brown's Schooldays*. Happily, such atrocities do not happen at Headfort or most modern schools. From the very outset, successive Headmasters and staff have been vigilant in watching out for bullying in all its derivatives, and curbing it when found. Despite this, most staff meetings during all three eras of the School's existence have included on the agenda concern about one or more children who appeared to be having a hard time and were perhaps being targeted by others.

Bullying these days is more likely to be of a verbal, rather than a physical, nature. Yet it can be deeply insidious and requires careful treatment. The author was on several occasions approached by a child or his parent and informed that the child was being teased or intimidated by another pupil. Often there would follow the plea, 'but please don't say anything to the offender, or it will only make things worse for the victim.' Of course, if one honours that request, one's hands are tied and the situation will not improve. The perpetrator must be confronted and persuaded, firstly by appealing to his good nature, and secondly, should that fail, by substantial sanctions, to discontinue his unkind behaviour. All of the staff must be alerted to the menace and generally the problem is resolved.

Naturally most antisocial actions, including bullying, will take place out of the sight and hearing of members of staff. In such situations a diligent set of Prefects and Dormitory Captains can be invaluable. They too are sometimes alerted by the Headmaster when bullying is alleged or suspected, as they may be in a better position than the staff to discover whether there is a case to answer. Occasionally a particular child irritates the others, either because of arrogance or some other aspect of his personal behaviour. In such cases, the child himself must be told that his own conduct is partially responsible for the other children's negative reaction towards him; he must be helped to change his ways. At the same time it may be necessary to explain to the multitude that, although the victim might irritate them, they are being unkind to persecute him.

Nowadays schools have definite written policies to alert all parties to the danger of bullying. Headfort is proactive in educating the pupils themselves about its perils.

Homesickness

It is a very fair claim that most Headfort children are happy most of the time. And so have they always been.

However there are of course episodes of unhappiness and homesickness. It can be quite a shock to the system for a small child to find herself or himself in a strange environment. All is unfamiliar. She encounters a peculiar specimen, called a Headmaster who, as P.G. Wodehouse might describe him, appears as a ghoulish fellow, about nine feet high, and with the sort of eye that could shuck an oyster from fifty paces. You know, the type of cove who dines off broken glass and metamorphoses into a werewolf when the moon is full. One past pupil from the 1950s recalls that his parents used to stop for a picnic on the way back to School at the start of each term. They would always pour a Baby Power's whiskey into their son's tea to give him Dutch courage to face the ordeal ahead.

Many new pupils take to boarding school instantly (without a shot of alcohol), and never display any sign of apprehension; however, others who may be spending their first night away from home, might require a little time to adjust. The situation is worse for their parents. Quite frequently a new child and his mother may part on the School steps, each of them in tears. The unfortunate mother will not be there to see, in twenty minutes time, that her daughter or son is having a whale of a time in the dormitory and being a damned nuisance.

Sometimes a child may take longer to settle and, just occasionally, he never does. It was the long-held belief of the author that those who arrived in the middle of the prep school cycle tended to take longer to adjust than the eight-year-olds. The latter, who were in the vast majority, had so much attention and affection lavished upon them that they were soon 'up and running'; whereas new pupils arriving as ten- or eleven-year-olds might find that the pecking order was to an extent already established and after a few days people tended to forget that they too were new.

It is probable that this opinion is less valid nowadays than before, because more children arrive at Headfort at an older age and also, with the advent of day pupils and weekly boarding, the majority of children see far more of their parents than did their predecessors.

Displaying creativity during break

New Board Members

Three new members joined the School Board at the beginning of 2012: present parents, JO-ANNA TOWNSHEND and ALLEN KRAUSE, and TOM COLLINS, a professor of education.

Headfort Green

Under Mary Kelly's leadership, Headfort participates in the National Green Schools programme that aims to promote responsible behaviour towards the environment. Headfort was awarded a Green School flag in March 2011 at a ceremony in Croke Park for its work on Litter and Waste management; their Action Plan detailed novel ways of dealing with waste.

Since September 2011 the children have been working on Energy, the second theme listed in the Green Schools programme. They participated in an Energy Workshop, conducted by Dr Sophie Nicole from the Sonairte Centre in Laytown, a sustainability and ecological-education centre.

Members of Headfort Green grow organic produce in an area behind the stable yard that was used for target shooting in years gone by.

The sheer fun of Headfort

Let us draw the story of Headfort's sixty-three year history towards its close with news of the School's second skiing adventure during the 2011 Christmas holidays. The party, led by Henry Clesham, comprised both novice and expert skiers; they went to Le Grand Bornand in the Savoie region of France. It is an ideal resort with a healthy snow record and is only an hour's drive from Geneva airport.

Skiing trip, 2012

The hosts at the hotel, 'Les Ecureuils' ('the squirrels' – a rich source of vitamin B12 apparently) coped easily with the invasion, feeding them well and steering them in the direction of the skating rink and toboggan slopes, après-ski. Other evenings were passed playing Michael Bolton's inexhaustible collection of games.

'Brilliant' was one of the children's summation of the holiday.

A past pupil's memories

A pupil who left Headfort in 2006 recalls a few memories from her time at the School:

> During my third year at Headfort we produced *The Empress of Blandings*. I was given the important role of the backside of a pig, the Empress herself. The play was one of my favourites: I and the girl who played the front of the pig had to learn to coordinate our movements. In one scene the pig receives an injection from the vet and I (as the back legs) had to kick out in discomfort, and squeal. The plays at Headfort were always great fun, directed by Mr Goulding and Mr Bolton, as everyone took part in them and the excitement backstage was immense.
>
> One night when I was about eleven my dorm decided to sneak out of the windows and climb into the moat that surrounds the school (luckily not filled with water). We crept along until we reached the windows of another dorm where we knew they were awake, telling each other scary stories. When we rapped on their windows, their screams were so loud that Matron came sprinting to see what the problem was. By the time she reached our dorm, we had hidden in our beds, muddy from the outdoor escapade.
>
> Riding was one of the main sports at Headfort. We were allowed to miss classes for a day's hunting. The riding teacher, Miss Maher, would take a group of girls out with the Meath Hunt a few times a year. These were some of the best times at school.
>
> In order to raise funds for the survivors of the Sri Lankan tsunami in 2004, we were sponsored to spend the whole day in our pyjamas. Some of the teachers got involved as well: Mr Dix arrived in his pyjamas and Mr Mac stripped off his suit and wore his pyjamas at morning assembly.
>
> The circle at the front of the building played an important part in our lives. Every morning we would walk around it for fifteen minutes to get some fresh air.
>
> Two events from my final year were the most anticipated of my Headfort career. One was when the Upper Sixth girls camped in Mr Dix's garden, and the other was the Leavers' Party. The camping was brilliant. We brought an enormous amount of food: marshmallows, chocolates and biscuits, and we stayed awake for hours, scaring each other with ghost stories.
>
> For the Leavers' Party on the final day we went 'bog jumping'. This involves jumping into pools of thick, black mud. It was incredible fun. Afterwards we cleaned ourselves in buckets of water, ate a barbeque and did some Irish dancing. When we finally returned to school, we had a midnight swim

in the freezing pool, and then stayed up watching films. It was my best night at Headfort, but it made it so much harder to leave the next day!

Parents' memories

A set of parents whose two sons and a daughter were at Headfort during the 1980s and '90s paid this handsome tribute to the School:

> … there was a sense of anticipation as we neared the School. We would come to see the children, or to watch them playing games or to see the marvellous plays that were put on over the years. There were the first days of term, with the eager bustle of new faces and new arrangements; then the last days of term when there was the anticipation of holidays to come. Finally, the last day of all, when there were tears, and a sense that life would never be the same again.
>
> But more important than what we thought of the School is what our children thought. Our daughter, even before she went, recalls that she thought Headfort was 'the coolest place on earth'. Her anticipation was heightened by her first major sporting achievement, being victorious in the brothers' and sisters' Sports Day race, largely due to her elder brother having thwarted the handicapper by moving her to within a couple of metres of the finishing line. All three children loved every moment of their time at Headfort: life evolved around sport and matches, building forts, skating, riding bikes, tuck, midnight feasts, weekend trips (races, ice-skating, museums), and there was some work thrown in!
>
> Now, as past pupils, they have wonderful memories of a School that gave them such a sound preparation for the rest of their lives; of a School that was in a way removed from the real world, but that taught them manners and a code of conduct that has stood them well in that real world. The friendships that they made at Headfort have endured to the present day.

Stop Press

As this book goes to press comes the welcome news that the Headmaster has appointed Michael Bolton Deputy Headmaster, and Neville Wilkinson Senior Master, both effective from the Autumn Term, 2012.

Tim Macey has been appointed Chairman of Headfort School.

A hammock in the Forts

Summertime at Headfort

There is a mystique about Headfort in summertime. The benign old mansion breathes its karma upon all who dwell in her: a sense of timelessness, of immutability that determines the future condition of all sentient beings.

Rhododendrons of myriad hue emborder the playing field. Alone in the centre stands the sacerdotal square, redolent in its variegated, twenty-two-yard strips; upon some of these, battle has already been waged; one, with stumps proud, awaits today's game; others' time will come. The patriarchal Big Tree that has hosted so many match teas in the past, sways gently as it oversees its protégés. The fading scorebox, chronicler of heroic deeds of yore, is initialized, as before every game. Horses glance superciliously over their fences, trying, like Americans, to interpret the ritual that is cricket.

On the field, little boys and girls disport themselves gaily. They gambol like gamesome lambs, each with his unique gait. The sun glints off the roller in the long grass; children's shirtsleeves flap in the light breeze and their hair is softly ruffled. Their faces intensify as they prepare to play.

There is a transience to this lyrical scene, as though the world's heart has missed a beat. Here is a canvas that old men take with them to their deathcouch; a world devoid of factories, diseases, mortgage payments, serial killers; a world in which nobody suffers, and all one's woes are anaesthetized in an extraordinary, escapist balm; a world of leather and willow, circumscribed by a boundary line. Shooting sticks and umpires' coats are intrinsic elements, as are jugs of Pimm's and deck chairs and esoteric commentary.

Too soon must one recede from this Utopia and submit again to the strictures of the 'real' world. But for the moment, let us enjoy heaven on earth at Headfort for as long as we may.

The future

There is constant evolution. Headfort flourishes as it enters the second decade of the twenty-first century. After nine years in office, Dermot Dix is preserving the principles upon which David Wild built the School, yet setting them in a modern context.

As one old fossil drifts into the twilight, it is his joy that the present Master Mason should be a chip off the old block, matured in the Headfort fault line, and assisted by elements of the purest granite that the fossil has garnered along the way. Upon such rock, the future of this precious monument lies assured.

David Wild in church, sporting his Headfort tie till the last

ACKNOWLEDGMENTS

P.G. Wodehouse dedicated a book to his daughter Leonora, 'without whose never-failing sympathy and encouragement this book would have been finished in half the time.'

In my case, without the never-failing sympathy and encouragement of so many people this book would not have been finished, nor begun, at all.

James Jackson, former Chairman of Headfort School, was the prime mover. He wanted six or seven pages of history to include in a folder of general information about Headfort. The number of pages has grown like a strawberry from Chernobyl.

Dermot Dix and Henry Clesham, past pupils both, were bombarded with many of the book's incarnations. They patiently read, criticized, advised. Henry supplied photographs.

Jack Sweetman, who taught at Headfort almost from the beginning, fed me material that none other could supply. When even his extraordinary memory failed him, Edith was generally able to fill the void.

The perennial John Leyden supplied esoteric snippets of information from the early 1970s onwards.

Victor de Raeymaeker lent encouragement from Belgium. And, of course, he granted me permission to use his incomparable sketches, many of which we still retain, despite his having left Headfort twenty years ago.

Neville Wilkinson, past pupil, present teacher, gathered archival material. He even rescued a barrow load of historic files from the back of a trailer that was destined for the dump – on the orders of Cathal McCosker. And he gave me valuable criticism.

I pestered Mike Bolton incessantly.

Grania and David Shillington supplied numerous insights from the many years that they were Headfort parents and they wrote the charming paragraphs, entitled 'Parents' memories', that appear towards the end of Chapter Seventeen.

Peter Lyons, without whom there might be no School, was the receptacle of many queries.

Dick Blakiston Houston supplied me with details of the restoration to the house and especially the renovation of the Ballroom.

Six of the nine months that I have taken to write this book were spent in South Australia. During that time, as well as before and after, many past pupils have fed me information and anecdotes from their time in the School. Should there be anything that is amusing in *Your Children are not your Children*, it is their contributions that have supplied it. They are:

Michael Barrow, Micky Chamberlayne, Grattan de Courcy-Wheeler, Horace de Courcy-Wheeler, Alan Cowley, Martin Cowley, India Dunn, Killian FitzGerald, Shane Gallwey, Peter Haworth, Jeremy P. Hill, Hardy Jones, David Kearney, Domini Kemp, Noel McMullan, Dan Minchin, Simon Mitchell, Frances Monaghan (née Stuart-Mills), William Morton, Hugh Newell, Richard Nugent, Mark Pery-Knox-Gore, Hugh Pheifer, Miles Podmore, Ferdinand von Prondzynski, Laurence Swan, Alan Sweetman, Rupert Tubbs, Tim Whitley, Guy Williams, Andrew Willis, Edward Wilson.

Of these, Frances Monaghan (née Stuart-Mills) and Hardy Jones are the only original pupils from the Summer Term of 1949. They each painted a picture of Headfort as it was in the very beginning. Hardy supplied me with the first clothes list.

Peter Haworth sent me photographs of some of the early, key figures in Headfort's history. Hugh Newell found scans of the crest that was awarded for colours at games, and also menus from the dining room.

The Headfort crest, awarded as 'colours' for games

My Australian friends, Catherine and Nathan Sim, who spent part of their honeymoon at Headfort, have allowed me to use the splendid photographs that they took during their visit. Other photographs that show the vibrant life of the School today were taken by Liz and David Pratt-Jarvis. Liz helped me to scan some of the photographs and images. Emma Finnegan assisted with the School database.

Mary Maher launched herself into the massive task of alerting past pupils, their parents and friends of the School to the arrival of the book. Jo-Anna Townshend and Michael Bolton also devoted themselves assiduously to this task.

Gerry Barron allowed me to print his photograph of the BRM Aero NG4 aeroplane.

Tony McLean allowed me to print his wonderful photograph of the wingèd horse Pegasus, with two riders aboard, in the Front Hall of Headfort at the launch of the Irish Pony Club's 2012 'Minimus' competition.

Richard Barber, author of *The Story of Ludgrove* (2004), granted permission to quote two anecdotes from his beautifully produced book about my old prep school.

Tim Goulding allowed me to borrow lines from his book *The Viper Lounge* (2011).

Miriam and Ham Goulding read an interim draft of the text and each offered constructive criticism.

Barbara Wild, the widow of David, spent a day with me in Adelaide and spoke fondly of her life with David, as well as supplying biographical details and photographs.

Charles Lysaght has written a Foreword that is far too generous – as, I suppose, I knew it would be.

Past pupil Antony Farrell of The Lilliput Press was quick to respond when I approached him about publishing the book. His son Seán, to whom I had taught English some sixteen years ago, has turned the tables on his old Headmaster by serving as editor. They both gave me oodles of sound advice. Another Headfort alumna, Sarah David-Goff, is Lilliput's Publicity Officer. She too has worked hard to promote the book.

To each one of these people I extend my warmest gratitude.

Appendix A

HEADFORT LOCATIONS

THE CIRCLE

As one emerges through the front door of the house, one crosses the drive onto 'the circle', a grass patch of that shape which, from time immemorial, has been used for the children's 'morning walk' after breakfast. In summertime children hasten outside and parade around the circle, deep in conversation with their friends, rather as racehorses patrol the paddock before leaving for the starting line. Come winter, however, and the member of staff on duty must assume the skills of a prestidigitator to scour the house and ferret out children from every conceivable hiding hole. In cold weather the circle becomes a less attractive arena.

A group of riders walk past the circle

THE LUCY MARTIN GATE

The Lucy Martin Gate is the gateway to the Lawn and the modern tennis courts. The actual wrought-iron gate is in a state of sad disrepair nowadays, yet it lends its name to a well-known Headfort location that includes The Seven Sisters, a remarkable configuration of Western Red Cedar.

The Seven Sisters, near the Lucy Martin gate

The present Headmaster performed an obvious, beneficial operation early in his reign – one that previous Headmasters had not had the wit to visualize – namely to construct a roadway near the Lucy Martin Gate, enabling service vehicles to drive behind the stable yard to the south side of the house. This development has opened a range of opportunities. (He bequeaths the credit for this idea and its execution to Dick Blakiston Houston).

THE LONG WOOD WALK

The Long Wood Walk holds less significance nowadays than formerly, because only a small part of it lies within the School's property. It used to be the duty master's, or mistress's, soft option during break in the two winter terms, or

during wet weather, to despatch the children to complete a circuit of the Long Wood Walk. The walk would become a veritable quagmire, and gumboots were essential attire.

'Is it gumboots and Long Wood Walk, Sir?' would enquire a small boy, as a host of children gathered around the trolley in the downstairs corridor for their mid-morning snack.

'Is *what* gumboots and Long Wood Walk, Ponsonby?' would reply the master on duty. Or, perhaps, more pedantically,

'Parse that sentence, boy.'

Urn in the American Garden

THE LAWN

The Lawn is an optional playground for the children on the south side of the house, an alternative to 'the pitch'. It tends to be used by those who do not wish to kick footballs or hit cricket or hockey balls, but prefer to indulge in less physical pursuits, although it is the site of the School's two tennis courts.

Formerly, all children were required to watch School cricket matches. Boys were encouraged to maintain a scorebook, and a runner would deliver the names of opposing batsmen and bowlers from the scorebox to the spectators who were spread out on tartan travelling rugs – an item on the School clothes list. A prize was offered for the tidiest and most accurate recording. Some would observe the play with interest: others would prefer to read a book. At a certain time, generally to coincide with the afternoon snack, the master on duty would present the option of retiring to the Lawn, a release that non-cricketers would gratefully accept.

The glorious rhododendron bushes that adorn the steep bank above the lawn form a popular backdrop for outdoor classes in the Summer Term.

THE STABLE YARD

The stable yard is one of the most popular locations at Headfort, especially for the riders who spend every permitted moment, and several that are not, tending their ponies there. The stable yard is also home to the roller-skating rink, the squash court and the new theatre.

THE TOPIARY

Headfort's yew Topiary is an elegant, formal region that in previous regimes was regarded as too precious to permit the presence of children. Today the Headmaster encourages children to play among the keenly tended conifer bushes during 'Junior Playtime'.

The topiary, taken from the roof

THE FLOWER ROOM

The Flower Room is an unattractive, airless cavity underneath the stairs on the bottom landing. It was originally used by the Housekeeper for storing flowers that had been cut from the garden, prior to their arrangement into elaborate displays in the Ballroom, the Front Hall and elsewhere. However it also bore an array of 'pigeon holes' wherein the children's black Sunday shoes were stored. In the Early Years, a manservant, initially Bill Kirwan and latterly Johnny Grimes, would polish these couple of hundred shoes by hand every Saturday and then shine them with a buff mounted on a Black and Decker drill. Thus Headfort children would march to church on Sundays in radiant footwear.

The Headmaster of the Middle Years deemed that this pampering of the children was excessively Fauntleroy-ish, and so he required all those in the five senior forms to polish their own shoes, each form performing the task on a given morning every week after breakfast. The shoes of the pupils in the two junior forms continued to be cleaned for them, because it was thought that the distribution of black shoe polish would extend too liberally beyond the actual shoes, should eight-year-olds be let loose with the waxy, colloidal emulsion.

The practice has discontinued in Headfort Today for two reasons: firstly, only a minority of children attend the churches in Kells because most of them go home at weekends; and secondly styles in footwear have evolved over the years and very few modern children own a pair of formal black shoes – parents find it a costly luxury to buy such garments for a solitary outing on Sundays.

Today the Flower Room is used as the 'tuck' cupboard.

Appendix B

DRAMATIC PRODUCTIONS OF THE LAST THIRTY YEARS

1981–2	*Under Milk Wood* – Dylan Thomas
1986	*The Old Boys* – William Trevor
1988	*Amadeus* – Peter Schaffer
1999	*Juli(a) Caesar* – William Shakespeare
1990	*Forty Years On* – Alan Bennett
1991	*The Sound of Music* – Rodgers & Hammerstein
1992	*The Empress of Blandings* – P.G. Wodehouse
1993	*To Kill a Mockingbird* – Harper Lee
1994	*The Plough and the Stars* – Sean O'Casey
1995	*The Scarlet Pimpernell* – Baroness Orczy
1996	*Just William* – Richmal Crompton
1997	*Saint Joan* – George Bernard Shaw
1998	*Toad of Toad Hall* – Kenneth Grahame/A.A. Milne
1999	*Macbeth* – William Shakespeare
2000	*Leave it to Psmith* – P.G. Wodehouse
2001	*The Jungle Play* – Rudyard Kipling
2003	*Alice in Wonderland* – Charles Lutwidge Dodgson (Lewis Carroll)
2004	*David Copperfield* – Charles Dickens
2005	*The Empress of Blandings* – P.G. Wodehouse
2006	*Not Quite William* – Richmal Crompton
2007	*Bugsy Malone* – Alan Parker
2008	*A Grim Night for Hans Christian Anderson* – H.C. Anderson/J & W Grimm
2009	*The Queen and I* – Sue Townsend
2010	*The Canterbury Tales* – Geoffrey Chaucer
2011	A series of form plays in which every child in the top five forms featured
2012	One-act form plays by the top three forms

Appendix C

LIST OF HEADFORT PUPILS

There follows a list of all Headfort pupils with their date of arrival in the School (where known) from 1949 until 2011. 'M', instead of a date, indicates a Montessori pupil. Please inform the School office of any omissions or errors.

Ignacio Abando 1999, Nicholas Abando 2000, Jose Abando 2000, Luke Abudarham 1993, Zachary Adebayo-Oke 2008, Omotomiwa Adeyefa 2008, Robyn Aitken 2008, Maria Jose Alarcon Baena 2004, Mercedes Alba Castillejo 2009, Mercedes Alba Castillejo 2009, Sarah Aldelemi 2008, Juan Pedro Alvarez 1993, Alvaro Alvarez 1995, Marcos Alvarez 2006, Robin Amoore 1953, Michael Amoore 1955, Clara Andrada 2003, Isobel Andrews-McCarroll 2009, Charles Appleby 1953, MW Aprahamian 1962, John Aprahamian 1964, P St L Aprahamian 1966, Cristina Arboli de Parias 2008, Jaime Arbona 1998, Patricia Aristegui 2006, Harry Arkwright 2010, Mark Armstrong 1987, Jim Armstrong 1962, Sam Armstrong 1965, George Armstrong 1968, Ben Armstrong 1999, Jack Armstrong 2001, Camilla Armstrong-King 1986, Julian Armytage 1956, Alexander Arnott 1987, Andrew Arnott 1985, Nicolas Arreciado Ballester 2009, BR Ashe 1959, HC Augustin 1951, Conor Austin (M), RHH Baird 1959, Ignacio Bajo Ysasi 2009, Piers Baker, Leticia Baldrich O'Farrell 1992, Rodolfo Baldrich O'Farrell 1994, Olympia Baldrich O'Farrell, CR Ball 1960, Alexis Baltardive 2011, John Bamford 1979, Marta Banus Pallares 1991, Alvaro Banus Pallares 2005, Baratin, Ana Barbadillo 2004, Rafa Barbadillo 2009, Garth Barlow-Graham 1953, Rodney Barlow-Graham 1953, Fernando Barquin Martel 2011, Nicholas Barrington 1950, Jonah Barrington 1950, RLD Barrow 1956, Peter Barrow 1961, EGC Barrow 1959, MS Barrow 1956, Juliet Barrow 1980, Lukey Barrow 1981, Rhona Barry 1979, Mark Barry 1980, NCG Bathurst 1964, RG Bathurst 1965, LJ Baugh 1964, CB Baugh 1966, Penelope Baugh (M), Daniel Baugh 2011, Serge Bauvet 2001, Henry Beadle 2007, VN Beamish 1962, Brian Beare 1952, DF Beare 1955, Andrea Beca 2003, Christopher Bective 1967, Christopher Begg 1985, Anthony Bellew 1980, Antonio Benjumea 1998, John Bennet 2006, Charlotte Bennet 2006, Cyprien Benoit 1988, Basile Benoit 1987, Luke Benson 2007, Angelique Beresford Ash, Pedro Bermudez 2007, Charlie Berridge 1994, Alejandra Bertran 2007, Jose Bertran Salazar 2005, RH Best 1961, MC Bevan 1956, Kim Bielenberg 1970, Andrew Bielenberg 1967, JS Birmingham 1958, Callum Blackburn 2008, Benjamin Blackburn 2008, CPB Blackwell-Smith 1950, Jack Blakiston Houston 1997, Kit Blakiston Houston

1999, Leticia Blakiston Houston 2001, Poppy Blakiston Houston 2002, Harry Blakiston Houston 2004, RP Blakiston Houston 1956, Michael Blakiston Houston 2006, Jasmine Blenkins-O'Callaghan 2006, Ines Boada 2003, Manuela Boada 2011, Sofia Boada Castellanos 2005, Macarena Bohigas Munoz-Rojas 2011, OJH Bonham 1962, Francis Bonham 1964, Johnny Bonham 1969, Oliver Bonham 1962, Ignacio Borrero 1998, Esperanza Borrero 1999, Luis Borrero 2005, Charles Bostock, Laetitia Bouron 2011, Christopher Bowly 1949, Cliona Boyce 1988, Rupert Boyd 1969, ARC Boyd 1966, Timothy Boylan, Dennis Boyse 1949, Anthony Brabazon 1986, Arthur Brabazon 2006, Daniel Braddell 1984, Emily Braddell 1986, Edward Braddell 1990, Kye Bradshaw 2007, FM Brady 1958, David Brady 1960, Dara Brady 2001, Emma Brady 2001, MR Brassey 1961, Christopher Brazier-Creagh 1954, JW Brittain 1969, Harry Brooke 2002, Matthew Brooke 2004, Archie Brooke 2001, Laurie Brown Ellis 1997, Holly Browne 2009, Jamie Brownlow 1970, Aidina Brownlow 2005, Elinor Brownlow 2006, William Brownlow 2005, Quentin Bruley des Varannes 2006, Jonathan Brunton 1996, John Bryce-Smith 1953, Adrian Bryce-Smith 1983, JS Buckley 1961, Charles S Buckley 1993, Georgina Buckley 2001, James Bullman 1999, PFB Burkitt 1963, TD Burkitt 1964, EMP Butler 1955, GAM Butler 1965, Tara Butler 1988, David Butler (M), Stuart Byrne 2004, Kim Byrne 2006, Louise Cabot 2006, Hannah Cadden 2002, Daniel Caffrey 1984, Aaron Caffrey 1983, Jamie Caffrey 1988, Sarah Caffrey 1987, Julian Cafolla 1996, Alex Cafolla 2001, Christopher Cahill 1997, Patrick Cairns 1965, JDR Cairns, Neville Callaghan, Jessica Callan, Robert Callow 1993, Euan Callow 1997, Lewina Callow 2002, Henrietta Cameron 1979, Jamie Cameron, William Campbell 2001, David Campo Ruiz 2006, Carmen Campos Illanes 2005, Javier Campos Lopez 2005 Sean Canning 1973, Liam Canning 1973, Eamonn Canning 1975, Diarmuid Canning 1977, DSP Cant 1950, JPN Cant 1953, Marcella Carew 1977, Keri Ann Carolan (M), Declan Carr-Robinson 2011, Dorian Carrell 1983, PA Carril, Emilio Carro 1985, Mamen Carro 1985, C M St J Carter 1968, Shauna Carter-Paice 2007, HAS Cartwright 1953, PDC Caruth 1954, Richard Casey 1978, Brian Cash 1993, Neil Cash 1995, Deidre Cash, Andrea Castillo 2008, Jack Cavanagh 2007, Lauro Cervantes Tepos 2008, Manuel Cervera 1994, Elena Cervera 1997, Michael Chamberlayne 1950, Theo Chamberlayne-Daye 1999, Jake Chamberlayne-Daye 2006, William Chambré 1978, Tom Chambré 1985, Kate Chambré 1987, Jolie Chang (M), Marta Charlo Pumar 2009, Tomas Charlo Pumar 2009, Teresa Charlo Pumar 2010, Rory Chavasse 2011, Simon Chawner 1978, Marcus Chawner 1979, Adrian Clarke 1980, Jason Clarke 2008, Darren Clarke 1982, Campbell Classon 2008, M Cleeve 1955, Charles Clements 1968, Nat Clements 1971, Hal Clements 1974, Tim Clesham 1960, Henry Clesham 1961, Brian Clesham 1964, Chris Clesham 1969, Miles Clower 1984, HFG Cobden 1957, NDG Coburn 1967, Simon Cocksedge 1959, Kate Coffey (M), Olivia Coffey (M), Sophie Coffey (M), Emer Cogan (M), Susan Coghlan 1986, Sasha Cole 2010, Carina Coleman 1982, Paloma Colon Hidalgo 2004, Isabel Colthurst 2001, John Colthurst 1999, Olivia Colthurst 2003, Charlotte Colthurst 2000, Stuart Conlon 2001, Alannah Connell (M), Karen Connolly 1985, Tina Connolly 1994, William Conolly-Carew 1983, Jose Conradi 2003, Blanca Conradi 2005, Roisin Conroy 2004, Laragh Conroy 2005, Amber Conroy 2007, Lily Conyngham 2005,

AE Cooke 1954, JFC Cooke 1960, Patrick Cooper 1968, Jonathan Cooper 1969, Emily Cooper 1991, Paddy Cooper 1994, Rowland Cooper 1997, Charlotte Cooper 2006, Sean Cooper 2010, AK Cooper 1966, Victoria Cooper 1998, David Cooper 1999, John Cooper 1999, Patrick Copeland Guinness 1988, Julian Coquet-Benka 2006, Eimear Corcoran (M), Ciara Corcoran (M), FDW Cornwall 1956, Alexander Cosby 1984, Phillip Cosby 1987, Kate Cosgrave 2001, Cameron Cosgrove 1998, Romain Cosson 2008, Macarena Costales 2004, James Couldridge 2004, Kate Couldridge 2004, DP Counihan 1971, Edward Coveney 1987, Martin Cowley 1973, Alan Cowley 1973, HA Cowper 1955, Maurice Cox 1977, Oliver Cox 1990, Rebecca Cox 1980, W Craig 1962, IHM Craig 1962, Richard Craik-White 1960, Allen Crampton 1999, James Crampton 1999, Mauritz Crasemann 2007, Benedict Crasemann 2008, Maxime Crasemann 2011, Owen Crinigan 1999, Arlynejane Crinion 1995, Gian Croft Pearson 1949, SJS Cromie 1950, Charles Croome Carroll 2006, Vernon Crowley, Mark Cubitt 1972, David Cubitt 1974, Hugo Cubitt 1975, Amy Cusack (M), Ryan Cusack (M), David Cushnahan 1994, Sean Cussen 1972, Jonathon Daley 2006, Christopher Daley 1993, Eamonn Daly 2004, Mairead Daly 2002, Laura Daly 1975, Tara Daly 1976, Michael Daniels 1971, Bertram D'Arcy 1990, Thaddeus D'Arcy 1991, James Darlington-Cramond 2005, Theodore Dautresme 2005, PE David 1953, Andrew Davidson 1952, CJL Davidson 1955, AML Davidson 1962, James Davis-Goff 1997, William Davis-Goff 1988, Sarah Davis-Goff 1990, Henry Davis-Goff 1994, RW Davis-Goff 1963, David Dawnay 1981, Sebastian Dawnay 1983, George Dawson 1954, Jason Dawson 1974, Lucy Day 1996, Alexander Day 1996, Clemence de Bary 1999, Pia de Bournazel 2010, Pierre de Bournazel 2011, Savinien de Bryas 2006, Marie de Bryas 2008, Octave de Bryas 2009, Salome de Bryas 2011, WHD de Burgh 1966, HDJ de Burgh 1962, JD de C Minchin, Augustin de Cambourg 2004, Horace de Courcy-Wheeler 1968, JRD de Courcy-Wheeler 1957, Grattan de Courcy-Wheeler 1960, SGI de Courcy-Wheeler 1963, GHA de Courcy-Wheeler 1965, Leopold de Croy 1996, Constance de Diesbach 1987, Alexis de Germay 2010, Alicia De Ibarrondo 2002, Maria Rosa De La Chica 1982, Mariano De La Chica 1982, Rodrigo De La Chica 1982, Alejandra de la Oliva Parias 2008, Patricia de la Oliva Parias 2011, Paz de la Oliva Parias 2011, Diego De La Pena 2004, Anthony de la Poer 1949, Nigel de la Poer 1953, Rupert de las Casas 1968, John de Montfort 1971, Roger de Montfort 1972, Simon de Montfort 1963, Piers de Montfort 1966, PCL de Montfort 1967, Frederick de Montfort 2009, Patricia de Parias, Karel de Raeymaeker, Gaspard de Roquefeuil 1998, Leonore de Roquefeuil 2001, Elvire de Roquefeuil 2008, Teresa de Simon Lomo, Renaud de Tilly, Griselda de vere Walker 1988, JD Dean 1960, RC Dean 1961, Mark Deane 1965, Peter Deane 2004, Harry Deane (M), Pia Deane (M), Enrique Delgado Ruiz-Gallardon 2010, Santiago Delgado Ruiz-Gallardon 2010, Richard Dennis 2007, Guillaume Desmarez 2011, David Devine 1988, Miguel Diaz-Maurino Carrera 2008, Arturo Diez Gutierrez 2002, Alex Dillane (M), HF Dillon-Malone 1970, Dermot Dix 1971, RI Dixon 1949, Corinna Dixon 1986, Alex Dobrovolsky 2002, Sophia Dobrzynski 1975, Patricio Domecq 2003, Pedro Domecq 2004, Pilar Domingo 1985, Rory Donleavy 1988, Rebecca Donleavy 1987, Leah Donlon (M), Cian Donlon (M), DAC Doran 1961, Dermot Dorgan 1996, PE Dorman 1954, Lucy

Douthwaite 1983, MG Dover, Margaret Downey, Mark Doyle 2007, Aoibheann Doyle (M), Jim Dreaper 1958, Bridget Drew 1996, NSW Duff 1971, James Duff 1999, John Duff 1999, Robert Duff 1999, Lord Dunalley 1956, India Dunn 2003, Charlotte Dunn 2007, Patrick Dunn 2009, Gigi Dunn 2010, Annie Dunne 1997, Ben Dunne 1997, Alexander Durdin-Robertson 1988, Mathew Durdin-Robertson 1994, Harry Durdin-Robertson 1995, JCF Dutton 1966, Anna Edmondson 1983, David Edmondson 1986, Mark Egan 1993, Laura Jane Egan (M), Robin Egerton 1970, W Elliot 1955, Natasha Elliott 1976, PR Enraght-Moony 1961, Karen Erskine Crum 1985, Gabriel Escudero Munoz 2010, Juan Carlos Esquinca 2002, Javier Esquinca 2002, JE Eustace 1955, Caroline Eustace 1975, RAC Evans 1958, WH Evans 1960, C Evans-Tipping 1957, PM Everard 1952, Ciara Fagan (M), Adam Fairclough, James Fanshawe 1970, Herve Didier Farre Zaragoza 1998, Bridget Farrell 1990, Seán Farrell 1993, John Farrell 1954, Antony Farrell 1959, Claire Farrell 2011, James Farrell (M), Stephen Fäsenfeld 1977, Andrea Fäsenfeld 1981, Franz Fäsenfeld 1982, Reza Fazel 1976, Morgan Fehily 1981, OC Fenton 1953, Tim Ferguson 1970, Elena Fernandez Garcia-Saavedra 2010, Sofia Fernandez Garcia-Saavedra 2011, Luis Fernandez-Vega 1997, Anthony Ferrier, Maria Feu 2002, Stephen ffrench Davis 1975, Katy ffrench Davis 2007, Dermot ffrench Davis 1972, Dominic ffrench Davis 1973, Michael ffrench Davis 1977, Clara ffrench Davis 2006, Townley Filgate 1997, John Filgate 1983, Caroline Filgate 1987, Eva Filgate 1988, Alex Filgate 2001, Alexander Filhol 2003, DH Filmer-Sankey 1958, CJT Filmer-Sankey 1966, Joanna Finnegan 1995, Saran Finnegan (M), Charlie Finucane 2005, Millie Finucane (M), Killian FitzGerald 1978, Maria FitzGerald, Jamie Fitzhenry 2002, George FitzHerbert 1982, Harry FitzHerbert 1982, Trevor FitzHerbert 1970, Malcolm FitzHerbert 1975, David FitzHerbert 1978, William FitzHerbert 1998, Allegra FitzHerbert 2000, Octavian FitzHerbert 2002, Luke FitzHerbert 2003, GHT Fitzjohn 1966, Ryan Fitzpatrick 2002, Zara Fitzpatrick 2007, Brian Fitzsimons 1998, Pamela Fitzsimons 2006, John Robert Fletcher 1966, Richard Fletcher 1970, Florence Flipo 2009, Richard Flood 1990, Sophia Flood 1997, Brian Foley 1985, Danny Foley (M), Gregory Forshaw 1980, Michael Forshaw 1981, Georgina Forshaw 1983, Howard Fox 1978, Dillon Fox (M), John Frankland 1958, William Frazer 1993, JS Freeman 1967, FCAJ French 1965, MAM French 1969, Justin Furnell 1971, Michael RV Gabbett 1956, Peter Gallagher 1996, Rossa Gallagher 1996, Matthew Gallagher 1985, Patrick Gallagher 1985, GR Gallie 1965, EC Gallie, JBP Galloway 1957, WPP Galloway 1959, Shane Gallwey 1985, Felipe Galvez Roca 2011, Edward Galvin 1985, Vanessa Galvin 1989, James Galvin 1990, Margaret Galvin 1991, Olivia Galvin 1987, Ava Galvin (M), Paolo Garavelli 1977, Davide Garavelli, Laura Garcia Redondo 1986, Leonore Garnier 2006, Alejandro Garrido 2006, JL Gates 1955, Grace Gavigan (M), Ellen Gavigan (M), Tom Gavigan (M), MA Gethin 1961, Malise Gibney 1971, Natasha Gibney, DW Gibson-Brabazon 1954, Thomas Gilbert 1977, Rory Gilbert 1978, Raymond Gilmore 1981, Seanin Gilmore 1981, Grainne Gilmore 1983, NPC Giltsoff, RNJD Giltsoff, Ivan Golitsyn 2007, Nicolas Gonzales del Campos 2006, Sofia Gonzalez 2006, Ana Gonzalo de la Puerta 2011, Michael Good 1982, Eleanor Good 1984, RSM Goodbody 1955, RN Goodbody 1960, TB Goodbody, Colin Goodwin 1981, Simon Goodwin (M), William Gossip 1991, John Patrick Gough 2007, Andrew

Gould 1993, MJ Graham 1964, Adam Grant 2005, Fergus Grant 1994, Edward Grant 1983, Julian Grant 1984, Alexander Grant 1994, AF Graves 1968, MF Graves-Johnston 1956, Davina Gray 1991, Roger Greene 1959, James Greene 1986, Danny Greening 2000, Daisy Grehan 1999, Stevie Grehan 2001, Christopher Grew 1978, Jonathan Grew 1967, Bruno Griffin (M), JD Griffith 1965, PD Griffith 1967, Juliet Grogan 1980, Alexander Grubb 1994, Georgina Grubb 1988, R de C Grubb 1956, N de C Grubb 1958, Natasha Grubb 1994, Hippolyte Guigon 2009, Tom Guinness 2002, Malachy Guinness 1995, Patrick Guinness 1964, Patrick Guinness, Jasmine Guinness 1987, Celeste Guinness 2002, Lorcan Guinness 1998, George Guinness 2009, Thomas Guinness Taylor 1997, Caspian Guirey 1980, RPD Gun-Cuningham 1968, Julian Gun-Cuningham 1969, JA Gun-Cuningham, Max Gurney 2009, Hugo Gurney 2009, Regina Guttierez 2006, ADBP Hackett 1949, Tadgh Hagan (M), Cillian Hagan (M), Rachael Hague (M), Hadrien Hahn 1991, Berenice Hahn 1996, PG Hall 1954, R Hall 1954, RMA Hall 1962, Anna Hamilton 1991, Nicholas Hamilton 1989, Alex Hamilton 1996, James Hamilton 1993, Edward Hamilton 1995, Ion Hamilton 1964, Evelyn Hamilton 1969, EWJ Hamilton, Eliza Hancock 2008, Lucy Hancock 2010, Emily Hannon-Rubotham 2004, Jessica Harcourt-Tillis (M), Georgina Harris 1984, Julian Harris 1986, DCW Harris 1951, JA Harris 1953, MT Harris 1962, Brian Harvey 1961, Meghan Hatherell 2006, Peter Haworth 1953, Marcus Hayden 2009, Elizabeth Hayden 2006, James Hayden 2007, Anna Hayden 2010, Joss Hazell 1977, Ralph Hazell 1979, Jack Hazell 1987, Olivia Hazell 1985, Amira Healy (M), Clare Heary 1997, Alizee Heems 2003, Axelle Heems 2006, Clemence Heems 2008, Sebastian Hennessy 1984, Paloma Hepburn Jimenez 2006, Marco Herbst 1986, JE Herdman 1959, Nigel Herdman, AC Herdman RN 1954, TM Heron 1963, NJ Herriott 1952, Holly Hesnan 2009, Kate Hesnan 2010, Aurora Higgins 2011, Kirsten Higgins 2009, Soren Higgins 2009, Mary Hoare 1988, Henry Hoare 1990, Phoebe Hoare 1996, Phoenix Hoare 1996, CW Holden 1950, DG Holden 1950, John Horsman, AMF Horsman 1966, GAA Horsman 1968, PH Horsman 1969, RA Horsman 1971, JM Hosken 1956, TEF Hosken 1957, Orlando Hughes 1983, Rachael Hull 1989, Lucy Humphries 2009, Giles Hurley 1986, Otto Hurley 2006, Louise Hurst 1985, Jonathan Hurst 1986, Maria del Camino Hurtado Dominguez 1994, Geoffrey Huskinson 1986, Charles Hyland 1985, Joanna Hyland 1982, Alexander Iles-Nyberg 2008, Alexander Irwin 1973, Rhianna Ives 2005, Olivia Jackson 2002, TMR Jackson 1954, Anthony Jackson 1979, Shane Jackson 1980, Aude Jambu-Merlin 1993, Flore Jambu-Merlin 1996, Tristan Jambu-Merlin 1998, Tanguy Jambu-Merlin 2007, Jeremy James 1974, Caroline James 1977, Dominic Jameson 1969, DJM Jameson, Hans-Reiner Jauch 2008, Diego Jaureguizar 1994, Alvaro Jaureguizar 1998, Konrad Jay 1967, Alexander Jay 2000, Nicholas Jay 2000, Dominic Jenkins 1974, Hilary Jenkins (M), Imogen Jenkins (M), Luke Jennings 2007, Rachael Jeon 2007, AE Jessel 1949, RN Jobson 1956, Shane Jocelyn 1999, Stevie Johnson 1994, CS Johnson 1967, January Johnson 1988, Olivia Johnson 1992, Jonathan Johnston 1978, Richard Johnston 1978, Christopher Johnston 1978, Clodagh Johnston (M), Heather Johnston (M), Alastair Jones 1952, Alan Jones 1949, Hardy Jones 1949, Leslie Jones 1952, Alastair Jones, Nicholas Judd 1972, M Judd, Anthony Kamm 1949, Sophia Kauntze 1982, Nina Kauntze

1988, Annie Kavanagh 2006, Megan Kavanagh (M), Bailey Kavanagh (M), Timothy Keane 1976, DJD Kearney 1960, Leah Kehoe 2006, David Keize, Opeline Kellett 2005, David Kelly 1975, Andrew Kelly 1979, Jonathan Kelly 1979, Sonja Kelly 1981, Johanna Kelly 1988, MA Kelly 1953, Marcus Kelly 1979, Michelle Kelly 1989, Suzanne Kelly 1989, EJ Kelly, Domini Kemp 1983, SJM Kempster 1954, Daisy Kende, Brian Kennedy 1993, BJ Kennedy 1950, RE Kennedy 1950, John Kennedy, RA Kenny 1952, MS Kenny 1953, Alex Kenny (M), Arian Keogan-Nooshabadi 1997, Aoise Keogan-Nooshabadi 2003, James Kerr 1973, JF Keys 1957, Robert Keys 1979, Tanaka Khoza 2004, Philip Kidd 2000, Robin Kilroy 1968, James Kilroy 1981, Sebastian Kindersley 1975, N Kindersley, Gerald Kindersley, Selena Kindersley 1979, Ciaran King 1976, Eoghan King 1976, Daniel King 1988, Benjamin Kitchin 1999, Sean Koberl 1992, Klaus Krause 2008, Genevieve Kyle 1983, James Kyle 1986, GV Laird 1967, JAS Laird 1953, RS Laird 1966, Roger Laird 1971, Theodore Lambton 1998, Niall Lamont 2004, Piers Landseer 1974, Alex Langan 2009, Phoebe Langham 2008, John Langham 1969, Rupert Langham 1971, Isabella Langham 2010, PJ Lanigan-O'Keeffe 1963, RS Lanigan-O'Keeffe 1965, AM Lanigan-O'Keeffe 1961, T Lanigan-O'Keeffe 1964, Philip Lauterbach 1978, Finbar Lavarack 2002, Iseult Law 2004, Alicia Law 2001, Emma Law 1997, Poppy Law 1998, Hamish Law 2003, Sarah Lawlor, PA Lawrence 1956, Maxime le Gouvello 1999, Louis le Gouvello 1999, Geoffrey Leahy 2000, Lauren Leahy 2002, India Leahy 2003, Edward Lefroy 1975, Langlois Lefroy 1973, Nicolas Leger 2001, Cyprien Leger 2002, Philippine Leger 2002, Patrice Leger 2002, Mathias Leger 2010, Coco Leitch 2002, Sebastian Leitch 2002, Michael Leonard 1984, Nicholas Leonard 1991, Matthew Leonard 1995, James Leonard 1996, Maurice Leonard 1970, Noel Leonard 1970, Hannah Leonard (M), Conor Leonard (M), Astrid Leroux 1999, John Leslie 1977, James Leslie, Jean Levy 2007, JC Lewis-Crosby 1957, Huei Lim 1997, Ern Lim 1998, Ping Lim 2000, Christopher Lind 1972, David K Lind 1973, Beetle Lindsay-Fynn 1993, MAK Linton 1966, Cristina Llanos 1999, Alfonso Llorens 2002, Lester Lloyd 1995, Ciaran Long 2008, Jasper Long 2010, Alvaro Lopez 1999, Rosario Lopez 1999, Rocio Lopez 2002, Eva Lopez Lumbreras 2010, Jorge Loring 1993, Javier Loring 1994, Cristina Losada 2000, MD Lougher-Goodey 1951, Nicholas Lowry 1969, Peter Lowry 1972, Inigo Lozano Parias 2006, Philip Lush 1968, P. Lush, Gerard Lynch 1982, Jack Lynch (M), Grattan Lynch, Kerri Lyons 2005, Patrick Lyons 1986, Dagmar Lyons 1981, Francis Lyons 1980, Peter Lyons 1984, Alastair Macauley 2000, Hamish Macauley 2001, Craig Macdonald 2000, Colin Macdougald 1966, Tim Macdougald 1973, PN MacEwen, Lisa Macey 1990, Alanna Macey 1990, Conor MacGillycuddy 1967, Stevie Macken 1984, Jamie Macken 1989, Duke of Macklenburg 1965, A MacLacklan 1949, Antony Macnaghten 1980, Philip Macnaghten, PAC Madden 1954, MHD Madden 1954, Freddie Madden 1988, Igor Maestre 1998, Ana Clara Maestre 1998, Pelayo Maestre 2000, Tom Magnier 1989, John Paul Magnier 1995, Michael Magnier 1996, Simon Magnier 1977, Julie Magnier 1979, Mikaela Magnier 1998, Lucy Maher (M), Jamie Maher (M), Myles Mahon 1988, Blaithnaid Mahon (M), Dominick Mahony 1970, Edmond Mahony 1980, Honor Mahony 1984, Luke Mahony 1988, Edmund Mahony 1969, Marcos Mahony 2006, William Maire 2003, Molly Maire 2005, Joshua Maloney 2008, Oliver Maloney 2009, Francesca Mangan

(M), PJ Mansfield 1969, Millie Mantle 1998, Lucy Mantle 2001, Valeria Manukovskya 2008, Laureline Marras 2008, David Martin 1989, Oliver Martin 1983, Clive Martin 1983, Andrew Martin 2002, John Martin 1975, Theophile Martin 2007, Ignacio Martinez-Mejias 2008, Julia Martinez-Mejias 2008, Georgina Martyn (M), Ines Mata O'Donoghue 2010, Lewis Mathews 1999, Jasper Mathews 2000, Duncan Mathews 2003, Josh Mathews 2003, Conall Mathur-Dix 2004, Alexander Mattei 1968, Roberto Mattei 1971, Ailbhe Matthews 2009, Ben Matthews (M), PT Maxwell 1966, Darius Mazahery 1999, Simon McAleese 1975, Thady McAleese 1975, Robert McAleese (M), Lucy McAleese (M), Oscar McAuley 2007, Grainne McAuley, James McCafferty 1971, JD McCafferty, James McCaldin 1982, Peter McCaldin 1955, Alicia McCaldin 1985, Max McCaldin (M), Harry McCalmont 1964, Tom McCarren 2011, Eoin McCarthy 2003, EM McCarthy, Oliver McCausland 2006, MFS McCausland 1960, AFS McCausland 1963, Arlen McCausland 2008, Sean McClory 1987, Ben McCloy 2006, CJA McCluggage 1967, Philip McCutcheon 2000, Conn McDermot (M), Roan McDermot (M), Hugo McDermott 2007, Oliver McDermott 2009, John McDonnell 1973, James McDonnell (M), Ross McDowell 1990, Alistair McDowell 1995, Lisa McDowell 1997, Jackie McDowell 1998, Nicola McDowell 1993, JG McDowell 1965, Jonathan McDowell 2000, Conor McElhinney, Shane McElhinney, Morgan McEntee 1991, Niall McEntee 1996, Amy McFarland 2000, Max McFarland 2002, Rory McFarland 2003, Stephen McFarland 1978, Harry McGeough (M), Ben McGeough (M), David McGonigle 1966, Nicolina McGrath 2005, Gerard McGuinness 1979, Patrick McGuire 1971, EA McGuire 1968, Bailey McHugh 2002, Maeve McHugh 2002, Hannah McHugh (M), Christian McKeever 2005, Daisy McKeever 2006, Baris McKenna 2003, Danny McKeon (M), WN McKinley 1963, David WJ McLerie 1969, Robin McLerie 1972, Noel McMullan 1952, PD McMullan 1953, KM McMullan 1955, HD McMullan 1961, Rebecca McMullan (M), Jack McNulty 2010, William McNulty 2010, Hannah McNulty 2010, Philip McRoberts 1980, Bruce McRoberts, Alexandra McVittie 1983, HG Meade 1965, G Meade 1969, Sean Meaney 2010, Breeach Meehan (M), Cecilia Melcon 1985, Cecilia Melero Alarcon 2005, Gabriela Melia 2006, Diego Melia 2008, Marita Menacho 2002, Rosarita Menacho 2004, MPV Mercer 1971, Brett Merry 1968, Hugo Merry 1968, Fernando Jose Messia Popcev 2010, Lauren Meyler 2004, Jamey Mierins 1977, Kathryn Mierins 1977, Hugo Mills 2000, William Minch 2006, Emmet Minch 2002, JB Minch 1964, Dan Minchin 1955, Simon Mitchell 1986, Ian Mitchell 1949, PED Mitchell 1963, AEM Mitchell 1965, Andrew Mitchell 1997, Lisa Moeran 1989, Robbie Moeran 1992, Prince Akbar of Moghul 1993, Prince Babur of Moghul 1993, Rodrigo Molina Fernandez 2010, Tom Molony 2011, Frances Monaghan, Shane Monaghan, Declan Monaghan, James Montgomery 2007, PTE Moody 1970, Victoria Mooney 2009, Kristian Mooney 2009, Henri Mooney 2011, David Jonathan Moore 1981, Arthur Moore 1958, John Daniel Moore 1987, A Moore 1991, Javier Morales 2003, Victor Morales 2006, Cristina Morales 2008, Peter Moran 1991, Tomas Morenes y Leon 1986, Felipe Morenes y Leon 1988, Jose Moreno 1998, Guilana Mori Aguilar 2007, Jack Moriarty (M), Harry Morris 2004, Freddie Morris 2008, Kitty Morris 2011, Jamie Morton 1995, Patrick Morton 1996, Alexander Morton 1994, Thomas Morton 1996,

Stewart Morton 1998, William Morton 2001, James Morton, Lord Henry Mount Charles 1959, Rodrigo Moya 2006, George Mulholland 2001, RCM Mulholland 1962, Frank Mullen 1984, Sean Mulligan (M), JPD Mullins 1956, Ronat Mulvihill 1998, Anna Mulvin 1996, Yanina Munck-Fagan 2007, Rocio Munoz Gonzalez-Adalid 2009, Marisa Munoz Gonzalez-Adalid 2009, Michael Mura 1974, Charlie Murless 1967, Jaime Muro 1999, Antonio Muro 2002, Mariana Muro Morenes 2005, Gavin Murphy 1994, CCR Murphy 1967, RN Murphy 1969, Michael Murphy 2007, Caitlin Murphy (M), Aoife Murphy (M), Louis Murray Brown 2001, Isabelle Murtagh (M), Shane Musgrave 1976, Christopher Musgrave 1968, Sasha Musgrave 1975, Sophie Myerscough 1992, Jamie Myerscough 1987, David Myerscough 1998, NRWB Myles 1962, James Naper 1957, Merrik Naper 1989, Alex Naper 1990, Isabella Naper 1992, Nicholas Naper 1992, Edward Naper 1994, Charles Naper 1958, Francis Naper 1961, JJ Naper 1998, APMJ Naughten 1953, Gretta Neary 1997, JB Newall 1955, Hugh W. Newell 1957, PEI Newell 1958, EGB Newell 1961, Fionn Ni Anluain (M), Nat Nicholson 1993, NP Nicholson 1956, Christopher Nicholson 1978, Ellen Noonan (M), SH Norman 1955, Harriet Norris 1997, William Norris 1997, Lucy Rose Nugent (M), Katie Nugent (M), Richard Nugent 1955, Ruairi Nulty 2008, Finn Nulty 2009, Claire Nulty (M), Pedro Pablo Nunez Martinez 2009, Jose Pablo Nunez Martinez 2010, Ana Nunez Martinez 2011, Katie Oakes 2004, Alvaro Obregon Simo 2008, Max O'Brien 2006, Raoul O'Brien 2006, Sholto O'Brien 2006, TJ O'Brien 1966, Lucia O'Brien 2002, Emily O'Brien 2005, Abigail O'Brien 2007, Ava O'Brien 2011, James O'Brien (M), D O'Brien, Roger O'Callaghan 1991, Henry O'Callaghan 1993, Gary O'Callaghan 1987, Aran O'Carroll 1979, Tara O'Carroll 1980, Conn O'Carroll 1981, Katie O'Connell 1975, Sinead O'Connell 1998, Lauren O'Connell 1999, Max O'Connell 1999, Claire O'Connell 1978, Edward O'Connell (M), Alicia O'Connor 2006, Meriel O'Connor 1987, Helena O'Connor (M), Eoin O'Conor 2003, Hugh O'Conor 2006, David O'Doherty 1952, Robert O'Doherty 1982, Catherine O'Donohoe 1984, Teige O'Donovan 1970, MTG O'Donovan, Lee O'Driscoll 2002, Tomi Odunowo 2004, Olivier Offman 1985, Stephen O'Flaherty 1970, Golden Ogbonna 2001, Violet Ogden 1997, A Ogilvy 1972, Robert Ogle 1962, Isaac Ogoo-Logan 2009, CPD O'Gowan 1953, Patrick O'Hara, James O'Hara, Sean O'Hara, Maxwell O'Keeffe 2008, Iarlaith O'Kelly-Lynch (M), Alexandra O'Leary 1998, Julie O'Mahony 2000, Sarah O'Mahony 2003, Tim O'Mahony, S O'Neill 1961, WH O'Neill 1962, ARM O'Neill 1971, Oisin O'Neill 2008, Jason Onyeka 2010, Alfonso Orbea Pazos 2002, John Ordway 1974, Peter Ordway 1972, Rebecca O'Reilly 1994, Farrell O'Reilly (M), James O'Reilly (M), Riannagh O'Reilly (M), Raquel Orejas 1996, Miguel Orejas Iban 1982, Diana Orejas Iban 1983, Alvaro Oriol 2010, Iria Oriol Rotaeche 2011, Ana Ortiz Florez 2009, Rafael Ortiz 2003, Antonio Ortiz 2004, Begona Ortiz 2006, Ben O'Shea 2011, Aoife O'Shea (M), Oliver Osthus 1978, John Osthus 1977, Bernard O'Sullivan 1976, Thomas O'Sullivan 2003, David O'Sullivan 2007, Christopher O'Sullivan, DJB O'Sullivan, Delia Otero 2007, Zara Owens (M), Patrick Oxmantown 1978, Maria Pablo Romero Lopez 2007, Carmen Pablo-Romero 2005, Guadalupe Pablo-Romero Parias 2008, Paz Pablo-Romero Parias 2008, R O'M Page 1959, Victor Palhon 2010, Gregor Palmstierna 1976, Gabriela Pando Pando Sanchez 2011,

Humberto Parias 1982, Miguel Parias, Oliver Parkinson-Hill, Jeremy Parkinson-Hill, B Parkinson-Hill, Michael Parsons 1992, Nikolaus Pass 1998, Caroline Patton 1986, Robert Patton 1958, David Patton 1957, Nick Patton 1987, RAG Pearson 1956, Virginia Peck 2002, Mercedes Pena Hernandez 2007, Manuel Pena Hernandez 2011, PLR Pennefeather 1957, Tomas Peralta 2004, Pablo Peralta Palacios 2009, Freddy Pereira 1998, David Perry 1949, RPG Perry 1951, Flora Pery-Knox-Gore 2008, Callum Pery-Knox-Gore 2008, Mark Pery-Knox-Gore 1963, Igor Petrenko 2009, Cecilia Pfeiffer 2004, Nicholas Pheifer 1973, Hugh Pheifer 1975, Arthur Phelan 1985, Charlotte Phelan, Sean Phelan 2006, Patrick Phelan 1979, Jack Phelan 2007, Eleanor Phelan (M), Pen Pickersgill 1997, Jasper Pickersgill 2002, Owain Pickersgill-Mallaney 1992, Anna Pieper 2009, Freya Pierce 2008, Hubie Pilkington 1999, Jack Pilkington 2004, JRR Platt 1954, Emily Plunket 2000, Olivia Plunket 2002, Randal Plunkett 1994, Oliver Plunkett 1994, Miles Podmore 1972, Mark Podmore 1974, Alexander Poklewski Koziell 1973, Marina Pollock 2004, Josephine Pollock 2004, Johnny Pollock 2009, Leah Pollock (M), CJ Pooler 1968, RG Pooler, Pablo Portes Navarro 2009, Ana Portes Navarro 2011, HCS Potterton 1964, Sarah Potterton 1976, Elliott Potterton (M), Barry Potterton, Ben Potts 1985, Rachel Potts 1985, Naivasha Pratt-Jarvis 2005, Arthur Preston 1998, Eliza Preston 1998, Claudia Preston, Mario Prieto 2000, Stefan Prinz 2007, Michael Prittie 1969, Bella Purcell 2006, Wolfe Purcell 2006, Oliver Quinn 1979, Diego Ramos Garcia 2010, Alistair Rauscher 1997, SM Rawnsley 1963, DC Rawnsley 1964, Francisco Ray Gonzalez 2005, KMF Rea 1963, RCF Rea, Mark Reade 1995, Richard Reade 1958, DJ Reade 1963, Rodrigo Rebora 2004, Harry Record (M), Kumar Reddy, Ingrid Redmond 1990, Ian Redmond 1988, MRM Reed 1950, Catherine Reid 1998, Thomas Reilly 1978, Caroline Reilly 1986, Luke Reilly (M), Callum Reilly (M), Tristan Reneaume 1996, Inigo Rengifo 2007, Rex Reubens 2010, Santiago Revilla 2006, Carla Reyes 2003, Paul Reynolds 1973, AF Reynolds 1962, RE Reynolds, FM Reynolds, Georgina Ribelles 2002, David Riggs 2008, Aaron Riggs 2009, PC Ritchie 1952, D Roberts, Albert Roberts, Velma Roberts 1981, Joanna Roberts 1982, Mathew Roberts 1988, PJ Robertson 1962, Max Robinson 1989, Luis Rodriguez 1997, Ana Rodriguez-Arias Olleros 2009, Lawrence Roe 1996, Oscar Rogan (M), Nadia Rogers 2005, Michael Roller 1973, Ian Ross 1981, David Ross, Sarah Rountree 1985, Vanessa Rountree 1987, Archie Rowan Hamilton 2006, Tara Rowan Hamilton 2006, Jake Rowan Hamilton 2008, Charles Rowan Hamilton 2011, Oliver Roydhouse 1989, Ana Rubio 1985, Marta Rubio 1985, Alejandro Ruiz Caro 2010, Blanca Ruiz del Olmo 2002, Carlos Ruiz del Olmo 2008, Robin Russell 2003, DN Russell 1957, Desmond Ryan 1991, Cornelius Ryan 2006, Archie Ryan 2011, Will Ryan 2011, Fernando Salido 1988, RD Samuelson 1961, Eduardo Sanchez 2002, Raquel Sanchez-Friera 1984, Olga Sanchez-Friera 1984, Fernanda Sandoval 2002, Antonio Santos 2006, Emilio Scala 1997, Alexander Schmarsel 2001, Benedikt Schuessler 2011, FC Schwab 1949, Hannah Schwartz 2006, Patrick Scott 1995, Radley Searle 1956, John Searle 1959, Peter Searle 1960, David Searle 1965, Radley Searle 1979, Jason Searle 1980, Etienne Secretan 2005, Seth Seth-Smith 2003, Ora Seth-Smith 2007, Edward Shackleton 1996, Robin Shackleton 1998, Viola Shackleton, RDC Shattuck 1969, RHM Shaw 1954, R Shaw 1961, AJ Shears 1954, Susan Shekleton 2009, Philip Shekleton 2009,

James Sheridan 2001, RD Sheridan 1965, Florence Sheridan 2006, Tommy Shillington 1980, Christopher Shillington 1987, Clare Shillington 1989, PC Shillington 1953, Milo Shirley 2006, Philip E Shirley 1964, HS Shirley 1970, S Shirley, Marie Sichel-Dulong 2009, Alexander Simmons 1982, Ben Simmons 1992, Will Simmons 1992, Raoul Simpson 1987, William Simpson 1972, Marcus Simpson 1973, Edward Simpson 1976, JG Skrine 1961, Patrick Slevin 2001, NA Slevin 1972, EV Slevin, WJH Sloan, Oliver Smith 2000, HL Smith 1958, Carl Smith 1975, Gordon Smith 1977, Alejandra Smith Burrull 2006, Maria Solis Benjumea 2009, GM Solomons 1962, Jaime Soriano 2003, Marion Soudre 2003, Jean Soudre 2005, Ivan Soukhine 1998, Jeremy Speid-Soote 1949, Cosmo Spence 1971, John Spicer 1978, Patrick Spicer 1979, Kevin Spicer 1980, Jack Spicer 2008, Gwendoline Spicer 1977, Joanna Spicer 1984, Clare Spicer 1985, Roly Spiller 1991, Henry Spiller 1993, Deedee Spokes 1984, Doug Spokes 1984, Arthur St George 1988, Henry St George 1990, Michael Stafford 1992, Louise Stafford 1993, Catherine Stammschröer 2006, Alexandra Stammschröer 2007, Stephanie Stammschröer 2009, Richard Stammschröer 2011, Morgan Stanley 1999, Marcus Stapleton 2006, TP Starling 1954, MJ Starling 1959, GM Starling, Christy Staunton 2005, Rory Staunton (M), Harry Staunton (M), Theo Staunton (M), Sam Sterling 2004, Andrew Sterling 1971, Natasha Sterling 2004, PWHK Stevenson 1966, Alexander Stewart 2006, Hugo Stewart 2001, Ludovic Stewart 2007, Louisa Stewart 2004, WG Stickland, Sam Stoney 1971, James Stoney 1978, RAV Stoney 1965, Alan Stoney 1966, W St GV Stoney 1967, Fania Stoney 1978, Harry Stoney 2011, Milo Stuart-Arkins 2004, Frances Stuart-Mills 1949, Elizabeth (Christine) Stuart-Mills, 1954, Alister Stuart-Mills, IA Stuart-Mills, Siobhan Stuart-Mills 1958, Konrad Suchodolski 2006, Jonathan Sullivan 2005, Maria Sullivan 2005, CD St J Sullivan 1957, Robert Sullivan 2005, Tristan Swan 1980, Laurence Swan 1956, Charles Swan 1976, Alan Sweetman 1965, PJ Sweetman 1951, Daniel Swift 2010, Aurelio Tagua 2006, Patrick Talbot 1994, NS Talbot 1950, WEDB Talbot 1950, Henry Talbot 2000, MNO'C Tandy 1963, PSO'C Tandy 1963, AC Tarry 1961, JL Tarry 1966, Joe Teesdale 1958, Lynn Temple 1959, Charlotte Temple 1992, Patrick Temple 1994, Rosy Temple 1998, RM Temple 1967, Robin Thompson 1949, Brian Thompson 1949, RJ Thompson 1955, BP Thompson 1964, Katie Thompson 2009, KL Tierney 1949, Heuston Tilson 1978, Perri Tilson 1978, Victoria Tindal 1981, Lucy Tindal 1987, Mathew Tindal 1983, Charlie Toal (M), Diego Torre 2004, Daniela Torre 2007, John Tottenham 1963, Charles Tottenham 1965, Robin Tottenham 1985, Fred Tottenham 1986, George Tottenham 1987, Joanna Tottenham 2005, Edward Tottenham 2006, Geoffry Tottenham 1970, CRB Tottenham 1971, M Toulemonde 1949, B Toulemonde, Isabelle Townshend 2007, Oliver Townshend 2008, Henry Traill 2006, Anna Traill 2002, Alexandra Traill 2004, Ben Traill 2006, Antony Tregoning 1951, Julian Tregoning 1955, Christopher Tregoning 1960, Coralie Treherne 2005, Nina Treherne 2008, Richard Trevithick 2007, Nicholas Tubbs 1975, Rupert Tubbs 1973, RDG Turbett 1967, AA Turney 1957, Rodrigo Turrent 2007, Orla Tynan 1998, Tristan Tyrrell 1990, Simon R Umfreville 1955, Peter Umfreville-Moore 1949, AC Umfreville-Moore 1949, Natalie Uriguen 2000, Anita Uriguen 2005, Carla Valero Quintana 2011, Victor Valero Quintana 2011, Eva Valles Torices 1983, Cesar Valles Torices, Davy van Geerke 2006, Angus van Schoenberg 1974,

Tom Vance 1957, Charles Vance 1989, Monica Vargas Gonzalez 2007, Luis Vazquez 2004, Ana Sofia Vazquez Martinez 2010, Juan Vega 1992, Alfonso Vega 1994, RJ Velzeboer 1957, Ferdinand von Prondzynski 1962, Robert Wachman 1979, Gillian Wachman 1983, Sarah Wachman 1986, Katie Wachman 1987, DJ Waldron 1954, HEC Walker 1950, CA Walker 1955, Roy Walker 1986, Jane Walsh 2009, Shannon Walsh 2001, John Walsh 2009, Eddie Walsh 2011, Nicola Ward 1975, Caolan Ward (M), JJJ Ward, William Ward 1972, Barley Ward Thomas, Jonathan Wardell 1986, Rebecca Wardell 1990, TGD Wardell 1962, MH Wardell 1965, Marcus Waring 1950, Suzannah Watson 1989, AS Watson 1970, Sam Watson 1993, Rosalind Watson, Toddy Watt 1972, Bradley Weatherhead 2008, DL Weaver 1960, AS Weaver 1965, RJ Welbourne 1970, J Welsby-Deakin, Richard Wentges 1963, Sophie Wentges 1996, Rosemary Wentges 1999, Hannah Wentges 2002, MJHE Wentges 1965, Charlotte Wessolowski 2011, James Westendarp 1993, Mervyn Whaley 1953, Richard Whaley 1955, Sam Wheeler 1985, James Wheeler 1994, TKT Wheeler 1968, ARB Whitaker 1969, Tim Whitley 1967, Ben Whitley 2009, R Whitworth 1960, Sam Wiggins 2006, Charlie Wiggins 2006, Grace Wilbur 2003, David Wilby 1978, Charles Wilby 1979, Thomas Wilkes 1979, Rupert Wilkes 1977, Neville Wilkinson 1979, Nigel Wilkinson 1981, Pr Wilkinson 1954, Nicholas Wilkinson 1984, Harry Wilkinson 1985, Mark Wilkinson, Simon Williams 1968, David Williams 1973, Marcus Williams 1980, Patrick Williams 1976, Petra Williams, Charles Williams 1988, Griselda Williams, 1988, G St J Williams 1958, Emily Williams 1988, DA Williams Ellis 1967, Andrew Willis 1990, Jeremy Wilson 1978, Edward Wilson 1949, RJ Wilson 1959, AJ Wilson 1959, CG Wilson 1964, NS Wise, Nicholas Wolfe 1988, William Wood 2002, Cameron Wood 2004, Jack Woods 1996, Robert Woods 1996, Poppy Woods 2005, Derek Woods 1961, WA Woods, Bethaney Woolley 2005, Chloe Woolley 2005, CW Wordsworth 1954, PJ Wordsworth 1957, James Wright 1981, Nick Wright 1961, NP Wright 1963, DC Wright 1966, Hector Wright 2009, Chris Yoo 2007, Sam Yoo 2007, Jenny You 2007, AW Young 1969, Patricia Ysasi Lara 2011, Christina Zhang 2009.

INDEX